Reproducing Rape

Dedicated to the memory of Jim Schenkein

REPRODUCING RAPE

Domination through Talk in the Courtroom

Gregory M. Matoesian

Polity Press

First published in 1993 by Polity Press in association with Blackwell Publishers

Editorial office:
Polity Press
65 Bridge Street
Cambridge CB2 1UR, UK

Marketing and production:
Blackwell Publishers
108 Cowley Road,
Oxford, OX4 1JF, UK

ISBN 0 7456 1036 6
ISBN 0 7456 1171 0 (pbk)

A CIP catalogue record for this book is available from the British Library.

Typeset in 10 on 12 pt Garamond by Hope Services (Abingdon) Ltd.
Printed in Great Britain by T. J. Press Ltd, Padstow, Cornwall

This book is printed on acid-free paper.

Contents

Human societies present a new phenomenon of a special nature, which consists in the fact that certain ways of acting are imposed, or at least suggested *from outside* the individual and are added on to his own nature: such is the character of "institutions" which the existence of language makes possible, and of which language itself is an example. They take on substance as individuals succeed each other without destroying their continuity; their presence is the distinctive characteristic of human societies, and the proper subject matter of sociology.

Émile Durkheim, *The Rules of Sociological Method*

Encounters are sustained above all through talk, through everyday conversation. In analysing the communication of meaning in interaction via the use of interpretative schemes, the phenomenon of talk has to be taken very seriously, as constitutively involved in encounters.

Anthony Giddens, *The Constitution of Society*

Preface

During the Fall of 1991 and Winter of 1992, two spectacular and well publicized trials and one equally well publicized senate hearing catapulted the issue of rape and sexual violence into the center of public consciousness in the US. The William Kennedy Smith, Mike Tyson, and Clarence Thomas cases revealed the deepseated yet ambiguous sexual conflict between men and women. But still, after all the ritualistic name-calling from the various partisans about who was right and who was wrong, who was telling the truth and who was lying, we are still left more puzzled than ever about the nature of sexual crimes against women. Did she consent? Did she say no? Did he have sex with her against her will? Did he use force? How do we know?

I don't think we can begin to answer these perplexing questions until we look at them in a new way, until we study the interaction among law, language, and power. As I mention in the pages to follow, the legal system is not necessarily about truth and falsity, but winning and losing, and that, in turn, depends largely on which side can best manipulate language. This position is critical for understanding rape and reforming the legal system because, contrary to popular belief, the court does not determine if there was consent or nonconsent from an individual woman's or man's point of view, at least not directly, but determines instead if she consented to patriarchal standards of sexuality, sexual access, and sexual availability. These are two different orders of questions and should, I believe, be kept separate. One is about a subjectivity; the other is about an objectivity. The first question is about what went on in the minds of the victim and the accused; the second is about the social institutions of law, patriarchy, and especially language as forms of domination. In this work, I address only the second question. In particular, I address the role of language in the rape trial: how language functions as the symbolic embodiment of social values, as a strategic instrument of domination and, along its most Sacksian dimension, as a sequentially organized inference generating machine. I address how the woman's experience of rape is transformed into consensual sex through the social organization of courtroom talk. As the reader will soon see, I propose to accomplish this task through an integrative exercise which draws abstract theoretical concepts into the fold of empirical data and analysis. I look at the areas of patriarchal violence, social theory, and the law from the fascinating micro-detailed world of trial talk-in-interaction.

I owe a special debt to those people who made this work possible, especially to my teachers in the fields of both sociology and linguistics for tolerating my split academic personality: Ed Brent, Peter Hall, Ken Benson, Mary Jo Neitz, Warren Handel, Hugh Barlow, and Jim Henslin in sociology; and Don Lance, Jim Schenkein, Chad McDaniel, and Louanna Furbee in linguistics. I would also like to thank my legal "advisors" Michele Matoesian-Taylor and Judge Andreas Matoesian for putting up with endless questions on legal procedures and other matters. I would also like to thank the people at Polity Press, especially Ann Bone for her meticulous copy-editing. My best friend Henry Bangert kept me from going crazy during the past few years, so a very special thanks to him. Finally, I would like to thank my parents, Gregor and Kenarr, whose generous support made this work possible in the first place. I dedicate this work to my wife Helen and son Nicky, and to my good buddy, Willy "hey Joe" Champlin.

Introduction

This study offers a nuts and bolts view of the constitution of power and social structure as they live and unfold during the course of linguistic performance – during the performance of knowledge. From this vantage point, social life is constituted as a socially structured and moral interpretative reality within a sequentially powered framework of talk-in-interaction. More fundamentally, the constitution of social life involves not just the performance of knowledge but the pre-existing collective circumstances which constrain and enable those performances, recursively regenerating the conditions for future performances. The theoretical question I address in this book is a complex one: How is social structure embodied in and reproduced through social action? How is the social order constituted through the mutual and simultaneous elaboration of structure and action?

Rape trial talk is the empirical site for pursuing this theoretical goal. More specifically, I look at how rape is reproduced or "discovered" during the defense attorney's cross-examination of the victim. Cross-examination is an adversarial war of words, sequences, and ideas, a war in which the capability to finesse reality through talk represents the ultimate weapon of domination. When considering the reproduction of rape as a criminal social fact, I am looking at how a woman's experience of violation is transformed into routine consensual sex through the organization of courtroom linguistic practice, and not at how that violation is subjectively experienced through the meanings and intentions of individual victims, rapists, or administrators of justice. In very tacit and taken-for-granted fashion, language categorizes, objectifies, and legitimates our interpretations about social reality, sustaining some versions while disqualifying others, and conceals the hierarchical arrangements and sexual differences between men and women. Language is a system of power for those who control it, and, in the context of the rape trial, talking power transforms the subjective violation of the victim – the victim's experience of sexual terror – into an objectivity: namely, consensual sex.

Both popular and social scientific conceptions of the rape trial have referred to this form of domination as a generic, blaming-the-victim process, a process in which the female on the stand is a mere passive recipient of blame-allocation strategies employed by the defense attorney, in particular, or the victim of a patriarchal legal system which structures courtroom interaction in general, or, still more comprehensively, both. It is time to bracket these impressionistic and anecdotal glosses, and analyze in fine-grained, blow-by-blow detail the reproduction of domination as it unfolds *in situ*.

When envisioned as locally produced discovery, rape is constituted and reconstituted through a multiplex interweaving of sequentially driven, institutionally anchored, and patriarchally organized forms of talk: what I refer to as socially structured talk. The conjuncture of talk, patriarchy, and the legal system collide and fuse in courtroom cross-examination to create a richly layered mosaic of domination – a structurational totality. Although patriarchal modes of domination and legal disciplinary regimes represent analytically distinct social systems, they intersect during courtroom talk to fashion the penetrating thrust of blame attributions against the victim. Because of procedural and evidentiary strictures in court, blame work is conducted inferentially through powerful procedures of talk and sense-making practices. But access to these procedures is not equally distributed across social position. Attorneys and victims possess differential access to the procedures of talk. The defense attorney possesses the linguistic and sequential capital to make his/her account "count" relative to the victim. Attorneys control the topic, the syntactic form of questions, and the sequential resources with which to manipulate words, utterances, and turns as microtechniques of disciplinary power. When interlaced and synchronized with patriarchal ideology – ideas about sexual access and practice – these power mechanisms generate the accusatory sense of what happened during the rape incident; they thereby reproduce the constraining and enabling facticity – facts constructed locally in context – of both rape and the legal order.

Yet while the social organization of the court differentially distributes the procedures of talk, the defense attorney and victim still possess reciprocal opportunities for action, however asymmetrical those options may be (see Hall 1985; Giddens 1985). The constraining and reifying facticity of courtroom social organization and rape must therefore be reproduced, regardless of how prestructured both might *prima facie* appear, and if attorneys and victims are to reproduce their relations of autonomy and dependence, their asymmetrical relationship, they will have to achieve it within the context of live interactional performance. Systematically asymmetrical relations or modes of domination are not constituted structurally through social position, or culturally through social practices, but through the mutual elaboration of both in position practices.

In a different vein, this study marks a new departure for the study of both talk-in-interaction and rape. It is designed to anchor organizational talk squarely in the midst of social structure and power, and to situate that talk within a contemporary sociological theory: the theory of structuration. With few exceptions (such as Grimshaw 1981; Davis 1988; Boden and Zimmerman 1991), sociologists of language have refrained from any consideration of the complex interrelationships between language and power, and have concentrated instead on the formal properties of language use. Strategically, this made sound policy. We would never have learned as much as we have about the formal, sequential properties of talk if some scholars had not concentrated on these to the exclusion of all else. But if we do not transcend this policy we can never hope to unravel the multiplex interpenetration between talk and modes of domination.

Likewise, despite the explosive development of research on rape since the mid-1970s, there has been no analysis of the constitution and reproduction of rape in trial talk. Scholars in the area of rape studies have noted the pivotal impact of such talk for the reproduction of rape, especially considering its impact on victim reporting and its role in acquitting rapists in court, and policy advocates have engineered legal changes such as rape shield legislation in an effort to limit the defense attorney's access to the procedures of talk. These statutorial changes were designed to limit "blaming the victim" and provide various procedural and evidentiary safeguards for victims during defense cross-examination. While legislative reform was designed to limit the defense attorney's power of talk, and seemed *prima facie* to make good strategic sense, the outcome of such reforms has been limited at best. Ironically, while noting the relevance of talk during the rape trial and implementing legal changes on the basis of that relevance, scholars and policy advocates in the area of rape and rape reform have completely neglected the fine-tuned organization of language in real-time courtroom performance – interactional processes instrumental in the structuration and reproduction of this criminal social fact. Like most researchers, scholars writing in the areas of rape and language use live comfortably within their own academic habitats.

The alternative course, pursued here, is by nature a risky one. It entails crossing interdisciplinary boundaries and maneuvering across well-established yet diverse fields of inquiry: rape, gender, conversational analysis, sociological theory, and even the macro–micro problem. In so doing, there is always an inevitable danger of oversimplification. But I think the potential gain is well worth the challenge. I can breach formal constraints in ethnomethodological and conversation analytic forms of inquiry, and seek to address how talk is implicated in social reproduction. Relatedly, I can offset the narrow victimology bias found in the study of rape, and the methodological/empirical limitations found in interviews, pre-categorized coding schedules, and anecdotal or impressionistic accounts of blaming the victim – empirical techniques and conceptual approaches characteristic of contemporary research on rape. Instead, the real live discovery of rape through trial talk occupies center stage for this analysis.

The organization of the study is as follows. Chapter 1 starts with a brief consideration of the incidence and prevalence statistics on rape in the United States and then reviews various theoretical explanations of rape and sexual violence, including recent research on rape reform legislation and the role of law and the legal system as patriarchal legitimizing mechanisms. The next four chapters examine the properties of talk-in-interaction. Chapters 2, 3, and 4 trace the theoretical, conceptual, and methodological framework of conversational analysis, including the transcription techniques and data base for the present study, and describe the relevance of talk for rape and sociological theory. Chapter 5 examines the disciplinary power of the courtroom speech exchange system, illustrates the difference between courtroom and natural conversational systems, and shows how patriarchal ideologies are mapped on to sequential structures. This chapter illuminates the rhetorical skills of charismatic oratory found in courtroom talk, and illustrates in detail how the manipulation of words, the balance of utterances, and the rhythms of sequencing are rigorously implicated in discovering rape. Operating inferentially, these disciplinary and persuasive power devices capture the interpenetrating moments of talk and ideology. The inferentially implicative blame-sequences of cross-examination are transformed into full-blown accusations in the closing statement, and disparate strands of evidence are resurrected in tightly integrated and rhythmically interlaced sense-making packages. And chapter 6, the last chapter of the study, traces various concepts of social structure within the sociological literature, and situates rape trial talk within Anthony Giddens's structuration theory, illuminating the analytical power of the duality of structure when considering the reproduction of both patriarchal and legal modes of domination.

1

The Social Facticity of Rape

Rape is a widely prevalent and highly systematic aspect of American social life – a social fact. We can appreciate the extent of rape victimization by considering prevalence rates: the total percentage of women who will experience a completed or an attempted rape over the course of a lifetime. A. Johnson (1980: 145) gave a conservative estimate that, excluding marital rape, 20 to 30 percent of girls aged 12 at the time of the study would suffer an attempted or completed rape during the course of their lifetimes. In a much more sophisticated and comprehensive study, Diane Russell (1984: 47) discovered that the prevalence rate for women 18 and older was 44 percent, a figure including marital rape. And, more recently, Mary Koss and her associates found a prevalence rate of 27.5 percent in a sample of college women since the age of 14 (Koss et al. 1987: 166; see also Koss 1988, 1989; Koss and Harvey 1987; Warshaw 1988).

If we translate these prevalence figures into incidence rates, new rapes that occurred in a particular time period, and then compare them with official statistics, we can gain an even greater appreciation that the crime of rape has reached epidemic proportions. According to Koss, the incidence of rape victimization is 38 per 1,000 women (ages 18–24 in college) over a six-month time frame, 10 to 15 times higher than the National Crime Survey's (NCS) victimization rates of 3.9/1,000 women for ages 16–19 and 2.5/1,000 women for ages 20–24 (Koss et al. 1987: 168).

Diane Russell's findings are just as dramatic. She compared the incidence of rape victimization not only with NCS rates but also with the FBI's Uniform Crime Reports (UCR) for 1978, which only takes into consideration rapes and attempted rapes that are officially reported. The incidence of rape in the Russell study was 35 per 1,000 women compared with 5/1,000 in the NCS study and 1.71/1,000 in the UCR. Thus Russell found rape victimization rates 7 times higher than the NCS and 24 times higher than the UCR. Translating the incidence of rape victimization into the total number of rapes in the United States for 1978, Russell's figures come to true total of 1,611,144 rapes and attempted rapes, a figure radically higher than the UCR rate of 67,131 reported rapes (Russell 1984: 46–7).

Clearly, rape is a massively underreported crime. In Koss's sample of 3,187 women, 886 suffered a rape or an attempted rape, but out of this sample only 5 percent or 45 reported the incident to the police (Warshaw 1988: 50). Similarly, Russell (1984: 35) found that less than 1 in 12 or 8 percent of the 407 rape victims out of a sample of 930 women reported the crime to the police.

Why is there such a massive discrepancy between official crime statistics and feminist research findings? Why is rape so massively underreported? To answer these questions we must look to theoretical explanations for rape and sexual victimization.

EXPLAINING RAPE:
THE PSYCHOPATHOLOGICAL MODEL

Until the 1980s, the most frequent explanation for rape was that it was a rare and random act committed by a "small lunatic fringe" of the male population (A. Johnson 1980; Scully 1990). According to the psycho-pathological model, rapists are abnormal males, psychotics suffering from various forms of sexually psychopathic diseases – mental illness, uncontrollable sexual impulses, aggressive tendancies – and, as sick individuals, they require clinical assessment and psychiatric intervention and treatment. As the primary exponent of the psychiatric or disease model states: "Rape is always a symptom of some psychological dysfunction, either temporary and transient or chronic and repetitive . . . The rapist is, in fact, a person who has serious psychological difficulties which handicap him in his relationships to other people and which he discharges, when under stress, through sexual acting out" (Groth 1979: 5–6).

But looking back at the prevalence and incidence figures on rape, it is hard to deny Scully's (1990: 46) pointed critique of Groth: "the psychopathological model does not explain why women in some societies are the targets of so much uniquely male 'disease.'" Nor could we disagree with Russell's (1984: 65) observation: "How could it be that all of these rapes are being perpetrated by a tiny segment of the male population?" How is such an anomaly possible? What is the status of Groth's claim?

Indeed, if we look more closely at the facts of rape a quite different picture emerges. If rape were a psychopathologically isolated, random act committed by a few deranged men, we would not only have a difficult time explaining so much male "disease" through the prevalence and incidence figures previously cited, but we would also have a serious problem accounting for several complementary research findings.

First, according to Koss et al. (1987: 166; see Warshaw 1988), while 27.5 percent of women suffered either an attempted or completed rape, an additional 11.9 percent experienced sexual coercion (sexual intercourse obtained through male pressure and arguments) and 14.4 experienced some form of unwanted sexual contact – fondling or kissing against their will. While 46.3 percent of women suffered no sexual victimization, 53.7 percent experienced various forms of victimization ranging along a continuum from rape, on the one hand, to unwanted sexual contact on the other.

In a similar vein, Russell found that the extent of male sexual exploitation is quite pervasive, even beyond the rape prevalence figure of 44 percent. Combining incestuous and extrafamilial sexual abuse, 38 percent of the women in the Russell survey suffered at least one episode of sexual abuse before the age of 18, and, for both categories, males committed 96 percent of the offenses (Russell 1984: 285–6). Sexual harassment on the job or "legal rape" (MacKinnon 1979; Messerschmidt 1986: 145) is another area for looking at the extent of sexual exploitation. According to Russell (1984: 270), over a two-year period 42 percent of all female employees reported varying degrees of sexual harassment on the job. Once again, most of the perpetrators were male. Doubtless, if the study had questioned victims for prevalence data, the figures would have been much higher. In sum, then, there is a vast amount of male sexual aggression against females in American society, aggression ranging along a continuum from rape and sexual abuse on the one hand, to sexual harrassment and "hoot howls" on the other. The amount of aggression and violence against women is much more widespread and common even than rape statistics reveal.

Second, if rape were a rare and isolated act committed by and limited to a few sick men, we would expect it to be an act confined to strangers and readily recognized by victims. But rape is not, for the most part, committed by strangers, nor is it a crime that is readily recognized by victims. Koss (Koss et al. 1987; see Warshaw 1988: 11) found that 84 percent of female victims either knew or were acquainted with their assailants, and 57 percent of all rapes happened on dates. Despite these figures, only 5 percent of rapes were reported to the police, and only 27 percent of the women recognized or interpretated these actions as rape, even though they met the legal criteria. Russell (1984: 61) found similar results: only 17 percent of the rape (and attempted rape) incidents involved strangers while some 83 percent happened with acquaintances, dates, boyfriends, lovers, husbands, friends, relatives, or authority figures. And although rapes by strangers constituted only 17 percent of all rapes, they represented 55 percent of all rapes reported to the police (Russell 1984: 96–7). In all, only 9.5 percent of the nonmarital rapes and attempted rapes were reported (Russell 1984: 96). As we saw from Russell, when marital rape was included, less than 1 out of 12 or only 8 percent of the rapes and attempted rapes were ever reported to the police (Russell 1984: 35–6). As both Koss (1988: 20) and Russell (1984), and other researchers (see Messerschmidt 1986: 130–56; Herman 1989: 25) have noted, since official statistics like the UCR reflect only incidents of reported rapes, and since even victimization studies like the NCS fail to elicit data on date and acquaintance rape, these official figures grossly distort not only the true amount of rape, but also the type of perpetrators who are sexually assaulting women. The overwhelming majority of reported rapes are limited to classic or aggravated rapes, rapes involving a stranger and frequently some type of extrinsic force such as knives, guns, and beatings (L. Williams 1984; Estrich 1987).

Third, both the above points seriously undermine the notion that the rapist is a sick, diseased, or abnormal male. In fact, less than 5 percent of rapists have been diagnosed as clinically psychotic during the time of the rape assault (Scully 1990: 41; see also Walby 1990: 130; Lottes 1988: 194). Relatedly, Kanin (1984, 1985) studied 71 self-reported college date rapists and 227 males from the same population and found no pronounced evidence of criminal or psychotic behavior in the former when compared with the latter (see also Kanin 1975). The facts about rape, therefore, force us to consider this: sexual aggression, including the propensity to rape, is not only widespread but also normative sexual behavior or an extension of normative sexual behavior in the male population (Scully and Marolla 1985b: 253; Herman 1989: 28–9; Schur 1988: 178; Bart and O'Brien 1985: 96–8; MacKinnon 1987, 1989).

Bearing this in mind, Koss (1988: 10) found that 25.1 percent of the 2,972 men in her sample admitted to some form of sexual aggression against women: 10.2 percent admitted to unwanted sexual contact; 7.2 percent admitted to sexual coercion; 4.4 percent admitted to rape; and 3.3 percent admitted to attempted rape. Even here we must be extremely cautious when looking at male questionnaire responses, for, as Koss (1988: 19–21) discovered: "Most men (88%) who reported an assault that met the legal definitions of rape were adamant that their behavior was definitely not rape." This is not to say that males are necessarily lying or concealing information about sexual aggression, but rather that they may actually be more likely than females, first, to interpret routine friendly encounters as sexual and, second, to interpret sexual interactions as consensual, even if they involve various levels of physical force and coercion (Koss 1988: 21; Hansel 1988; Lottes 1988: 200–2; Scully 1990; Bart and O'Brien 1985: 92–9, 119; E. Goode 1990: 249).

Further evidence for the normativeness of rape comes from several recent social psychological studies. Jacqueline Goodchilds and her associates (1988: 245–70) conducted interviews with 432 Los Angeles adolescents from ages 14 to 18 to discover various circumstances in which male sexual force against females would be considered legitimate. The findings demonstrate that not all nonconsensual sex is interpreted as rape (Goodchilds et al. 1988: 255). For example, in response to the statement, "He spends a lot of money on her," 12 percent of females and 39 percent of males indicated that forced sex would be legitimate; 32 percent of the females and 43 percent of the males stated that forced sex would be legitimate if "they have dated a long time"; 21 percent of the females and 36 percent of the males said force would be legitimate if "he's so turned on he can't stop"; 18 percent of the females and 39 percent of the males stated that force would be legitimate if "she's had sexual intercourse with other guys"; 42 percent of the females and 51 percent of the males thought that force would be legitimate if "she gets him sexually excited"; 27 percent of the females and 54 percent of the males stated that force would be legitimate if "she's led him on"; 31 percent of the females and 54 percent of the males indicated that forced sex was legitimate if "she says she's going to have sex with him then changes her mind"; and 28 percent of the females and 39 percent of the males said that forced sex was legitimate if "she lets him touch her above the waist."

Studying self-reported rapists in college populations, Briere and Malamuth (1983) and Tieger (1981) provide evidence that many males would consider raping if they were assured they could get away with it. In a sample of 356 college men, Briere and Malamuth discovered that 28 percent indicated some likelihood of raping and using force, and 6 percent indicated a likelihood of rape but with no force. Tieger, in a sample of 179 males, found almost identical results: 37 percent responded that they might rape if they were guaranteed not to get caught. These findings highlight the socially structured interconnection among sexuality, aggression, and violence as the hallmark of masculinity in violent patriarchal societies.

Thomas Kuhn (1970) wrote that scientific revolutions may occur when prevailing theoretical models of reality are unable to account for and explain the occurrence of increasingly perplexing anomalies. In such cases, a new theoretical model or paradigm which can explain the discrepant findings becomes accepted by a community of scientific practitioners. Applying this to the recent research on rape, the psycho-pathological model of rape not only fails to articulate recent feminist findings on the prevalence and incidence of rape but also fails to incorporate research on the vast scope of male aggressive proclivities within a coherent and cogent explanatory framework; it leaves the great bulk of male aggression against females unexplained and grossly distorts the facts of rape. Just as crucial, when considering the psychopathological model it is well worth re-emphasizing C. W. Mills's (1959) distinction between personal troubles, problems appearing more or less randomly or infrequently and which permit individualistic explanations, and public issues, problems which afflict many people systematically over time and space and therefore require not psychological but social structural explanations.

EXPLAINING RAPE: THE STRUCTURAL FEMINIST MODEL

Recognizing these explanatory and scientific precepts, feminist studies on sexual violence and aggression move in a radically sociological direction. In contrast to psychopathological models which explain rape individual-istically as a disease, feminist models link rape to the social structural conditions of inequality between males and females in violent patriarchal societies. Within this explanatory framework, male violence constitutes a socially structured mode of domination in which rape and the fear of rape produce and reproduce patriarchal social organization – sustaining female subordination to males (Walby 1990). Interacting with other patriarchal social structures, rape and other forms of male violence against women function as institutionalized (and, of course, individual) mechanisms of social control, keeping women in their place, and operate in conjunction with the state and male ideologies to legitimate and conceal male terrorism against females (Brownmiller 1975: 5; Kelly 1988: 20–42; Scully 1990; Gordon and Riger 1989). Indeed, rape is not a violation of the social order but an enforcement of it (Connell 1987: 107). Rape is not outlawed as much as it is organized, regulated, and legitimated, such that it meets male standards and beliefs about sexual access (MacKinnon 1989: 179). In sum, according to feminist research, rape and sexual violence are sufficiently systematic and persistent across space and time, with sufficiently patterned outcomes throughout the legal system, to constitute a social structure (Walby 1990: 143).

More specifically, most sociological feminist studies explain rape along four overlapping dimensions:

(1) The incidence of rape varies with the structural and cultural organization of a society; for instance, the rate of rape varies inversely with the degree of gender inequality (Baron and Straus 1989), or rape is interconnected with sexual inequality and capitalism (Schwendinger and Schwendinger 1983). According to Sanday (1981), rape-prone societies, societies with a high incidence of rape, are characterized by male domination, high levels of interpersonal violence, adversarial relations, and sexual segregation between males and females. In such societies, rape is ritually and ideologically condoned, and males express their superiority over women and prove their manhood through sexual violence. By contrast, rape-free societies, societies where rape is either infrequent or absent, are characterized by sexual equality and mutual respect between males and females. In these societies, female decision-making is valued, and women's contribution to social life is viewed as sacred and complementary to males. Blumberg, in her macro theory of gender stratification, also discussed the incidence of male violence and oppression against females in terms of structural features of social organization. She found that in modes of social organization where females control (not just participate in) substantial economic resources, and are able to translate that power into political influence, overt forms of male violence against them will tend to be restrained (Blumberg 1984: 39). Similarly, Collins (1975: 230, 1988a) notes that when economic and political power, including the organization of violence, is concentrated in the hands of males, the use of force and violence against females will be high.

(2) The second locus of rape research looks at how differential sex-role socialization generates male personality traits of aggression, force, dominance, and competitiveness, while simultaneously producing female traits of passivity, dependence, and acceptance: rape "is a logical consequence of the lack of symmetry in the way males and females are socialized in this society" (Russell 1975: 274; see also Baron and Straus 1989: 6; Scully and Marolla 1985a). The propensity for sexual violence is normatively and asymmetrically programmed into male and female personality types through distinct gender-role socialization practices, including gender segregated peer groups (Bourque 1989: 75; Johnson 1988: 110–27; Thorne and Luria 1986; C. Adler 1985) and the different interpersonal environments experienced as boys and girls develop, especially the sexual division of labor in which females provide the role of

primary caregiver in society (Chodorow 1978, 1989; also see Messer-schmidt 1986: 188). Through different interactional practices and contexts, males are socialized to compartmentalize sex, to prefer sex that is aggressive, physical, and impersonal, and to seek sex outside of a relational and emotional context. Females, by contrast, are socialized to experience sex as an emotional and intimate experience, not just or even primarily a physical one, and to prefer romance, tenderness, and consideration in a commitment relationship – to prefer sensuality within the overall quality of the interaction (Baca-Zinn and Eitzen 1990: 249–54). The male model of sexuality is conquest with orgasm, a penetration oriented, all-or-nothing standard of sexuality (Russell 1975: 272; Russell 1984: 162; Schur 1988: 147). The female model of sexuality involves sex that does not necessarily culminate in penetration. It involves affection without a sexual component, a model of sexuality encompassing a much broader range of activities – talking, touching, holding, caressing – than the limited male model (see Rubin 1983; Finkelhor 1984). Following Russell, since males and females have different sexual preferences and desires, the stage is set for a sexually aggressive and dominant male forcing himself on or pursuing a sexually passive and submissive female. Adding to this the chronic sexual ambiguity of male and female interactions, where various signals are differentially and "ethnocentrically" interpreted, the script rather systematically unfolds in divergent and antagonistic directions, a dance of complementary schismogenesis (Bart and O'Brien 1985: 92–7; Hansel 1988; Lottes 1988: 200; Muehlenhard 1989).

That an underlying normative relationship exists between coercive and consensual sex strongly militates against the claim that rape is an act of violence and not sex. While rape is violence from the point of view of a female model of sexuality, it is a *non sequitur* to claim that rape is not sexual for males (or is just physical or symbolic violence) yet simultaneously reflects normative male sexual preferences (Scully 1990: 143; Hansel 1988). As MacKinnon (1987, 1989) has repeatedly emphasized, rape and other forms of sexual aggression represent sex – and doubtless preferred sex – for many males. When sexually aggressive traits are socialized into males, such behavior becomes a means of asserting masculinity, and thereby animates our culturally generated scripts of male–female interaction (Schur 1988: 143, 187; Herman 1989: 21). As one author puts it: "That sexual violence is so pervasive supports the view that the locus of violence against women rests squarely in the middle of what our culture defines as 'normal' interaction between men and women" (A. Johnson 1980: 146). And in a very similar vein: "American culture produces rapists when it encourages the socialization of men to subscribe to values of control and dominance, callousness and competitiveness, and anger and aggression, and when it discourages the expression by men of vulnerability, sharing, and cooperation" (Herman 1989: 32). Gender is not just about difference. It is about power. Male–female differences conceal the dynamically structured relations of domination and subordination embedded in those differences (MacKinnon 1987, 1989).

(3) Rape and sexual violence against women are reproduced and legitimated through culturally mediated interpretative devices which justify, excuse, and glorify male violence against females. Rape myths, techniques of neutralization, or, more generally, patriarchal ideologies provide the linguistic rationalizations and interpretive frameworks for assessing the rape incident: for making sense of what happened, and for legitimating the sexual scripts governing male–female interactions. More specifically, these patriarchal myths severely constrain the contextual discovery and reporting of rape by blaming the victim, by limiting our perception of rape to "real" rapes, that is, to the cultural stereotype of the rapist as a violent stranger jumping out of the bushes and attacking a woman, and by rationalizing rape through culturally approved sexual scripts which define males as aggressive and females as passive (see K. Wilson et al. 1983: 244–5; Herman 1989). Additionally, there is a close correlation between these rape supportive attitudes, attitudes which portray women as sex objects, and sexual aggression against women: "Men who more strongly hold such attitudes are more likely to report sexually aggressive behavior" (C. Adler 1985: 326). Burt (1980: 223; see also Burt and Albin 1981) studied the rape supportive character of patriarchal culture in the US and found that rape myths are deeply engraved and widely supported (by males and females) in American society: "A woman who goes to the home or apartment of a man on their first date implies that she is willing to have sex"; "in the majority of rapes, the victim is promiscuous or has a bad reputation"; and "a large percentage of women who report a rape are lying because they are angry and want to get back at the man they accuse." Additionally, Kelly (1988: 35–6) and Lottes (1988: 206–12) note the proliferation of other patriarchal myths: that "women enjoy or wanted sex," that "they ask for it," that "women lie/exaggerate about rape incidents," and that "rape only happens to certain women and is committed by strangers."

In a complementary vein from the symbolic interactionst perspective, Scully (1988, 1990) and Scully and Marolla (1984, 1985a, 1985b) note how the culture of patriarchal society provides both rapists and "normal" males with accounts and situated vocabularies of motives with which to rationalize, excuse, and justify their sexual aggression against females. Put more theoretically, the misalignment between culture and action is articulated in and through socially structured and culturally approved linguistic/interpretative devices which militate against and cognitively repress the untoward, indeed criminal, interpretations of their deviant misdeeds. Just as rapists are able to justify their acts to themselves, to mollify or release moral restraints against committing such acts, so also are they able to excuse or justify their acts to others, since aligning actions such as these are not just cognitive but are also communicative and therefore conversational mechanisms for assessing actions, ascribing blame, and redistributing responsibility (Emerson 1969). Some of the techniques Scully and Marolla (1984) list are the following: "women are seductresses," luring men into sexual contact with them; "women mean yes when they say no," and "a woman's no is really a societal not a personal no"; even though women initially resist, "most eventually relax and enjoy it"; "nice girls don't get raped"; and rape is "only a minor wrongdoing."

In essence, males and females learn a cultural language and an interpretative framework for understanding their sexual interactions and for shaping their expectations about those interactions – a hegemonic cultural framework woven into the fabric of male–female sexual inter-actions, a framework through which sexual violence is legitimated and reproduced (see Scully 1990; Herman 1989; Lottes 1988; Schur 1988).

(4) Last, male violence against women is institutionalized and legitimated through the legal system of the state: the state fails to intervene against sexual violence. This position is buttressed by the following facts. Rates of attrition in rape prosecutions are inordinately high, and even when prosecuted the likelihood of conviction is very low. Russell (1984: 284) noted that only 2 percent of rapes and attempted rapes resulted in an arrest, and, of these, only 1 percent resulted in a conviction. LaFree studied in detail the attrition process of 881 reported rape cases in Indianapolis, Indiana over a period of several years. Of these, an arrest was made in only 37.2 percent (328 total number) of cases, and only 11.8 percent (104) of the total resulted in a criminal conviction (LaFree 1989: 60).

Other researchers have discovered high rates of attrition in comparison with other crimes when rape cases go to trial. Holmstrom and Burgess (1983: 238) looked at 18 tried rapes and found the following: 10 were found not guilty; 1 case resulted in mistrial; 3 were convicted of a lesser charge; and only 4 were convicted of rape. Out of 109 total rape cases, only 8 cases – 4 trial and 4 plea bargained – resulted in a rape conviction (3 other plea bargains resulted in convictions on lesser charges). These low conviction rates are quite dramatic when compared with other crimes: 51 percent for murder/manslaughter; 48 percent for burglary; 36 percent for robbery; and 26 percent for aggravated assault (Holmstrom and Burgess 1983: 240). Z. Adler also studied rape cases going to trial and found that the conviction rate for those accused of rape who pleaded not guilty and went through an adversarial trial was "abysmally low." Out of a sample of 112 defendants, 32 pleaded guilty and were convicted of rape and a variety of other sexual offenses. The remaining 80 defendants – about 71 percent – went to trial. Of these, 44 percent were convicted of rape, 7.5 percent were convicted of other sexual offenses, 2.5 percent of the cases were retried, and 46 percent of the rapists were acquitted (Adler 1987: 43, 121). Although comparative figures relating those pleading guilty in rape cases to those entering guilty pleas for other serious crimes were not available for the year Adler gathered data, she notes that in 1976:

> 60 percent of those tried for rape offenses pleaded "not guilty." The corresponding figures for other serious crime offenses are significantly lower at 34 percent for homicide, 28 percent for all sexual offenses, and 12 percent for burglary. One is tempted to conclude that offenders and their legal advisers are well aware of the fact that they are more likely to get away with rape than with many other crimes. (1987: 6)

Indeed, these routinized modes of processing by the legal system represent the institutionalized decriminalization and legitimation of rape. These social facts illuminate the operation of the law not as a gender-neutral and free-floating institution but as a socially structured and gendered component of patriarchal domination – that is, as a system of male power, as an instrument of social control (see Smart 1989).

But, given this lack of legal intervention against rape – except in a very narrow range of instances – how is patriarchy embodied in the legal system? How is the law a gender-based asymmetrical system, and how is it systematically structured so that it fails to intervene against male violence?

An answer to these questions demands a consideration of when and in what cases the legal system *does* intervene on behalf of women. The legal system is more likely to prosecute and juries are more likely to convict in rape cases with the following characteristics: when the perpetrator and the victim are strangers, and some type of extrinsic force is used; when consent, intimacy, and prior sexual history are not introduced as issues in the case; and when the victim is a "nice girl" or a virgin, and has not been drinking, using drugs, "partying," or otherwise violating traditional female gender role behavior (Holmstrom and Burgess 1983; Z. Adler 1987; LaFree 1989; Estrich 1987).

But, as we have seen, the "aggravated, jump-from-the-bushes stranger" rape represents only a small minority of actual cases (Estrich 1987). Most rapes are not "real" rapes, but "simple" ones, rapes in which the victim and assailant are acquainted or intimate, and rapes in which extrinsic force or violence is absent. In simple rapes, judging consent from nonconsent is interpreted from *inter alia* the relationship between the victim and assailant, the context of their interaction, and the prior sexual history and overall moral character of the victim. As one noted legal scholar and law professor comments: "The relationship between victim and offender and the circumstance of their initial encounter appear key to determining the outcome of rape cases in virtually very study (Estrich 1987: 18).

Moreover, when issues of the victim's prior sexual history, moral character, and credibility are raised as relevant issues in courtroom cross-examination, distinguishing consent from nonconsent is judged according to patriarchal standards. When the relationship, degree of intimacy, and interaction between victim and assailant are raised as relevant issues in courtroom cross-examination, determining consent from nonconsent is interpreted from patriarchal standards. When this happens, the female's experience of violation is disqualified, since male hegemonic ideology is institutionalized or built into the very structure of the legal system and the law (Smart 1989). This is how the law shapes the social order to legitimate and conceal male domination in society, making that order appear normal and natural. This is how the law mystifies social reality and how it functions as a form of hegemonic ideology, while simultaneously appearing objective, rational, and gender neutral at the surface. Failing to take into account the female's experience of violation, the law and the judicial system institutionalize a decriminalized position on rape. As Estrich notes, this happens through the

> judicial imposition of male standards of conduct – school boy rules – on the women victims of simple rapes. Gender neutrality suggests that rape law can be made and enforced without regard to the different ways men and women understand force and consent. That might work if the governing standards were defined by the understanding of most women. But all experience suggests that if there is only one standard, it will be a male standard. (Estrich 1987: 82)

And, in a very similar vein:

> In male supremacist societies, the male standpoint dominates civil society in the form of the objective standard – that standpoint which, because it dominates in the world, does not appear to function as a standpoint at all. . . .

The state incorporates these facts of social power in and as law. Two things happen: law becomes legitimate, and social dominance becomes invisible. (MacKinnon 1989: 237)

If a woman agrees to intimacy, for example, then in effect she consents to sexual intercourse. Because of this convergence between the law and patriarchal culture, the legal system constitutes a gendered mode of domination and a strict disciplinary regime, a system which enshrines male predatory sexual activity as the normal model of sexuality while disqualifying the female's individual and cultural experience of rape. The act of rape is, in essence, transformed into consensual sex (Smart 1989); "Rape and intercourse are not separated by any difference between physical acts or amount of force involved but only legally by a standard centered on man's definition of the encounter" (MacKinnon 1989: 150).

Thus women will not report, attorneys will not prosecute, and juries will not convict acts of rape because the definition is based on male not female standards of violation, and according to that dominant standard, the interaction between the victim and assailant appears more like consensual sex than a crime of rape (MacKinnon 1987: 88; Smart 1989); "the injury of rape lies in the meaning of the act to its victim, but the standard for its criminality lies in the meaning of the act to the assailant. Rape is only an injury from women's point of view. It is only a crime from the male point of view" (MacKinnon 1989: 180). The law is, indeed, a powerful mechanism for conferring legitimacy, and, even more than that, a form of knowledge which is exercised as strict disciplinary power.

Responding to this structural bias in the legal system, feminists have implemented rape reform statutes in an effort to lower the inordinately high rates of attrition in rape prosecutions (see Marsh et al. 1982; Loh 1981; Estrich 1987; Temkin 1986; Spencer 1987; Rowland 1985; Polk 1985). These reforms have resulted in sweeping changes in corroboration requirements, resistance standards, and past sexual history evidence in order to increasing reporting, arrest, and conviction rates and to improve the treatment of the victim in court. But rape reform was designed to be more than just instrumental in its impact on the legal system. Reforms were not only designed to recriminalize and deter rape, but to also redefine and alter cultural myths about it. Yet despite these goals, rape reforms have met with only limited success. While rape reform has had some symbolic impact on society, such legislation has not increased overall rates of convictions or plea bargains substantially, nor has rape shield legislation, which was designed to prohibit introduction of the victim's sexual history during the trial, affected defense attorneys' trial tactics (Marsh et al. 1982: 53; Largen 1985: 283–4; Polk 1985). This is quite ironic, since rape reform, especially rape shield, was designed to have an immediate and direct impact on trial proceedings, primarily by constraining the defense attorney's cross-examining powers and reducing the discriminatory and traumatic treatment typically endured by the victim on the witness stand. But as Holmstrom (1985: 194) bluntly notes: "rape reforms have not affected trials." In essence, the instrumental impact of rape reform on case outcomes has been minimal (Horney and Spohn 1991).

To summarize so far. The four interrelated explanations I have discussed above view rape as a social structural component of patriarchal domination in society. As a social structure, rape is a systematic and widespread form of sexual terrorism which functions to control and subordinate women. Far from being an isolated act committed by a few psychopathically deranged men, rape is a culturally conditioned and ideologically supported social fact, a form of social power sanctioned by the state and institutionalized into the structure of law and the legal system. The vast majority of rapes are, indeed, not violations but enforcements of the social order.

THE MISSING RESEARCH AGENDA IN THE SOCIOLOGICAL STUDY OF RAPE

Yet feminist scholars have completely neglected one area in the study of rape, one which is merely taken for granted or presumed in their studies, but nonetheless crucial for understanding and explaining the constitution of sexual violence. Let me introduce this area in the following preliminary way. Connell (1987: 184) claims a close and dialectical interrelationship exists between hegemonic masculinity (the ideology of male domination) and patriarchal violence: violence backs up ideology as ideology justifies violence (see also Kelly 1988). MacKinnon also discusses in detail a similar type of dialectical relationship between hegemony and force in relation to the law: "The law is a particularly potent source and badge of legitimacy, and site and cloak of force. The force underpins the legitimacy as the legitimacy conceals the force" (1989: 237)

I think that both these Weberian formulations are more or less accurate (see Hall 1985: 312), though MacKinnon's argument is more relevant for purposes here – if recast in a much different fashion. Her equation expresses a close connection between authority and coercion, between force and hegemony: ultimately and irremediably, the force or absence of force in rape – and, derivatively, consent or nonconsent – is shaped by and channelled through patriarchal ideology. Much more generically, the interpretation and discovery of rape are organized around the patriarchal standpoint. Hence, the force and coercion in rape are systematically concealed through the institutionalized power of the law. When closely scrutinized, however, this equation expresses and exposes more than just that there is a close connection between force and legitimacy: that force underpins legitimacy or that force packs the iron fist inside the velvet glove of consent. I think a much more radical and operational observation is necessary here, to wit: patriarchal ideology shapes our interpretation and drives the discovery of what constitutes force and absence of force, consent and nonconsent (and derivatively rape or consensual sex) in the first place.

If this is indeed true, then it follows that the next relevant question to pose is: What medium assembles and implements this hegemonic ideology? What mechanism generates and organizes the criminal facticity of rape? If rape is systematically transformed into consensual sex in the legal system (Smart 1989: 36), if rape functions systematically as an enforcement of the social order, where and how does this process occur? The criminal reproduction of rape is organized in, through, and around courtroom talk-in-interaction. More operationally, if rape is routinely and systematically transformed into consensual sex, then courtroom talk represents an excellent site for examining how the victim's experience of violence (nonconsent) is delegitimized and decriminalized in real live performance. Courtroom talk captures the moment-to-moment enactment and reproduction of rape as criminal social fact.

Researchers in sociology and related field have demonstrated that rape designates a social fact but have completely neglected the structuring mechanisms which contribute to its reproduction in the first place – how rape myths and patriarchal ideologies operate through courtroom talk to constitute the interpretative framework for discovering the interaction and relationship between the victim and assailant, that is, for discovering consent or nonconsent. That rape researchers have completely neglected courtroom talk is even more remarkable since rape reform was a direct response to abuses in the defense attorney's treatment of the victim during cross-examination, treatment which suppressed reporting and acquitted rapists when the case went to trial (Marsh et al. 1982). Although the legal system functions as a vast mode of domination, with many more plea bargains than trial cases, the criminal trial nevertheless represents the system's most public and symbolic front-stage performance (see Maynard 1984).

Virtually all rape researchers have treated talk as an unexplicated resource, but not as a substantive topic in its own right (for instance LaFree 1989; Z. Adler 1987; Holmstrom and Burgess 1983; Toner 1977;

Rowland 1985). They have treated talk as an unexplicated resource for ushering in proposals for applied legal reform, in particular, for enacting rape shield provisions, permitting evidence on rape trauma syndrome, and reducing or removing what is generically referred to as blaming the victim, courtroom rape, or rape of the second kind during defense cross-examination (Marsh et al. 1982; Heiman 1987; Borgida et al. 1987). But aside from their emotional impact, anecdotal and impressionistic glosses about blaming the victim say literally nothing about the organization of courtroom talk-in-interaction, talk through which rape is discovered and reproduced as a criminal act. As yet, no researcher has treated courtroom talk as a strict and autonomous system of disciplinary power in its own right: that is to say, as a system with its own internal logic, interacting with, yet in large measure independent from, patriarchal ideology in the rape trial (but see McBarnet 1984 as an exception). Generating inconsistent testimony, for example, functions as a generic courtroom tactic, and operates across a broad spectrum of offenses – murder, robbery, bribery – having nothing to do with patriarchy, even though drawing on patriarchal ideology in the rape trial. In a very Foucauldian way, while the legal system interacts with and draws on patriarchy in the rape trial, as it does with other social structures like class and race, it is not reducible to patriarchy, or to any other social structure, but functions instead as a distinct micro-mode of domination, a strict disciplinary system possessing an internally autonomous logic of knowledge, epistemology, and talk (see Foucault 1979, 1980). To make matters even more complex, courtroom talk, like talk in other institutional contexts such as medicine, politics, and therapy, draws on and modifies our culturally inherited linguistic and conversational practices.

This distinction between topic and resource, the "missing" research agenda of rape trial talk, has crucial consequences not only, as we have seen, on theoretical grounds, but also for the application of social policy relating to the formulation and enactment of legal legislation. I mentioned earlier that, despite the fact that rape reform was designed to have a direct and immediate impact on trial procedure, such legislation has not, for the most part, affected trials (Horney and Spohn 1991): the victim's sexual history still enters courtroom testimony (Z. Adler 1987); innuendos about her moral character and credibility still surface during cross-examination (Largen 1988: 284); irrelevant information which may prejudice and undermine case outcome still plagues the victim's days in court; boring and incantatory details of the case still resonate during the trial (Tempkin 1986: 19; Holmstrom and Burgess 1983: 210); and, perhaps most crucially, trial tactics still remain unchanged (Marsh et al. 1982: 52; Holmstrom and Burgess 1983).

I do not disagree with any of these points. I do, however, plead for more intellectual rigor and more attention to empirical research when addressing such problems. Just how do defense attorneys introduce sexual history and irrelevant information which may undermine case outcomes? How do they bring the victim's characteristics into court to subtly impugn her credibility? How is blaming the victim generated through the procedures of talk? How and why have courtroom tactics remain unchanged? For it is unclear how or why trial tactics have remained unchanged, since there has not been enough on what they look like and how they operate in finely honed linguistic performances in the first place. The "mere" recitation and incantation of "boring" details in courtroom talk, which Holmstrom and Burgess, and Largen lament, might well organize the sonorous rhythmic design found in charismatic discourse (Atkinson 1984; Drew 1990, 1992; Heritage and Greatbatch 1986). Talk rests deeply implicated when addressing such issues, as it does in discovering the relationship and interaction between the victim and assailant – as it does in constructing moral character and hence reproducing rape. Yet despite the recent explosion of research in the area of rape, researchers have not broached any of these crucial questions, much less answered them.

One last point bears re-emphasizing. Estrich (1987) and others have discussed the critical import of the interaction and relationship between the victim and assailant when discovering rape. In this regard, Loh states that:

> It is not meaningful in an empirical sense to speak of consent independently of its observed basis, and this basis consists of the actor's conduct, the victim's conduct, and the social conduct in which the act occurs. . . . Acknowledging that consent is the "crucial issue," the Code directs attention to the antecedent social relationship or contact between the parties as part of the chain of causative events leading to the offense. In other words, the prior social interaction is an indicator of consent in addition to the actor's and victim's behavioral interaction during the commission of the offense. (Loh 1981: 48)

Now social interaction as constitutive or even *indicia* of consent or nonconsent bears a bit of elaboration, for it might appear *prima facie* that the issue of consent is or should be a relatively straightforward affair. If a woman says "no" that means no. And if a male has sexual intercourse with a female despite her remonstrations to stop, then rape has taken place as the ineluctable facticity we should all like and think it to be. But the social world of law, like the less exotic worlds we all live in, is not an unproblematically factual world. The social world of the courtroom is a political, micropolitical, and, above all else, a moral interpretative reality largely organized around talk-in-interaction. For the date/acquaintance rapes under consideration in this study, rape is not – nor could it ever be – about discovering "just the facts." Facts are always constructed, always interpreted. They are alway moral. Rape is always reproduced through the constitution of moral character.

If a verdict of guilt or innocence hinged on a simple and straight-forward "yes" or "no" to the question "Was there consent?" there would be no need for trials. But the offender's "yes" and the victim's "no" to that question are only assessable, only make sense, in the context of their social interaction and relationship. And discovering that social interaction surrounding the incident (social interaction about the victim/assailant interaction and relationship) happens – is formulated, constituted, and organized – through courtroom talk. If these points are accurate, then it follows that the transformation involved in treating rape trial talk as a topic instead of a resource allows us to pose as problematic the question (put forward in apposite and succinct fashion by MacKinnon 1987:88): "does this event look more like consensual sex or like rape?" And let me hasten to add, it allows us to ask according to whose standard it looks like rape or consensual sex, and how that standard operates in talk.

In summary, the structures of talk-in-interaction generate the moral-inferential parameters which govern our interpretation of the rape incident, in particular our interpretation of the relationship and interaction between the victim and defendant, and propel, in conjunction with patriarchal ideologies, the assessment of blame and ascription of responsibility for that incident. In the criminal trial, applicability of statutes, relevance of evidence, and rules of procedures must be interpreted and enacted locally *in situ* (H. L. A. Hart 1961). Rape is reproduced through the assembly of thousands of facts which are mobilized and synchronized through the design of sequential-syntactic structures, and through the organizational network of courtroom participants, including the power relations structured into and negotiated within that network. Through artful linguistic maneuvers and elegant conversational devices, through the complex and emergent design of sequential-syntactic structures, the local (indexical) particulars about the rape incident are assembled and fashioned into powerful blame implicative inferences against the victim. In the following chapters I shall introduce the relevance of courtroom talk for discovering rape through vigorously empirical demonstrations, and, by so doing, illustrate in more general terms how talk can illuminate and recast sociology's question of social order.

2
Introduction to the Sociology of Talk

As a theoretical introduction to the sociology of talk, let me offer a few preliminary observations about talk in general, and talk and rape in particular, in a more or less informal fashion, since the relevance of either may not be transparent in any relatively straightforward sense. First, what is the warrant and import of studying talk? And second, what is the sociological relevance of such study? Both questions can be answered with a rather innocuous and ostensibly noncontentious remark: sociology ultimately studies, or at least covertly addresses, social action as it relates to the question of social order – that is, to the persistence and reproduction of coordinated patterns of activity (Alexander 1982; Alexander and Giesen 1987: 10–12; Skidmore 1979: 17–18; P. Cohen 1969: 18–34; Heritage 1984: 15; Sharrock 1979: 477–566; P. Hall 1972, 1987; Turner 1988; Cuff and Payne 1984: 25; Parsons 1937; Smelser 1986: 34; W. Goode 1986; Zelditch 1986: 108–9). I will turn to the issue of talk and social order later on, but for now I wish to broach the question of and relationship between talk and social action.

According to Jonathan Turner (1988: 4) and Peter Hall (1987: 3), the "basic unit of sociological analysis is interaction," not individual action. As I noted in the previous chapter, when a man rapes a woman, quite obviously such social interaction occurs. If and when (if she survives) she decides to report or not to report a rape, then social action occurs, for she must interpret the act committed against her as a crime, and she must also prospectively interpret the possible actions, reactions, and inactions of significant and generalized others – including the police, attorneys, and jury – as a result of her allegations. Further social action occurs as the police and medical examiners scrutinize and interpret forensic evidence, the crime scene, and the coherence and cogency of the victim's testimony;

witnesses must be interviewed, and various strands of evidence reconstructed to generate, corroborate, or undermine a particular version of the events that transpired. If the case is "founded," then interaction occurs between the police and the prosecuting attorney's office, both of which are concerned with the organizational contingencies and exigencies of their respective social positions – the organization's constraints on their actions and decisions. Consequently, the case is interpreted not only in terms of evidence but also in light of *inter alia* the credibility of the witnesses (including the victim and rapist), case load, plea negotiations, and most importantly, the prosecution's categorization of the case in terms of possible favorable or unfavorable disposition (Frohmann 1991; Sanders 1980; Warshaw 1988: 138–42; LaFree 1989). Needless to say, such interpretations operate through and occur within social interaction. Finally, if the case goes to trial, social interaction occurs between the various participants in the proceedings. As I noted in the previous chapter, central to the decision-making process in the trial is the interaction and relationship between the rapist and victim prior to and during the incident. Because of this state of affairs, a great deal of the formal judicial proceedings is organized around (1) "discovering" the interaction that occurred during the incident, and (2) moral categorization work which trial participants employ to "discover," negotiate, and secure the victim's incumbency in the categorial identity of "rapable/unvirtuous" woman, on the one hand, or "unrapable/virtuous" woman on the other (MacKinnon 1989: 175; MacKinnon 1982, 1983, 1987; Schur 1984: 150–5; Schur 1988: 184). It is in this sense that rape, as a form of social organization, is describable as a discovery. The tools for making this discovery consist of coordinated social interaction.

The point I wish to make is this. If sociology in general and the social organization of rape trials in particular involve the study of social action, it becomes glaringly transparent that such action generally, though of course not invariably, happens through talk-in-interaction.

More pointedly, talk operates in natural conversation or some other type of speech exchange system, such as classrooms, interviews, trials, to mention but a few contexts. As J. L. Austin made incontrovertibly clear, talk does not merely describe some state of affairs, nor does it simply refer to events in terms of truth or falsity. But instead, under the appropriate felicity conditions, talk *performs social action* (Austin 1975: 6): advising, accusing, blaming, pronouncing, sentencing, questioning, answering. Moving far beyond Austin, I hope to secure the finding here that the interest and warrant of studying talk for sociology, on the one hand, and the sociology of rape, on the other, is not an interest in language *per se*, but an enduring preoccupation with the sequential interlocking of social activities as the infrastructural constitution of social order (Boden and Zimmerman 1991).

Since solutions to the question of social order are orthodoxly posed as general theories of society, as interactions between large-scale or small-scale systems of groups, institutions and positions, or, more generically, in terms of consensus or conflict (Porpora 1987, 1989), the practical production of social order as an empirical question is indeed difficult to conceive, yet quite convenient to ignore (Lee 1987: 20; Sharrock and Anderson 1986, 1987: 293). In methodological – even epistemological – terms there are a number of problems with this type of analytic strategy, not least of which is the often tacit according of privileged status to theorizing, to the relative neglect of researchable materials with which to address – much less test – large-scale questions of social order. The high levels of abstraction at which these theoretical problems are routinely expressed severely limits the ability for research, and leave us hovering in a no-man's-land of indecision about the relationship between theory and research. It also doubtless reflects the dissatisfaction with which Merton (1957) grappled long ago, and addresses recent interests in the necessity of developing a social theory of data (Lieberson 1985: 229). In any event, these problems provide a *prima facie* argument for an approach to the question of social order based on an integration of theory with research materials. The questions then become, "not what data do we need to answer this question but what question can this data answer?" (Sharrock and Anderson 1987: 300). In a similar fashion, Button and Lee (1987: 3) advocate examining the "social organization of materials [data] in an attempt to describe and understand that nature."

On a theoretical and ontological level, any question of social order must address the fact that modes of domination (Bowles and Gintis 1986: 23; Porpora 1989, 1987: 118), patriarchy for instance, are organized through the categorization and normatization of action in social systems (Turner 1988; Giddens 1984; Collins 1988b). The facticity of social structure as an objectively constraining social fact stretching across time and space is achieved in mundane interactions through the categorization, routinization, and normatization of actions, actors, and relationships (Turner 1988: ch. 11; Turner and Collins 1988; Shibutani 1986: 149–50, 37–40). Shibutani has phrased this question most succinctly:

> In the study of sustaining processes we are interested in social transactions that are repeated over and over in a similar manner . . . The study of such processes centers on an interesting question: Since nothing ever happens twice in the same manner, how is such stability possible? What regularities are there in the execution of transactions in which the normative framework

does not appear to change? How and under what conditions are fairly enduring patterns of coordinated activity maintained? (1986: 27)

The production and reproduction of these relatively enduring structures involve the collaborative coordination of socially organized methods of talk to generate, stabilize, and negotiate our categorized interpretations of social actions. As taken-for-granted modes of practical consciousness, these methods of talk reflexively "avoid calling reality into question" (Collins 1988a: 285; Garfinkel 1967). In the fine-grained context of interactional processes, they crystalize the obdurate and reifying facticity that modes of domination such as patriarchy possess (Porpora 1987, 1989; Walby 1989), and structure our reigning moral interpretations to reproduce the "female fear" as a mundane yet traumatic feature of everyday consciousness and experience (Gordon and Riger 1989: 1–22; Walby 1989: 224–5).

More specifically, categorization work refers to the sociocultural methods through which members classify actions, actors, and events, and assembly unique instances into pre-existing and therefore socially structured categories (Jayyusi 1984; Sacks 1972). In dynamic, inter-actional detail, social structure is produced and reproduced through public displays of moral assessment and performance: talking normative requirements of categorial incumbency. Descriptions of the victim's and offender's actions are produced, contested, and negotiated over the course of talk-in-interaction to discover their incumbency in the adversarial pair offender/victim, on the one hand, and the standardized relational pair boyfriend/girlfriend or consensual sex partners, on the other (see Jayyusi 1984). This mundane moral order organizes our descriptive practices and our constitution of facticity.

If our descriptive practices simply corresponded or referred to some external state of affairs, if there were some one to one mapping or isomorphism between events and our descriptions of them, then our task would consist of revealing this objective order. But the social world does not operate this way. Our descriptive practices are not disinterested reports that referentially mirror or correspond to some external reality. They are, instead, intimately motivated, practical and moral actions. They are produced with an eye toward the interactional work they can accomplish: for blaming, for delivering judgments and providing infer-ences, for ascribing blame and allocating responsibility for our actions. They are thoroughly enmeshed within and chronically subject to ordinary exigencies of the task at hand, of getting the job done. The sense, facticity, and objectivity of our classifications of mundane reality are produced as the ongoing interactional accomplishments of members. As Jayyusi notes, categorization work involves:

> the detailed study of the production, use and practical implicativeness of different categorizations within the moral order . . . ones that specifically and explicitly are used to display moral standards and do moral work. Such categorization work is, clearly, descriptive and ascriptive and involves both judgmental and inferential practices . . . in the very way that certain types of activities are produced the morally implicative character of certain types of activities is being oriented to. (1984: 11)

And further, she notes that when describing actions,

> What we can observe in such instances is *intertwining of description and judgment in an integral manner* – it is not that one provides (or is provided by) a description on which one can then build a judgment of the phenomena presented in the particulars of that description; rather it is the case that the very way that a set of specifics or a single specific (hence a person) gets described is embedded in and displays judgmental work, and *moral judgmental work. Categorizations can be made to function at once as inferences, descriptions and judgments.* (p. 45, emphasis in the original)

The irremediable interlacing of and gestalt-like unity between description and moral interpretation strongly militates against the notion that courtroom participants could ever base their judgments on purely legal, technically relevant, or evidentiary information – on just the facts. What counts as evidence, relevance, or procedural propriety must be selected and interpreted by courtroom participants on a moment-to-moment basis, as actions unfold in real interactional time and in the fine-grained density of talk.

But the moral order which organizes our categorization work is not gender neutral. The moral order is organized around and driven by power. Patriarchal moral inferences are inextricably interwoven with and therefore not isolable from mundane descriptive practices. More formally, patriarchy is a hegemonic system of ideological categorizations and normative standards governing the performance – interpreting the meaning – of male/female sexual encounters. It is a hegemonic system that cloaks its subjectivity and conceals its relativity under an objective stance of gender neutrality. It is an impressive and oppressive mode of domination, a complex web of hegemony woven into the very fabric of courtroom interaction. *The rape trial is generated through an institutionally anchored and patriarchally driven system of power, a two-tiered, socially structured mode of domination that is both a resource for, and a product of, talk in action.*

Thus locating the social order in systems of interrelated activities produced by members in the course of mundane or exotic interactions is pivotal to explicating the mechanics – *the how* – of producing and reproducing stable or changing structures of social action (P. Hall 1987, 1980: 7; Giddens 1976). Ultimately, contiguous social actions – one person talking and then another in recursively modeled structures – are linked via step-by-step movements to reproduce larger patterns of social activity. The import of analyzing this infrastructural site of the practical production of social order is foundational because "at the end of the day, neither cooperation nor conflict can be managed by actors who cannot engage in coordinated activity" (Heritage 1984: 305) and because "those structures of social interaction . . . would be invariant to the revolutionary transformation of a society's institution" (Zimmerman 1978: 390).

According to Schegloff, this analytic strategy of conceiving and posing the question of social order is quite radical in its implications.

> The organization of turn-taking, of sequences, of repair, to take three kinds of organization which I believe are generic to talk in interaction . . . are social organizations of talk-in-interaction. They constitute as fundamental a social organization as there is: the one that underlies the very constitution and co-ordination of social action . . . There is another, one could argue anterior, problem of order, for which the constitution and recognition of courses of action *per se* are the central problems. (Schegloff 1988a: 97–9)

Fundamentally, the real-time analysis of social activities provides, first, a necessary corrective to the reifying tendencies of much social theory and research (Giddens 1976; Maynard and Wilson 1980), and permits, second, access to the formal properties of interaction "rather than limiting analysis to outcomes of those developments – for example, who finally 'won' an argument, or who had the 'last word' in making a decision" (West and Zimmerman 1982: 508) – as if processes could simply be "read off" from (or even bear a relationship to) outcomes.

In the rape trial context, as we have seen, a substantial body of literature has analyzed the effects of evidentiary and statutorial change in the processing of rape cases, especially the role of rape shield legislation which prohibits defense attorneys from raising issues about the victim's sexual history and similar types of irrelevant character evidence (Bourque 1989; Polk 1985; Marsh et al. 1982; Loh 1981; Estrich 1987). This literature looks at input variables such as rape shield to establish causal linkages with output variables such as increases in conviction rates, on the one hand, and impressions of judges or attorneys about the effectiveness of input and output variables, on the other. Presumably such complex linkages allow legal researchers to analyze the effects of legal change on blaming the victim, and thereby study, however indirectly, the contribution of rape trial interaction to the reproduction of gendered modes of domination.

But, as mentioned before, glib pronouncements about blaming the victim reveal literally nothing about how this practice is implemented in courtroom talk. Nor do judicial impressions about trial practice constitute surrogate data for the real live performance of courtroom action. Instead, the major question to broach is this: What are the interactional processes and discourse objects to which rape shield inputs are, allegedly, applied and through which output variables are, presumably, affected? This "black box" has, ironically, never been raised as a problematic focus of inquiry before now, being merely taken as given, even though inputs must be implemented and outputs produced in real live courtroom performances.

What would the study of rape look like, however, under the auspices of these theoretical and empirical recommendations? Since these issues are taken up in chapter 5 and 6 of the study, I offer only a brief glimpse for now. A mere cursory glance at the trial data reveals the omnipresence and omnirelevance of talk as locking on to questions of meaning – of local here-and-now definitions of the situation: questions are asked and answered; accusations are made and rejected/accepted; definitions are proffered and agreed with, modified, or rejected; misunderstandings are displayed and corrected; and objections are raised, sustained, or overruled. These and other types of sequentially occurring social actions will be found in trial talk in particular, or any spate of talk more generally.

This sequential infrastructure of talk embodies the local context for interpretation and sense-making processes. Still more accurately, each speaker's action is "doubly contextual," first because each current action is shaped by and understood in reference to the immediately prior action, as well as the large organization of conversational activities in which it participates, and second and simultaneously because each current action renews the context for producing and interpreting a fresh next action (Heritage 1984: 242). The following segment serves to illustrate this sequential interpretative sense of context.

(2.1)   Trial 1
0618   **DA:**   You were <u>attracted</u> to Brian weren't you.
0619   (5.9)

0620   **V:**   I thought he was a nice (2.3) clean looking (.) man
0621   **DA:**   He was <u>attractive</u> looking <u>correct</u>.
0622   (1.5)
0623   **V:**   °Yeah.

Though I will discuss this segment in more detail later in the study, suffice it to say here that this piece of cross-examination illustrates in a rather dramatic yet still transparent way the "context-shaped" and "context-renewing" properties of sequential actions. The response of the victim (V) to the defense attorney (DA) shifts the topic from her possible attraction to the assailant, along with the blame-inferential implicativeness such an ascription would pose, to the more neutral – less personal – assessment about his looks. But that response engenders a quick adjustment on the part of the DA as he attends to this new shift in topic. In the switch he upgrades and reformulates the victim's prior assessment from "nice clean looking" to "attractive looking", modifying her previous assessment while salvaging part of his original question, since "attractive looking" is much more inferentially blame-implicative than the more neutral "nice clean looking"; it achieves considerable categorization work for the defense attorney's competing version. The interactional task that this work serves to handle includes supporting or undermining a particular version of events. The victim's possible attraction to her assailant, or even her perception of his looks, involves categorization work specifically designed to create a disjuncture between the victim's actions on the one hand, and the requirements of normative and socially structured incumbency in the category victim on the other. But the rub is this. The fit between her actions and victim incumbency is assessed not by virtue of her standards, but according to male definitions through which rape is organized, interpreted, and legitimated (MacKinnon 1989: 182–3).

Most relevant to the points about "local" sequential interpretative context, each action is understood by reference to the larger configuration of actions which both precede and follow it and within which it participates, including the immediately prior action (Heritage 1984: 242). We interpret the victim's first response in relation to both the prior question and the rather lengthy silence preceding (and within) her first answer. The DA's second question is interpreted and understood by virtue of its placement after his previous question and the victim's response. The shift in topic, the subsequent reformulation and upgrade of the description in the next turn, and the ensuing agreement of that reformulation are interpreted, understood, and produced by virtue of sequential positioning. As it interpenetrates with formal courtroom procedure, patriarchy reproduces itself in live interactional color. In exactly this fashion sequential context provides a critical interpretative resource for the constitution and recognition of social action.

In sum, the context-shaped and context-renewing properties (Heritage 1984: 242) of each action function incrementally and processually to establish the sense of action in recursively contextualized gestalt-like processes. The meaning of each action temporally unfolds and retroactively "looks back" on this action-by-action basis. In so doing, the documentary method of action-creating-the-sense-of-context-as-context-creates-the-sense-of-action in repeating cycles of mutual elaboration operates as a fundamental sense-making practice (Garfinkel 1967: 78; Mannheim 1964; Handel 1982: 47). In the rape trial, construction of moral character, ascription of blame, and allocation of responsibility for the incident – the categorization work – are methodically and cumulatively achieved through this inferentially implicative and dialectically organized web of action sequences.

In courtroom cross-examination, in particular, much of the talk is topicalized around what was talked and – just as crucially – not talked about between the rapist and the victim prior to and during the incident. Due to its public institutional quality, talk represents the intersubjective display of discovery "artifacts," and is *indicia* of the nature of the rapist/ victim relationship, the moral character of actors, and hence the categorization of their actions, each of which, in turn, contributes massively to the sense of "what happened" during the incident.

For example and quite warrantably, "intimacy" might be assessed not in terms of subjective experience or feelings, but rather as an organization of talk – as a categorization of normatively accountable actions – with dominant male ideology embedded in and interlaced throughout such actions. Doing intimacy, doing consensual sex, or doing rape emerges from observable activities (Sacks 1985: 20) – as in the following three fragments.

(2.2)   **DA:**   ...What did you en Brian talk about?

(2.3)   **DA:**   ...Talk about what he did for uh living?

(2.4)   **DA:**   O.K. considering a ten <u>minute</u> conversation with John °before Brian arrived° (1.4) <u>What else was talked about?</u>
                    (6.7)
          V: °It was jus-° (.) conversational type things.
                    (1.4)
          DA: Well what <u>was said</u> to make you fee:::l (.) so (much) at e::ase with these two people? That you would go <u>off alone</u> with one of them?

In these examples, the cumulative sense of the victim's action – the assessment of her moral character – emerges from turn-by-turn talk, from utterances anchored in context-shaped and context-renewing sequential structures, and from conventional action categorizations which are built into or mapped on to those sequences. If the relationship between the victim and assailant is the critical interpretative resource for reproducing rape, then "what was talked about" and "what was said" – talk about talk – emerges as the primary vehicle for securing the uptake of what happened.

The selection and assembly of particulars which produce competing versions of the incident (Smith 1983: 333; also see Smith 1978) are not an uninterested "working out" of the facts. Descriptions of the incident of rape are reflexively tied to that very same incident, for the descriptive asymmetries embedded in and filtered through these sequences are markedly moral/political: the sexual behavior of the male is, for the defense, normatively appropriate consensual sex, while that very same act embodies, for the prosecution, a violently criminal sexual assault perpetrated by the male against the female. Viewed in this light, the rape trial, like other adversarial trials, is not about truth or falsity, but winning and losing. In a narrow vein, all that is available for discovering rape, intimacy, or consensual sex operates through an endogenous organization of sequential activities which assembles descriptions of the scene and conventional moral assessments of actors and their actions. In a much broader vein, whose subjectivity, the male's or the female's, "becomes the objectivity of what happened" is irremediably enmeshed in multiplex systems of power (MacKinnon 1989: 182–3).

At the outset of this section, I posed a pair of questions: what is the import of studying talk and what is the sociological relevance of such a type of study? Bearing these considerations in mind, I think that we are now in better position to offer the following hypothesis: patriarchy, as a mode of domination, is inextricably interwoven with and legitimated by what I refer to as *socially structured forms of talk*: who gets to say what, when they get to say it, and how much they get to say is contingent on and negotiated within the social organization of the courtroom system, the distribution of power among its participants, and the larger structure of patriarchy within which these actions are embedded. And if the above hypothesis is accurate, how does the notion of socially structured talk operate? In this regard, I seek to discover and illuminate how the covert practices of talk-in-interaction embody the structurational properties of domination. In a courtroom context, the constraining facticity of rape is reproduced over space and time. Patriarchy as a system of power and hierarchy (MacKinnon 1982, 1983, 1987, 1989) interpenetrates with and is superimposed on conventional moral interpretations to shape and organize our thoughts, feelings, and actions – in sum, create the meaning – about this crime. Such categorization and normatization of actions are infused in talk. Much more opaquely, I suggest that these processes conceal the hegemonic status of male ideology, treating it as objective and gender neutral, and, simultaneously, seal the sense of facticity so necessary for interpreting actions, actors, and events. Social structure is both a resource for, and a product of, this interweaving of talk, categorization, and normatization (see Turner 1988: 149–72; Giddens 1976, 1984).

More thoroughly, patriarchy as an *abstract structure* of domination is instantiated by or tracked into the *mediate organizational structure* of courtroom talk. The former, with its ideological perquisites of male hegemony, represents the social structure of domination; the latter, with its attendant differential/asymmetrical distribution of speaking rights, constitutes the institutional structure of domination. Together, both structures represent the intersection of and interaction between patriarchal and courtroom modes of domination. Much more generically and theoretically, I address the following hypothesis: *The driving coupling mechanism of socially structured talk represents the mundanely transparent operation of the duality of structure. Ascription of blame and allocation of responsibility derive from sequentially powered and patriarchally driven moral inferential practices.* I seek to explicate the underlying dynamics of this mechanism.

These abstract structures of cultural hegemony operate covertly. Since the use of force is costly and inefficient, systems of structured inequality ultimately rely on mechanisms of legitimation to maintain obedience (Kerbo 1982: 374; Della Fave 1986: 476). Put most generally, since systems of inequality do not operate automatically, various devices are employed to justify existing social arrangements. Put most specifically, women and men must be convinced that rape is morally right, that rape is casual/consensual sex, and that it constitutes not a violation of the social order but an enforcement of it (Connell 1987). As Warshaw's recent study illustrates, both men and, to a lesser degree, women believe in the moral sanctionng of victims. This state of affairs doubtless reflects the extremely low rates of reporting, or even lack of recognition that the experience is indeed rape (Warshaw 1988: 46, 50, 3) or both (Gordon and Riger 1989: 2).

In an analytic excursion into the mechanics of legitimization, Kerbo (1982: 386) very felicitously notes that for elites the "trick is to exploit non-elites without them recognizing it" (although I doubt that this process operates as an organized conspiracy). In the case of rape, how are women exploited? How is it possible that women and men fail to recognize it? As mentioned previously, the relationship between victim and assailant before and during the incident, the question of consent, and the moral character of the victim are critically interwoven with rape culture (Herman 1989), male definitions of reality, morality, sexuality, and most importantly, male power. Talk encapsulates and categorizes rape as an ambiguous act of both sex and force (Warshaw 1988: 131). It establishes the inferential parameters that are necessarily required to discriminate normal sex from the crime of rape (Warshaw 1988: 139; Sudnow 1965).

As we saw in chapter 1, the reality of acquaintance rape continues to be unknown, ignored or denied by most people, despite the fact that 70–80 percent of all rapes fit into this category (Warshaw 1988: 3, 12). That women and, presumably, men fail to identify these experiences as rape involves the interpretation of actions, a process necessarily involving talk and power. Even when such recognition occurs there are still strong constraints against reporting the act to official authorities, for as Gordon and Riger (1989: 2) note: rape "is a fear much worse than fear of other crimes because women know that they are held responsible for avoiding rape, and should they be victimized they know they are likely to be blamed." More relevant to the present study, the authors (ibid.: 57) embrace the position that the social organization of the court system contributes to the legitimization of the "female fear" as an unintended consequence of its mundane operation. Still more relevant, the "blaming" happens through talk.

In the case of rape, however, discriminating between force and legitimization indeed proves difficult, since both are collapsed into the discovery process in trial talk. In trial talk, the discovery of force and the legitimization of inequality are not isolable. As a hypothesis and therefore provisionally, the gist of this process operates as follows. First, because talk is a central device of legitimization and social control, male hegemony is largely produced and reproduced through it. Second, once force is collapsed into a discovery process via courtroom talk, it becomes reflexive to those very same discovery processes. Trial talk is the incarnation of rape. And third, since the discovery process involves legitimation of male hegemony, force, legitimization and the discovery process itself occur in a mutually elaborative and concealed moment of talk – what Sharrock and Watson (1988) refer to as action in a social structure. In this study I seek to explicate how this underlying reproductive mechanism operates.

I try to demonstrate that not only is the ideological supremacy of male hegemony threaded throughout victim cross-examination, but the talk that drives and structures such ideology in the first place is differentially and asymmetrically distributed across social position. Defense attorneys ask questions; victims answer questions. Defense attorneys set the agenda; victims follow the agenda. The concept of socially structured talk is designed to underscore the fact that such "talk tends to be structured or organized, which means that what is said, who says it, how it is said and with what effects is more or less determined" (P. Hall 1980: 25; also see Grimshaw 1981; Collins 1975). More accurately, talk is never quite determined, but rather negoitiated through the asymmetrical resources which actors bring to their encounters. Put most succinctly, I shall address how courtroom talk maps male hegemony on to formal interactional procedures, the intersecting parameter of formal and substantive mechanics of social organization.

Once talk and language are investigated as social action, *particular* social systems exhibit the hegemonic properties of social organization in process. The systematics of such processes or procedures provide empirical access to the structures of male control of female sexuality, and therefore to the legitimation processes of gender inequality. The examination of action in a social structure allows us to track the constitution of social inequality, and to see how modes of domination are negotiated and reproduced through ensembles of institutionalized methods of talking. Talk is *one* site for envisioning structure as "processual, contingent, and enacted" (P. Hall 1987: 33). But, perhaps most importantly, such an endeavor may allow us to understand how commonsense knowledge of social structure invades and organizes our individual perceptions and interpretations of reality.

In this introduction, I undertook the task of focalizing the import of talk for sociological theory on the one hand and for the sociology of rape on the other. In a sketchy way, the implications of these objectives – the organization and coordination of social action as talk-in-interaction – were spelled out and given a greater degree of prominence. Given the surge of interest in contemporary sociological theory toward integrating micro–macro levels and structure and action via structurational or meso theories (Giddens 1984; P. Hall 1987; Collins 1988b; Wiley 1988), the study of talk-in-interaction offers an empirical site to pursue these aims. This sketch has offered a glimpse of the yield.

Although such claims about talk might appear pretentious, and perhaps unwarranted, they merely complement ideas previously taken up. Some of the more interesting claims in the sociological literature include the following. Talk is "society's central institution for communication and generating understanding" (Lee 1987: 21); it constitutes "the most important vehicle of reality maintenance" (Berger and Luckmann 1967:

152); it represents the basic mechanism for socialization (Moerman 1988: 119; Heritage 1984: 235); and more substantively, it coordinates and constrains joint activity in society's basic institutions, such as politics (P. Hall 1972: 51; P. Hall 1979; Atkinson 1984), education (Mehan 1979), gatekeeping (Erickson and Schultz 1982) and, of course, legal systems (Atkinson and Drew 1979). With these points in mind, the analysis of talk is not just exotic sociology, tangential to basic sociological concerns. Rather, it is central to the production and reproduction of social structure, to the construction and objectification of social problems (Maynard 1988), and to the penetrating critique of social structure and power which C. W. Mills (1959) referred to as the sociological imagination (also see Collins 1975: 90–160).

I will return to these topics later in the chapter. But for now, starting with Erving Goffman and Harold Garfinkel, I turn to the idea that talk is an institutionalized system *sui generis* – a formal mechanics. I will then consider conversation analysis, the major progeny of their intellectual accomplishments.

THEORETICAL BACKGROUND: GOFFMAN AND GARFINKEL

In his article "The neglected situation" Erving Goffman (1972: 65) noted that talk is socially organized. It comprises a social system *sui generis*, replete with institutionalized mechanisms for *inter alia* distributing turns at talking, coordinating openings and closings of conversational encounters, repairing violations such as overlaps and simultaneous starts, and for managing the transition from one topic to another (Goffman 1967: 35).

In a contemporaneously similar vein, Harold Garfinkel (1967) coined the term "ethnomethodology" (EM) to refer to foundational studies of the interactional work/organized activities engaged in by "members" to produce the constraining social structures which are the objects of conventional or orthodox sociological inquiry. The external, constraining, quite general and stable/orderly properties of Durkheimian social facts are neither explanatory nor causal principles for Garfinkel, but are instead the indigenous accomplishments of members' concerted and collaborative social activities – occuring primarily, though not invariably, through talk in social interaction. As only he could put it:

> For Parsons Durkheim's aphorism is intact: "The objective reality of social facts is sociology's fundamental principle." . . . For ethnomethodology the objective reality of social facts, in that and just how it is every society's

locally, endogenously produced, naturally organized, reflexively accountable, ongoing, practical achievement, being everywhere, always, only,
exactly and entirely, member's work, with no time out, and with no
possibility of evasion, hiding out, passing, postponement, or buy-outs, is
thereby sociology's fundamental phenomenon. (Garfinkel 1988: 103; also
see Garfinkel 1967: vii)

That Durkheim's aphorism is steadfastly intact for EM as well as for
Parsons might seem surprising if not quite strange to many sociologists
who are enamored with misleading secondary accounts of Garfinkel's
work. Yet EM does not deny that social structure is an action-
constraining social fact. Nor does it deny sociology's study of causal
relationships between structural variables – social structure as statistical
regularities/relations among social facts. For Garfinkel, Durkheim's
objective social structure as a stable arrangement is transformed into a
procedural problematic: how is social structure achieved, and how is its
scenic objectivity accomplished? For Garfinkel, Durkheim's proposal to
treat social facts as things – as constraining social action – is in no way
contradicted by EM. The notion of social structure(s) as a causal
determinant of social action is transformed into a relentless preoccupation
with endogenous production problems: How do members make sense?
How are the formal structures of practical actions displayed and
employed as resources to produce forms of social order/organization?
For Garfinkel, Parsons's treatment of the central problem of social theory
as the existence and persistence of institutionalized patterns of interaction
and systematic relationships – the problem of order – is accepted. But
although Garfinkel accepts the problem, he totally rejects the solution:
the problem of order as the internalization of a common normative order
is transformed into analysis of the fine-grained, real-time coordination of
organized procedures of talking and social activities. Put more prosaically,
both conceptualizations of social order run together two different orders
of question: the reigning and constraining facticity of social structure on
the one hand, and the production of that facticity on the other. And if
these two are separated we are left with first, a presumption of order, and
second, a question about how that order is produced in the first place.
One takes social order as a principle; the other takes it as a phenomenon.

Ethnomethodology for Garfinkel is not, contrary to popular belief,
designed as a corrective, or competitor, or replacement or even critique of
traditional sociology. It is, instead, a foundational discipline. EM
analyzes the organizational properties of making sense, properties which
are irremediably employed in sociological and lay theorizing, but are not
studied by either (Garfinkel 1988: 108; Sharrock and Anderson 1986;

Sharrock and Watson 1988: 62). Just as Wittgenstein (1952) rejected a referential theory of meaning, but emphasized the function of activities in particular language games, so also does Garfinkel locate these organizational properties *in the internal relations between social activities.* Peyrot's ensuing remarks offer the most lucid definition of this theoretical position, in addition to being instructive for understanding conversation analytic versions of EM.

> Ethnomethodology deals with organizations of naturally occurring ordinary activities, which consists of the relations that obtain between the actions which participate in an organization. Thus, analysis is concerned with the *relation of action-to-action,* rather than with the relation of sign-to-referent. In the case of conversation, even though it is a language activity, ethnomethodology is concerned with the organization of the activity carried out through talking, not with the referent of talk. (Peyrot 1982: 269; emphasis in the original)

Unlike received versions of social order, such as found in Parsons, *inter alios,* the achievement of order and social organization is not an unproblematic given for Garfinkel. His investigations are specifically directed at the systematic methods underlying that achievement.

In their own distinctive yet complementary ways, with their own different theoretical goals and methodological devices, both Goffman and Garfinkel address in revolutionary fashion a "hitherto unknown domain of social phenomena" – the neglected situation. In so doing, both men provided the driving impulse and analytic mentality for pursuing the sociology of talk-in-interaction as a legitimate, indeed as a primordial, scientific undertaking (Schenkein 1978: 6). Moreover, this neglected situation is neither linguistic nor psychological for Goffman and Garfinkel, or for those sociologists who have pursued the program outlined by them, but is instead a realm of *socially organized activities.* In the 25 years since "The neglected situation" and "Studies," both of which outlined the programmatics of the interactional order *sui generis,* a vigorously productive/cumulative and radically empirical research program has developed within sociology pursuing the systematics of talk-in-interaction. It is the purpose of the present chapter and chapters 3 and 4 to describe that research. More specifically, I will describe, first, the theory, methodology, empirical findings, and concepts of conversation analysis (CA), plus cognate linguistic approaches to the study of talk, including the transcription techniques and methodology on which the present study is based. Following that, in chapter 5 I will illustrate how courtroom talk in the rape trial differs significantly from the natural conversation model, and represents a systematically variant speech exchange system.

CONVERSATION ANALYSIS: THEORY

In the above definition and brief discussion of EM, two terms were introduced, "member" and "interactional work/organized activities", both of which are technical, and both of which bear a bit of elaboration in the present context. "Member" does not refer to individuals, persons, actors, or more generally to any individualistic or subjective phenomenon, but refers instead to mastery of natural language.

> The notion of member is the heart of the matter. We do not use the term to refer to a person. It refers instead to mastery of natural language . . . We offer the observation that persons, because of the fact that they are heard to be speaking a natural language, somehow are heard to be engaged in the objective production and objective display of commonsense knowledge of everyday activities as observable and reportable phenomena. (Garfinkel and Sacks 1970: 342)

According to Garfinkel and Sacks, the interest in mastery of natural language leaves traditional studies of syntax, phonology, and semantics, for instance, to linguistics, and bequeaths to sociology the analytic task of discovering, describing, and explicating the formal organizational technology of talk as social action.

Following Durkheim (1982: 45, 59; Mandelbaum 1959), natural language use is envisaged as a social institution, as a system of conventionalized practices, as a social fact, and is analyzed as a topic in its own right. Conversational structures stand independently of any particular topic, of any particular configuration of interlocuters, and of any particular setting. Still more generally, they exist independently of the psychological/subjective proclivities and social attributes of conversationalists. It is in precisely this sense that such procedures constitute the formal *sui generis* mechanics – the institutionalized structural organizations – of talk (Zimmerman 1978, 1988; Heritage 1984, 1985; West and Zimmerman 1982; Schenkein 1978).

Yet still, members are agents in this interactional system. They employ these abstract/context-free conversational resources as they coordinate and co-organize temporally occurring interactional contexts (Schenkein 1978). As a local management system, members must employ these devices on a here-and-now basis. Members improvisationally manage what conversational activity to produce, when to produce it, and where, precisely, to place it. They must locally negotiate in the midst of some spate of talk current and future topics, how to change, maintain, or close topics, and which turn-taking options to withold and activate within specific micro-spatialized environments and during the split-second micro-moments of real time. And that is a morally sanctionable process. The logic of conversational action depicts a normatively accountable structure woven into the design of turns and sequences. Given a complaint, for example, a limited range of relevant next actions is empirically projected and normatively required in the next turn. Conversational organization is tightly organized. Social actions are systematically – nonrandomly – related to each other.

Relatedly, the phrase "interactional work" is designed to accentuate the fact that talk is the ongoing accomplishment of members as they transact their conversational enterprises. Conversational structures exist as systematic solutions for members pursuing various sorts of interactional tasks (Garfinkel and Sacks 1970; Schenkein 1978); for example, changing topics (Maynard 1980; West and Garcia 1988), inviting laughter and applause (Jefferson 1979; Atkinson 1984), opening and closing topics or whole conversations (Schegloff 1972; Schegloff and Sacks 1974; Davidson 1975), turn-taking (Sacks, Schegloff and Jefferson 1978), producing and designing complaints and complaint responses. These constitute technical problems that conversationalists manage through coordinated and collaborative actions. As West and Zimmerman put it:

> Conversation analysis is concerned with the social organization of conversational interaction, and conceives of the various situated manifestations of this organization as a set of methodical solutions to locally occurring technical problems that conversationalists must "solve." The orderliness of conversation is thus seen to be an achieved orderliness, an accomplishment of conversationalists on actual occasions of their talk. (West and Zimmerman 1982: 506)

Although CA investigates the systemic structural organization of talk, this does not designate a deterministic model of action, but refers instead to structures as normatively accountable frameworks oriented to and produced by members: "the normatively oriented to grounds for action and inference" (Heritage 1984: 244, see Handel 1982).

This inscrutable tension between structure and action in CA warrants several passing remarks concerning their nature. Natural conversation is not like a script which mechanically unfolds, but is thoroughly improvised by participants in systematically sustained and temporally –

moment-by-moment – aligned coordinated interaction. Therefore, since they permit orderly transformations or variations/modifications in sequential operations, the constraining and optional rules are best envisaged as *flexed opportunity structures*. These operations are necessarily vast in scope, first because rules are multiplex, which means that conversationalists may orient to different rules simultaneously, and second because they are achieved, which means that speakers can produce an array of sequential objects that can be formulated as being produced in accordance with some rule. It is, therefore, quite misleading to say that conversation systems are rule governed. Members actually produce or orient to rules; they are achievements. Rules are conventional reference points that actors orient to when solving coordination problems. If anything can be produced in accordance with a rule, then members can produce literally anything and that anything can be formulated as invoking a rule. So in social action conversationalists invoke, negotiate, and contest rules and that is then a rule for all practical purposes, for right now, maybe tomorrow, maybe next week or maybe never again. But conversation is very orderly, and routinely stable, such that options are basically conventionalized and normative.

This built-in flexibility forces us to consider talk as an abstractly structured, locally managed, and interactionally contingent option system. In conversation, members generate for one another a recursive series of options and constraints, operating and unfolding moment by moment, which channel the trajectory and shape the organization of talk-in-interaction.

Nevertheless, insofar as we speak of constraints, these are not necessarily obligatory in a grammatical-logical sense, but are morally constraining in a social fact sense. For instance and by way of contrast, there are obligatory syntagmatic and paradigmatic constraints in English regarding consonant clusters. Initially occurring consonantal clusters may have up to three consonants, the first beginning with an s, the second with a p, t, or k, and the third with an l, r, y, or w, such that we obtain split, strike, etc., but not fpl, stl, or spu. No other consonant cluster occurring in word initial position is acceptable. This is a strongly obligatory rule system, quite unlike the flexibility of talk. Lucy Suchman (1987: 80) captures this distinction in a most germane way when she notes that "the rules of conversation are neither strictly optional (their breach does have consequences) nor obligatory (they may be breached without a necessary loss of coherence). They are, however, inexorably meaningful."

To summarize, the theoretical imagery of CA pictures talk as a self-explicating and self-organizing (endogenous) system of interrelated social activities for producing the order of mundane conversation. CA is concerned with the systemic functions of and relationships between utterances and conversational objects through their positioning and participation within a sequential organization – it studies the sequential organization of natural language use (Heritage 1984; P. Atkinson 1988). Conversation analysis is the study of natural language in use as an internally organized and socio-sequentially structured system. Instead of focusing on the substantive/content particulars of some spate of talk, CA analyzes the invariant/transsituational properties of talk, which structure the particulars of any conversational encounter. These properties are the socially structured, not psychic, generating mechanisms for producing orderly talk-in-interaction.

Following Schegloff, the central problem of order in CA consists of the constitution of social order, the endogenous coordination of social action. In this analytic maneuver, the structural organization of sequential activities and objects is "analytically isolated" from the "what was said, by whom, and on what occasions" – socially structured talk – type of questions which we sociologically (and commensensically) pursue as the interesting topics about talk (Sharrock and Anderson 1987: 316). As mentioned previously, talk is not studied to gain access to other phenomena, but the formal structures of talk are elevated to topics in their own right. This excavation of "formal" from "substantive" mechanics of social organization does not preclude investigations into the interaction between social structures, such as race, gender, and class on the one hand, and conversational structures on the other. It does, however, extricate the relevance of the former for the latter in order to "examine pure turn-taking and conversational phenomena" (ibid.). A premature injection of socially structured or exogenous attributes on to conversational structure is eschewed, yet their possible points of articulation are not thereby rejected, merely superseded by demands for precise specification and explication of such interrelationships (Schegloff 1987, 1991; Zimmerman 1988).

This study is specifically such an exercise in articulating social and sequential structure. Employing this framework, I plan to demonstrate how courtroom talk contributes to the ongoing production and repro-duction of social structure, to the facticity of modes of domination, and to the phenomenon of rape as a source of structural constraint. Rape as the social organization of trial talk exists and persists as actors enact social structure in structurally driven and sequentially organized methods of talking. Ideology and power are harnessed and then riveted into situated actions as seen but unnoticed structural properties of social systems – as modes of practical consciousness – through the interaction between socially structured and sequentially organized forms of talk. In order to prepare for such an undertaking we need to explicate and illustrate in considerably more detail the mechanics of CA, the preoccupation with endogenous social organizations, and, perhaps just as important, the departure from meaning as reference – the mesmerizing yet fleeting lure which poses severe obstacles for achieving even a sense of what CA is about (see P. Atkinson 1988).

An empirical illustration and theoretical reprise

Discussions of CA possess an excruciatingly dense, if not inscrutable, character, which threatens to bog down entire analytic movements in conceptual mud right from the start. An unwieldly thicket of terms and phrases – referred to as devices, mechanisms, systematic functions, conversational objects, machinery, structures, rules, resources, procedures, sequences, activities, and self-explicating and endogenous organizations – are used more or less interchangeably to reveal the constitution of talk as a systematically produced, socially organized achievement. The following illustration is designed, therefore, to clarify the jargon with a look at some fairly mundane materials. Following that, I will return to sketch the methodological contours of CA modes of analysis.

As a start, consider the following conversational exchange, edited here for convenience and ease of exposition.

(2.5)

1	**A:**	You can't ever make up your mind and you
2		<u>DO</u> this all the time
3	**B:**	All you ever do is BI(h)chhh all°the time- you=
4		[ ]
5	**A:**	<u>ME</u>:::
6	**B:**	=bi(h)tchh at me about everything and you like to (0.2)
7		∞<u>BI</u>(h)chh <u>BI</u>(h)chh <u>BI</u>(h)chh∞((∞ encloses utterances that are mimicked with +nasal))
8	**A:**	<u>I</u>, DO NOT...

In *Forms of Talk* (1981: 43) Erving Goffman makes a distinction between a reply, an utterance that refers to the state of affairs formulated in the prior utterance, and a response, an utterance that refers to some other aspect of or presupposition embedded in the prior utterance (also see Goffman 1983). Similarly and more substantively, Harvey Sacks (1967: 11) notes that when making a complaint it is systematically possible that the next utterance may address not the topic of the complaint, but the act of complaining itself instead. And Robert Emerson (1969: 167) observes that when making an accusation, "actors open up their own motives, character, and action for assessment and review, with the distinct possibility that they will be found wanting." Complaints, accusations, denunciations and the like create an interactional groove for a return complaint as a complementary next action (also see Watson 1978).

Bearing these points in mind, a more technical and systematic appreciation of this interactional process is in order. The above segment portrays a type of conversational sequence in which the complaint is prior to and sequentially implicative for a second complaint in the adjacent turn, the former being a complaint by speaker A against speaker B, the latter being a riposte by speaker B against speaker A. Of special interest is that the second complaint parries the first by complaining about it; that is to say, it constitutes a mitigation/rejection and complaint simultaneously, both packaged within the same utterance and both delivered within the same turn.

The class of complaints epitomized by B's complaint – formally characterizable as a complaint about complaining – represents an elegantly designed and multiplex conversational strategy in which the impact of a prior complaint is mollified and its texture of relevance altered by topical and interactional transformations performed on it. That is, while one aspect of the prior complaint – the state of affairs it is predicated on or the complainable – is topically deleted, another aspect – flaws concerning the actions, motive, or character of the complainant – is taking up, is endowed with topical import, and is turned into a sequentially implicative object in its own right. As a consequence, the original complainant gets inveigled or finessed, as it were, into responding to the complaint about complaining, and thus abandoning pursuit of the prior complainable.

Now this is just one of the many options available when responding to a complaint, for B could have conventionally exploited an excuse, an apology or a rejection. To complicate matters more, the complaint about complaining (CAC) is merely a gloss for a number of devices routinely and warrantably subsumed under its auspices. Hypothetically, B could have responded to the prior complaint with a member "species" other than the "habitual" formulation. Some of the other members of the CAC device include: formulating the prior utterance as a complaint with an ulterior or malicious motive, such as "you're just complaining about his teaching because he won't go out with you"; formulating the prior utterance as a recusant complaint, such as the famous "nobody's complained but you"; and formulating the prior utterances as a sanctimonious or hypocritical complaint, such as "if you had worn a longer dress, you wouldn't have been raped."

More formally, the CAC is a quite general or transituational conversational device, which I refer to as a *topic slift*; it lifts the relevance of a reply to topic and slips in a response to flaws concerning the actions, motives, or character of the complainant in and through formulations (see Goffman 1981). As a member of the class of topic-changing devices in natural conversation, topic slifting constitutes a quick topic switch.

The device is a transituational or context-free mechanism. That is what I referred to as conversational structure. Structures exist independently of the context, identities of participants, and topic under consideration. As a structure, the topic slift is subject de-centered, and represents an underlying device, existing only in its instantiation. But this generating structure must be employed by members to achieve orderly talk. When activated it accomplishes an array of interactional tasks. The device changes topics, shifts blame and resonsibility, formulates the topic or action, switches defensive to offensive positions, and expands the sequence. It produces a realignment shift whereby A is now positioned as blame recipient, while B assumes incumbency as blame allocator, with its strategic advantages and perquisites. Even in such interactional conflict and disagreement, members coordinate and improvise their actions to maintain a constant state of alignment – to sift through and lock on to one of the multiple threads of relevance and weave together a mutually intelligible strand of action.

The topic slift represents one device for illustrating the relationship between actions which we discussed in some detail earlier, and describes how rules are actually employed in interaction. The CAC demonstrates how members do things with rules (or do things with felicity conditions), and coordinate the relevance between their joint actions. Put most prosaically, given a complaint, a potential next action consists of giving a rule for not replying to the complaint, and for responding to, for instance, the "chronic" complaining instead: "you complain all the time." Conversation is orderly, even though members operate on quite different levels of relevance, as they break and reform frames (see Goffman 1981: 43).

Of course, whether a topic slift succeeds or fails to accomplish a particular task, such as changing the topic, is an interactional matter, for the contingent nature of talk means that a CAC might inherit a response as a sequel and not a reply, such as "that's a non sequitur if I ever heard one." Thus rules are invoked, negotiated, and contested, and these are inherently interactional phenomena *from a conversation analytic perspective*, not structures. The rules or devices for generating conversation, such as topic slifts, are underlying structures, regardless of whether or not they are activated and regardless of substantive outcomes.

The CAC is embedded in an organizational sequence of activities, a microsystem in which it is placed and through which it participates, and interacts with other aspects of that organization. Some of the artfulness of that organization can be observed if we note that in order for a complaint recipient to employ the CAC he/she must possess recipient-designed knowledge of the complainant or the complainable to apply a slift, as the following illustrates.

(2.6a)

1	**A:**	...I can't understand the prices we're payin for gas even at the
2		discount places
3	**B:**	Complain Complain Complain
4		(1.2)
5	**A:**	uh- wh- Huh:::?

Prima facie absence of recipient-designed knowledge of the complainant blocks members from exploiting the constraints, for not only is the silence in line 4 inferentially implicative as "trouble," the two quick cut-offs and the stressed repair initiator "Huh?" from A are even more dramatic indicators of serious problems in B's CAC as well, since there is simply no way B can know of A's complaining behavior (radio call-in talk show).

In a very transparent sense then, the rule of application for doing topic slifting requires recipient-designed knowledge of the complainant, his/her actions, motives, character, or all of the aforementioned. Despite the rule's initial and impressive attraction, however, its scope and power are seriously undermined, indeed, even imperiled, once we scrutinize the prior sequence as it unfolds.

(2.6b)

6	**B:**	...People have been complaining about that all day. On and on ..
7	**A:**	...Uh Huh what do you think about skylab falling?

Notice that the CAC in line 3 treats A's complaint as the "last straw," as it were, in a long litany of contiguous complaints: the most recent instance of that long litany. More formally, it constitutes an *achieved saturation threshold*, a conversational resource that creates the felicity conditions and context for its own use and constrains what devices can be exercised in next turn. Thus the recipient design rule can be circumvented by a *depersonalized topic slift*, so that the complainant is not a unique complainant, nor even a bona fide one, but merely a category co-member of those who complain about a particular topic.

This brief sketch of complaint sequences in no way distinguishes the complexity of the conversational structures under consideration. It is, hopefully, illustrative of the theoretical and explanatory issues dealt with at the outset of the chapter. Just as germane to that endeavor, the sense of each action does not have to reach outside of the sequence in reference to some corresponding state of affairs out in the world. The sense these activities possess is not only self-explicating, but also self-organizing: the relationship between actions is constructed and designed out of conventional properties of utterances and sequences, not from exogenous variables outside of the talk. Put another way, CA is interested in how the formal *sui generis* technology of talk constitutes and organizes local conversational contexts: how actions are designed, recognized, and oriented to by participants, and how mutual intelligibility is achieved as participants provide one another with resources and constraints for producing and interpreting action (Pollner 1979, 1987; Sharrock and Anderson 1986: 67–8; Atkinson and Drew 1979: 30–1).

This endogenous organization of activities replaces meaning as reference and/or subjective experience, an analytic maneuver strongly influenced by and reminiscent of the later Wittgenstein. Sharrock and Anderson go on to capture the flavor of this analytic strategy:

> Conversation analaysis is . . . more concerned with utterances than with speakers and hearers. It is much less concerned with talk as a relation between persons than it is with conversation as a relation between utterances. It is . . . devoted to examining the ways in which utterances can relate to one another, with the ways in which utterances can make up interwoven patterns and with the ways in which utterances, in their interrelation, build up those patterns (Sharrock and Anderson 1986: 68)

Thus conversation analysis offers a distinct analytic strategy for the study of naturally occurring interaction, for studying *not why* some particular action was undertaken but *how* the systematic nature of talk-in-interaction emerges from and is generated by structural mechanisms, as Sacks's remarks illustrate, "The idea is to take simple sequences of conversation and tear them apart in such a way as to find the rules, techniques, procedures, methods . . . that can be used to generate the orderly features we find in the conversations we examine" (Sacks 1984b: 413). For Sacks, the discovery and explication of the technology of conversation is a movement towards an "empirically based grammar of natural conversation" (Schenkein 1978: 3), not in a causal or predicative sense, but in an explanatory framework based on the generating mechanisms and machinery that accounts for the orderliness of talk. Having recognized this, we can now proceed to develop a description of the methodological precepts designed to accomplish that task.

3
Methodology and Data Collection

Having abandoned the theoretical question of order and taken up instead the empirical question of the practical accomplishment of order, what methodology governs the task of such an undertaking? If the objective facticity of social order is no longer sociology's fundamental principle but instead sociology's primary phenomenon, what data are required to locate and track the methods of practical reasoning that produce a sense of social order and sustain the mutual intelligibility of social actions? Since these methods are institutionalized, there must be publicly displayed and collectively shared conversational resoruces for generating the orderliness of talk-in-interaction. And, moreover, if these structures of social actions are instrumental in the endogenous constitution of context, exogenous factors which are superimposed on interactions bear an unknown relationship to those very same interaction processes, which militates against scientific description/explication. It follows, then, that observation as a basis for theorizing is a prerequisite for a natural observational science of interaction (Sacks 1984a, 1984b; Zimmerman 1988).

The impact of such methodological strictures means that in practice "no detail of interaction can be dismissed *a priori* as insignificant or irrelevant" (Heritage 1989: 22). If that is indeed the case – and there is a great deal of evidence to suggest that it is – then only a technique which preserves even the most minute order of interactional detail would suffice. These constraints on data collection restrict CA to the use of audio and/or audio/video recordings of naturally occurring conversations in conjunction with detailed transcriptions of those recordings. This radical hyper-empiricism (Collins 1981a, 1981b) epitomizes the ontological and epistemological privileged status of observable data (see Keat and

Urry 1982: 19): it can be repeatedly analyzed in detail; it can be subjected to replication, modification and verification; and it can provide readers/ analysts with direct access to "uncontaminated" or "pre-filtered" data.

The data-driven approach of CA overcomes the limitations of traditional techniques of data collection in social science: (1) the use of memory, recollection, and intuition; (2) the idealization of premature or pre-specified categorization and experimental design; and (3) the pre-selected, pre-interpreted, and unexplicated descriptions of traditional ethnography (Atkinson and Heritage 1984: 2; Atkinson and Drew 1979: ch. 1; Heritage 1984, 1985). In contrast to these techniques, the microscopic analysis of original materials captures the process of interaction as the temporal unfolding of successive actions, not as end products, and reveals *how* something is said, not just *what*. Social action operates in this fine-grained detail. There is simply no way to capture with scientific precision, for example, the richly detailed and densely layered texture of talk in the rape trial through field notes, memory, recollection, interviews, or pre-specified coding schedules because the details of live interaction are "hidden by real time and ordinary sensibilities" (Schenkein 1978: 3).

Since a recording "freezes" time, as it were, analysts can repeatedly review/scrutinize interaction, resurrecting those details in unprecedented molecular levels of analysis. In fact, as both Heath (1986: 4) and Heritage (1984: 311) observe, just as the invention of the microscope led to a scientific revolution in biological science, the use of both audio and audio/video recordings in CA has yielded discoveries of social organization that were inconceivable 20 years ago, and in so doing has yielded a penetrating glimpse at the bedrock level of social structure.

Less spectacularly, CA is interested in what people actually do, in opposition to analysts' constructions or interpretations of what they do. Such a methodological stricture preempts the use of surrogate evidence for naturally occurring activity, as Goodwin notes:

> a consistent problem in the study of interpersonal communication has been the location of appropriate units for analysis. In general the objects participants within interaction in fact construct, such as actual utterances, have not been made the primary subject of analysis. Rather these objects have been transformed into other objects through the use of a category system. Analysis has then focused upon relationships between these categories rather than upon the phenomena emerging within conversation in the first place. (1989: 100)

And, further:

Instead of coding turns at talk as a way of investigating the characteristics of groups . . . conversation analysts focus on the process that makes such coding possible, the way in which human beings coordinate the talk of separate individuals through *turn taking*. (p. 89; emphasis in the original)

For the founder of CA, Harvey Sacks, the empirical and objective nature of data analysis is the necessary prerequisite for the scientific advancement of sociology as a natural observational science. In fact, the case could be argued that Sacks was more concerned with emulating natural science than with studying natural conversation. Consider the not too thinly veiled allusion in the following remarks, worth quoting at length.

my research is about conversation only in this incidental way: that conversation is something that we can get the actual happenings on tape and that we can get more or less transcribed; that is, conversation is simply something to begin with . . . I figured that sociology could not be an actual science unless it was able to handle the details of actual events, handle them formally, and in the first instance be informative about them in direct ways in which primitive sciences tend to be informative – that is, that anyone else can go and see whether what was said is so . . . Such materials had a single virtue, that I could replay them . . . It was not from any large interest in language or from some theoretical formulation of what should be studied that I started with tape-recorded conversations, but simply because I could get my hands on it and I could study it again and again, and also, consequently, because others could look at what I had studied and make of it what they could, if, for example, they wanted to be able to disagree with me. (Sacks 1984a: 26)

This is little more than tantalizing speculation, however, much beyond the scope of this study to address but parenthetically. Yet it clearly illustrates and tracks the logic of Sacks's methodological position as it interpenetrates with current CA practice (see P. Atkinson 1988). More relevant to my interests here, this system of data-driven analytic induction *informs* the methodology and data collections techniques of the current study. Yet while Sacks's methodological precepts inform this study, I find them inadequate for the study of social structure and power – a critical position I develop later in this chapter.

DATA COLLECTION AND TRANSCRIPTION TECHNIQUES

The transcription techniques illuminate the sequential properties of talk, for it is sequences and the component parts within them that are the basic units of analysis in CA (Heritage 1984; Zimmerman 1988). The concept of sequence simply means that contiguous social actions bear some form of nonrandom relationship to one another, beyond that of serial occurrence or temporal succession (Sacks 1987: 54; Schegloff 1988a: 114). By the same token, still larger forms of conversational organization are created through the successive layering of these temporally unfolding sequential actions.

The data for the present study consist of approximately 2,500 pages of court transcripts of actually occurring rape trials, and one full-length trial on reel-to-reel tape. The following is a brief summary of the trials included in the study. I have simply listed them as trials 1, 2, and 3, thus making reference more convenient for readers who wish to check case disposition or details when encountering an analysis of a particular data extract in the text.

Trial 1 People of the state vs. defendant 1979
The victim and assailant met outside the parking lot of a bar after closing time, and since they left together, I refer to this (loosely) as an acquaintance/pick-up rape case. The defense attorney is an experienced and charismatic criminal attorney in the particular area, while the prosecuting attorney (PA) is an assistant to the chief prosecutor. The trial is on reel-to-reel tape, and consists of the entire trial from jury selection to sentencing. Tapes were made by the state during the trial and run for approximately 20 hours. I transcribed the extracts of the tapes found in the text. Most of the analyses presented in this study come from this particular trial.

Disposition of the case: Acquitted of rape; guilty of robbery ($6.00); guilty of unlawful restraint (technically, a misdemeanor charge defined as knowingly and without legal authority detaining another person).

Trial 2 People of the state vs. defendant 1, defendant 2, and defendant 3 1977
Two females in a car were picked up by a group of nine males in two cars at a gas station, then driven to a remote wooded area and raped/sodomized. The trial consists of three of the males involved in the

rape, three defense attorneys, and two prosecuting attorneys. One of the prosecuting attorneys is the chief prosecutor, and one of the defense attorneys is the same one who won for the defendant in trial 1. Defined loosely, this is a pick-up/acquaintance type rape. The trial runs from jury selection to sentencing, and consists of six volumes of trial transcript covering approximately 1,700 pages of testimony. The trial is captured on official state transcripts only. Thus there is no tape recording of this trial.

Disposition of the case: All three defendants guilty of rape and deviant sexual assault.

Trial 3   *People of the state vs. the defendant 1980*
The victim, who was hitchiking, was raped after being picked up by the defendant. The trial runs approximately 500 pages of testimony, from pretrial motions to verdict. Jury selection is omitted from the transcripts. The trial is captured on official state transcripts only. No tape recordings of this trial are available.

Disposition of the case: Acquitted of rape.

The data are public access and have been provided by a large mid-Western US state. Even though the data are public access, I have changed the names of the victim and accused and some place locations in order to protect the privacy of those participants. I have transcribed approximately 100 pages of the reel-to-reel tapes using the transcription techniques developed by Gail Jefferson (see Schenkein 1978) and currently employed in CA, taking approximately 50–60 hours to transcribe one hour of tape. The transcription symbols constitute a modified orthography that captures talk as it sounds to the hearer, that is, how a lexical item is pronounced rather than the way it is written, and a set of conventions for displaying social actions and utterances in a naturalistic/qualitative fashion (see Schwartz and Jacobs 1979). According to Schenkein (1978: xi), transcript design produces a "reader's transcript – one that will look to the eye how it sounds to the ear."

I have developed two more symbols for the present study, one for clicks and one for mimetic components, both of which are presented below with the rest of the transcription conventions. The following makes use of the conventions in Button and Lee (1987), Atkinson and Heritage (1984) and Schenkein (1978).

TRANSCRIPT SYMBOLS

Simultaneous utterances

Double brackets denote utterances that begin simultaneously.

> **DA:** Right?
> =[[
> **PA:** Objection your honor

Continuous utterances

Equal signs denote no gap between one utterance and the next.

> **V:** No=
> **DA:** =But she drove right across some strange people's lawn didn't she?

Overlapping utterances

Single lefthand brackets mark the point where one speaker's utterance starts to overlap with a next speaker's utterance. A single righthand bracket may be used to indicate the end of overlapping talk.

> **DA:** (So) the word <u>pardying</u> (.) les go pardy, something like that ( ) correct? <u>not just go to uh pardy</u>=
> **V:**   [   ]
>   °mmhmm

Intervals

Timed intervals within or between utterances are marked in parentheses to indicate seconds and tenths of seconds. A period enclosed by parentheses indicates a gap or silence of a tenth of a second or less.

> **DA:** You were <u>attracted</u> to Brian weren't you.
>   (5.9)
> **V:** I thought he was a nice (2.3) clean looking (.) man.

Prolongation, cut-offs, volume, and stress

Colons are used to mark words or sounds that are prolonged or stretched. The length of the stretch is indicated by the number of colons. A dash indicates a cut-off/stop sound or word. Underlining is used to indicate stress or emphasis in a word, and capital letters are employed to indicate words, sounds, or utterances with increased volume.

> **DA:**   Did he force you to get in- to his automobe::l in the parking lot?
>
> **DA:**   <u>WHY</u>::::
>
> **DA:**   WERE the <u>ITEMS</u>

Where several words are stressed continuously then there is no break in the underlining. If the words are stressed in a staggered fashion there is a break in the underlining.

> **PA:**   <u>what she remembered</u>
>
> **DA:**   <u>WHAT WERE THE ITEMS</u>

A degree symbol (°) is used to make words or portions of an utterance that are spoken at considerably lowered volume compared with surrounding talk.

> **V:**   °No
>
> **V:**   °Yeah

Intonation and rapid delivery

Punctuation marks refer to intonation not grammatical features. A question mark refers to rising or upward intonation, not necessarily a question. A comma refers to continuing intonation, and a period indicates a stopping fall in contination.

> **DA:**   Did'ju know where Brian <u>worked</u>? when you left the parking lot that night?

Portions of an utterance produced at a faster pace than surrounding talk are marked with "greater than" and "less than" symbols.

DA: <u>WHAT HE WAS ABOUT</u> >except that he was good looking<

Audible aspirations and inhalations

Audible aspirations (hhh) and audible inhalations (.hhh) are marked in the portions of the utterance in which they occur.

J: =Yeah- uh- uh- (hhh) no- ah- ...

DA: (hhh) (1.0) Are you telling me that you...

Mimetic components and clicks

Utterances that are mimicked with +nasal are indicated with enclosed (†), and utterances mimicked with −nasal are indicated with enclosed ({ }). Dental or alveolar clicks, often indicated by the "tut tut" or "tch! tch!" sign of disapproval, are indicated by [C].

DA: Now what ha- (1.1) [C]...

Other transcription conventions

Transcription difficulties/doubt are indicated by parentheses enclosing a blank space ( ) when the word, sound, or utterance is inaudible, or by parentheses enclosing the word, sound, or utterance which is doubted.

DA: (then did)

Double parentheses indicate a description of a sound or activity.

((cough))

((audience laughter))

Arrows draw the reader's attention to a specific utterance in a sequence.

→V: I thought he was a nice (2.3) clean looking (.) man

Speaker designations

The following are used:

Judge = J
Victim = V

Defendant = D
Defense attorney = DA
Prosecuting attorney = PA
Court reporter = CR
Witness = W

CRITICAL NOTES ON THE DATA AND DATA COLLECTION

More than anything, the major merit of conversational data is this: it allow us to analyze the structuration of social reality in fine-grained processual detail and to track the moment-to-moment reproduction of the social order. Moreover, conversational analytic methodology and data collection techniques are designed to uncover the transcontextual properties of interaction, and to transcend the more orthodox socio-linguistic research agendas centered solely around linguistic variations, such as class or geographic location, and other exogenous variables like speaker personality and context. Although this approach to data indeed possesses certain built-in limitations, we need to be careful with criticisms that CA ignores context – or possesses a more or less cavalier disregard for it. Consider a classic piece of sociolinguistic dialogue between Dr Poussaint, a black physician, and a white policeman in Mississippi during the early 1960s (see Ervin-Tripp 1969: 91–165; and Schwartz and Jacobs 1979: 345).

Policeman:	What's your name boy?
Dr Poussaint	Dr Poussaint, I'm a physician ...
Policeman:	What's your first name boy? ...
Dr Poussaint	Alvin

While certain aspects of social structure and context – race, power, class, and history – appear relevant in this extract, ostensibly being imposed on the action from the "outside" as it were, the talk itself forms the relevance of these social categories and serves as a vehicle for their imposition. The context is actually being reproduced, negotiated, and contested in the talk. More accurately, context and talk are not two separate entities, where one or the other exerts some primary or independent influence on the other, but exist in a dialectical or mutually elaborative moment. To continue with a couple more illustrations, a professor illuminates the dominational reality of classroom context and its formal status when he/she addresses a student with an informal first name yet insists on receiving a formal address term like "doctor" or "professor" in return (or invokes the rules for address in the first place: when the professor insists on reciprocal exchange of informal first name address terms). And the same is true of courtroom talk. Talk and the legal institution context mutually elaborate each other when, for example, attorneys ask questions and witnesses on the stand answer them but not vice versa. More formally, the notion of speech exchange system captures the sorts of asymmetrical relationships and distinctive properties embodied in particular contexts – interviews, courtrooms, classrooms – yet still concentrates on the "bottom-up" reproduction of context.

LIMITATIONS OF THE DATA BASE AND FOCUS OF THIS STUDY

As I have mentioned, talk functions as a major symbolic medium through which culture operates, and through which meaning is shaped (Schwartz and Jacobs 1979: 349; Fine 1990: 128–9). As such, it offers a focal site for studying the enactment and negotiation of gender categorizations embedded within the patriarchal order. Turning to the legal order, I also operate under the assumption that language does not just passively refer to but actively constructs social reality, and since the legal system uses language, it by implication also involves the social construction of meaning. The legal system involves the social construction of facticity. As I have also mentioned, CA offers one of the most sophisticated and accurate methods of analyzing talk-in-interaction. Employing a conversation analytic approach to the data, I am primarily interested in capturing depth of insight into the social organization of rape trial discourse mechanisms, and the methods of classification/categorization of actors and their actions, rather than gross coverage of the data. I am interested in explicating the performance and reproduction of modes of domination through courtroom talk-in-interaction.

To be sure, conversational materials furnish an important method of analyzing the performance of domination, but such materials are not comprehensive enough, and anything beyond an exploratory study of this sort would need to include other types of data gathered from a variety of contexts: in-depth interviews, participant observation, and even experimental and laboratory findings. A study analyzing the performance of domination, and relying exclusively on a narrow range of conversational materials to do so – no matter how intensive and comprehensive – is still limited by several factors.

(1) Comparative analysis of other speech exchange systems. Many properties of courtroom talk are found in other contexts, including not just natural conversation but other formal systems such as classrooms, news interviews, and political speeches. Although I make reference to the relations between courtroom talk and other speech exchange systems, a much more comprehensive comparison from data employed in these contexts would be necessary before making more definitive claims (see Clayman 1989). Even more comprehensively, other trial contexts involving different types of crimes and civil suits would warrant analytical scrutiny and comparison, especially to disentangle the distinctive properties of patriarchal ideology from courtroom disciplinary practice.

(2) Nonverbal aspects of courtroom interaction. While some nonverbal and paralinguistic phenomena are available through courtroom tapes and transcripts of those tapes, including silence and intonation, a number of these relevant properties of courtroom interaction are simply lost without more sophisticated audio/video techniques: gaze, head nods, posture, dress, evidence displays, and body and facial synchronization between participants. The appearance of both the victim and defendant in court is also relevant to the discovery of rape. Dress length and style, bra or no bra, and weight are espcially relevant. In trial 1, for example, the fact that an attractive man was charged with raping an overweight and unattractive woman appeared to have some bearing on case disposition.

(3) Limitation of the study to rape cases of the date and/or acquaintance type. All of the trials in this study are limited to acquaintance, date, pick-up, or hitch-hiking types of cases. Thus generalizations may be limited to these rape categories and may not apply across the full spectrum of rape cases – stranger, marital, or statutory rapes. As Russell (1984) and Koss (1988) have noted, however, most rapes fit into the category of date and acquaintance type rapes, making the current data set representative of the vast majority of rapes.

(4) The contribution of ethnographic particulars for reproducing rape are irretrievable for inspection. Distal circumstances originate outside of the local production site of the trial yet still influence the course of local trial interaction (Mehan 1987: 293). Proximal circumstances, on the other hand, consist of structures which emerge out of the local production of interaction. Together, both distal and proximal circumstances contribute to the structuring of rape trials, and capture the structuring relevance of factors both inside and outside the immediate local productional site. For instance, the chief prosecutor may delegate a "bad" case, a case which has

a poor possibility of conviction, to a less experienced assistant, and may choose to invest a minimum amount of resources for such cases. In such distal circumstances, an experienced criminal defense attorney would have a clear advantage over the prosecution compared to those cases in which the chief prosecuting attorney directly devotes time and resources to winning a conviction. Two of the trials in this study illustrate this possibility. The chief prosecutor in the large midwestern county where these trials take place is a nationally recognized prosecuting attorney, having recently won a conviction in a famous murder trial. Additionally, several circuit court judges and criminal attorneys have stated to me that this prosecutor is an impressive and imposing figure in the courtrom. In trial 1, the case was delegated to an assistant prosecuting attorney, and subsequently lost to an experienced and charismatic criminal defense attorney. In trial 2, the chief prosecutor handled the case directly, and won against the very same defense attorney who won an acquittal in trial 1 (though there were other defense and prosecuting attorneys as well). These ethnographic particulars are only illustrative (in a very impressionistic way) of the proximal/distal distinction, yet highlight an important and inherent limitation of conversational materials (see Mehan 1987).

Another issue worth raising from a more participant observation direction is this: the formal study of talk focuses on overt or public displays of understanding but ignores many covert categories and subjective interpretations found in traditional ethnographic interviews, interviews which could bolster the evidence from conversational materials. For example, judges and attorneys decide the permissibility and relevance of various topics prior to formal trial proceedings during pretrial motions. This data remains unavailable for inspection since it is not included in the trial tapes. In one rape trial (not included in the present data set), for example, an unmarried victim was obviously pregnant but the defendant was not the father. During pretrial motions the prosecution agreed that while the defense could bring out the fact that the defendant was not the father of the victim's child, they could not broach her marital status: that she was unmarried. Despite this constraint, however, the defense attorney consistently addressed the victim as "Miss" during the trial.

I mention this example to make two general observations about ethnographic interview materials. A first observation is that, despite many of the limitations discussed previously, interviews elicit a number of important and necessary details about trial practice. Since the formal study of conversation concentrates on overt understandings, much of the rich texture of trial strategies and tactics is simply unavailable via the study of language use only. Much of what I have learned about trials has come from numerous informal but in-depth interviews with judges and attorneys. For instance, talking about a rape victim's appearance, one judge stated that: "If there is such a thing as dressing like a whore (.) SHE LOOKED LIKE A WHORE." Another sound reason for interviewing judges is that they frequently interview jurors personally after the verdict to compare notes, as it were. This type of data, quite obviously, represents a rich mine of information about the importance of many of the strategies and issues relevant to the outcome of the case, but remains unavailable from a mere inspection of courtroom transcripts or trial tapes.

The second observation I make about ethnographic materials is much more critical. When talking to judges and attorneys, either formally or informally, I have found that they consistently refer to noticeable or remarkable characteristics of the trial – what they thought were exciting, exotic, and funny tidbits about this or that trial. I found that while these official courtroom participants knew how to talk and use linguistic devices – how to perform competently in practical modes of consciousness – they simultaneously exhibited little (if any) *discursive* penetration into the fine-grained linguistic features of discourse; they *know how* without *knowing the how* in much the same way that many people *know how* to ride a bike but without *knowing* in a theoretical way the necessary ergonomic and geometric alignments (see Psathas 1980: 11; Coulter 1979: 21).

(5) Other social structures such as class, race, and age are potentially relevant organizing mechanisms for discovering rape. I do not discount the import of these structuring mechanisms, and as LeFree (1989) and others have noted, they interact and clash with both patriarchy and the legal system on multiple fronts. For example, on numerous occasions defense attorneys raise the relevance of age structures. Below, the term "pardying" designates an activity requiring sex, drugs, and alcohol among cohort incumbents the same age as the defendant and victim. The defense attorney is attempting to frame the rape incident in terms of what "naturally" happens when young people go out "pardying" and to thereby implicate the relevance of age co-incumbency between the defendant and victim for consensual sex.

> Trial 1: Defense cross-examination of victim
>
> **DA:**   What's meant among- (1.2) youthful people (.) people yer age (.) Brian's ((the defendant)) age by pardying?

And later on, still intonationally emphasizing the word, he asks:

DA: Is it not true (.) <u>pardying</u> (.) among people yer <u>age,</u> (1.1) <u>does not</u>
<u>mean go to a pardy.</u>

A similar instance of co-incumbent age categorization occurs during
the defense attorney's closing argument. Notice the self-correction/self-
repair organized around the transformation from "where people go:::
young people go::".

Trial 1: Defense closing argument
DA: Another thing
            (0.7)
      the defendant
            (1.1)
      who supposedly about to-
            (0.8)
      according to the- (.) <u>alleged victim here</u>
      is is- going to take her out and rape her someplace (.)
      takes her to uh <u>common PARKing area</u>
            (2.1)
      places where people <u>GO:::</u> young people <u>GO:::</u>
            (0.6)
      to engage in <u>some sort of NECKIN::G</u> >at the very least<

Parenthetically, this instance also demonstrates the organizing power
of patriarchy, primarily because "necking" naturalizes a trajectory from
touching, for example, to sexual intercourse – a trajectorial standard that
is not gender neutral, but, as shown in some detail, male governed.

(6) While the present study focuses on courtroom talk during cross-
examination of the victim and the contribution of such talk for the
reproduction of rape and the legal system, the questioning of other
witnesses – friendly or hostile – either during direct examination or cross-
examination also contributes toward the reproduction of rape. For
example, even during direct examination of the victim the prosecuting
attorney routinely invokes the relevance of drinking and using drugs,
however covert these references may be. In the following extract, the
prosecutor appears keenly sensitive to the patriarchal order when
inquiring into the victim's alcohol intake: summoning up the patriarchal
myth that when women drink or use drugs they automatically consent to
sex, that drinking is a liability in such cases, and that a woman's moral
rectitude via alcohol or drug use or both must be established before
moving into further testimony. And, just as important, such a view

contrasts dramatically with the belief that when men drink they are excused for raping (see Scully 1990).

> Trial 1: Direct examination of victim
>
> **PA:**   OK::: (.) about how many drinks did you have while you were there
>   (0.2)
> **V:**   I had two
>   (0.7)
> **PA:**   What were they?
>   (0.8)
> **V:**   Either beer or wine (.) I don't recall ( )

Of course, more routinely the prosecuting attorney clearly rejects and attempts to denaturalize the patriarchal order.

> Trial 1: Prosecuting attorney's closing rebuttal
>
> **PA:**   An:::d (.) I don't (0.5) take that (.) (I take offense) at (.) the statement that just because a young lady gets into a car with a man that she's immediately consenting to have <u>SEX WITH HIM</u>.
>   (0.7)
>   I don't think that's the case
>   (0.9)
>   It's not the case.

Ironically, the prosecution's attempts to denaturalize the patriarchal order do backfire. During direct examination, the defendant claimed that he could not achieve an erection on two separate attempts with the victim, and that therefore no penetration had occurred, despite the victim's "pressure" on him to have sex. Additionally, the defendant testified during direct examination that his failure to achieve an erection and have sex with the victim was because of guilt feelings about his fiancée and son, an important feature of this trial since no forensic evidence about presence or absence of semen was introduced during testimony. Following the defense attorney's direct examination of the defendant, the prosecuting attorney, in the extract below, fashions the patriarchal order as an interpretative device during cross-examination of the defendant.

> Trial 1: Prosecutor's cross-examination of defendant
>
> **PA:**   We've heard uh lot of testimony that (as to) all of these thoughts

about yer- (.) <u>FIANce</u> and yer uh- (0.5) uh- (1.5) son (0.7) however that didn't stop you from goin out in the field did it.
          (2.6)

D: Sir when uh woman approaches you (0.4) in such uh manner – uh man feels <u>OB</u>ligated.
          (1.5)

PA: He feels <u>ob</u>ligated he must go through with it whether he believes he should or not is that correct.
          (0.4)

D: To uh certain degree

          .

          .

          .

PA: So she was really pushin you right.

D: I can't say she was (.) Phhh <u>ushin me</u>...

PA: Did she:::- Did you ever think about (all) you would have to say is NO.
          (2.1)

D: The <u>thought</u> occurred to me N'Huh(hh) ((a high pitched laughter sound)) yes sir it did.

Continuing with the inversion theme, the prosecuting attorney, to some extent, actually reinforces that very same order: a male could be considered deviant for failing to refuse a woman's advances, even if married, especially since the defendant initiated the sexual interaction in the first place. Interestingly enough, the prosecutor's questioning strategy parallels and exploits the defendant's inversion of patriarchally driven gender identities, a not so subtle breach of the gender order.

In a slightly different vein, I noted in chapter 1 that a major feminist issue in relation to the legal system centers around the claim that defense attorneys dominate victims on the witness stand. Although most researchers claim this to be the case, more accurately and generally, attorneys and judges attempt to dominate – to varying degrees – all witnesses. Below, the defense attorney cross-examines a police officer about illegally questioning the defendant during transportation to the county jail, even though the defendant stated that he did not wish to answer any questions after being read his rights. Notice, in particular, that the defense attorney, first, interrupts the witness and, second, insists on a yes/no (nonelaborated) answer to the question.

Trial 1: Defense attorney's cross-examination of police officer

DA: And you asked those questions despite the defendant's statement

to you that he did not wish (0.7) to answer any questions (.) isn't
that correct.

(0.5)

W: Pertaining to the aw::::ffense I wasn't askin him any
questions (.) I was askin uh personal im- im- im formation

[[   ]]

DA: That's not the question Officer.

(0.4)

W: Well I didn't understand the question then

(.)

DA: You were asking questions.

(1.0)

W: That's correct.

More as a general comment, a final aspect of trial testimony I will
mention here, which accentuates the fact that adversarial trials resemble a
battle between opposing sides, involves partisanship between attorney
and client. Seen in this light, the legal system is not about doing justice or
discovering what happened from some mythical and privileged Archim-
edean vantage point but is about winning and losing. Adversarial trials are
battles of impression management relying on overt displays of partisanship.

> Trial 1: Defense attorney's direct examination of the defendant

DA: And how long did you remain inside the Grainary.

(0.9)

D: Until it clo::sed.

(1.4)

DA: Approximately what time was that.

(2.3)

D: Eleven-fifteen (0.5) I think

(0.4)

DA: Eleven-fifteen? (1.0) Brian are you nervous

(0.2)

D: Yes sir

(0.4)

DA: N'Heh OK(hhh) ((short chuckle))
Approximately what time did it close.

(3.1)

D: Eleven (0.5) uh- (.) One-fifteen? Did I say eleven I'm sorry.

Considering the above extract, notice that the defendant commits an
error regarding the time the bar closed, a source of trouble occupying the
ensuing sequence. The defendant states that the bar closed at "Eleven-

fifteen" when the correct closing time was actually "One-fifteen." Notice, in particular, how the defense attorney manages the trouble. First, the attorney employs a next turn repair initiator (NTRI) with questioning intonation: "Eleven-fifteen?" which gives the defendant (his client) an opportunity to self-correct the error in the next turn and thus bequeaths the interactional advantages that accompany such an opportunity. But the sequence does not turn out that way – at least initially. The repair is postponed with a type of sequence or detour which marks a meta-instruction about the possible reason for the mistake about the time and hence provides the relevant context for interpreting the error. The defendant's "nervousness" creates an interpretative frame that attempts to cut out or thwart other possible interpretations for the mistake: that the defendant does not know the time, that he is perhaps lying, or that, more generally, he is not a credible witness to the mundane events that transpired during the course of the evening. The recycled question results in a second error concerning the time, but the outcome turns out quite differently this time around. The second repair sequence is self-initiated and self-repaired by the defendant with an appended apology: "Eleven (0.5) uh- (.) One-fifteen?" As I will show later, the defense attorney is rarely so charitable and polite when the victim commits such errors. In fact, we will see that such errors and troubles during cross-examination of the victim are dealt with rather severely, and deal devasting blows to her credibility. Even more interesting, I will show how the defense attorney actually creates the context for these types of errors and troubles during cross-examination of the victim (as attorneys do with opposing witnesses in general, including the prosecuting attorney versus the defendant).

Given this discussion of the advantages and disadvantages of conversational data, the present work focuses primarily on the reproduction of rape and the legal system during adversarial cross-examination of the victim, including objection sequences. The rationale for this narrow focus is not just a policy position but a restriction imposed by the very nature of the data: the delicate and fine-grained quality of transcription techniques generates such a high density of conversational detail that literally thousands of utterances and conversational properties become available and analytically relevant. In taking such a microscopic lens to the structural properties of talk, I have necessarily limited the range of data, for analyzing anything beyond a small collection of data, recordings, and transcriptions of recordings would rapidly escalate to unmanageable proportions. Going beyond the data included here and stretching the data set to include ethnographic details like interviews, participant observations, and other aspects of contexts, or even a larger sample of transcribed trial talk would lose the subtle density of conversational behavior. Going beyond the local courtroom linguistic context would pose serious difficulties, even if other contexts were available, and if we talk about context in an analytic manner, I have few doubts that researchers will have to seriously contend with the methodological reality that each particular utterance and conversational property creates and elaborates context. Since there is no methodological calculus for deciding, first, what defines a context and, second, when relevant contextual features have been exhausted (could they ever?), I have few qualms about the relativistic yet broad notions of context employed here: utterances, sequences, membership and patriarchal categorizations, and the courtroom speech exchange system.

Before turning to introduce the formal concepts of conversation analysis, I must emphasize one general point: this study is not a pure conversation analytic endeavor. Even though I draw heavily on CA, primarily when looking at courtroom discourse mechanisms, this work departs from orthodox CA in several key respects. First, conversation analytic devices are woven into and considered from a structuration theoretical framework. Second, I put more emphasis on the syntax of questioning, and how syntax is interlaced with sequential mechanisms. Last and from a more structural sociological framework, although membership categorizations and classifications capture important facets of courtroom interaction, members' orientations clearly represent an inadequate grounding for understanding the larger courtroom picture. Since patriarchy prestructures many of our commonsense categorizations about rape, and conceals itself in those very same categorization practices, I move far beyond members' interpretations to unveil the deep structured forms of power that hyper-drive surface categorization practices, yet still focus on the complex interaction between them.

More succinctly and illustratively, granted that the prosecuting attorney rejects and contests patriarchal logic, he/she still has no equivalent to patriarchy to draw on during courtroom testimony: no form of hegemonic femininity equivalent to its patriarchal counterpart (Connell 1987: 183–8). This asymmetry between hegemonic masculinity and emphasized femininity functions to conceal the structured forms of power embodied in courtroom talk. While both defense attorney and prosecuting attorney draw on the strict disciplinary power of legal regimes – rules of relevance, evidence, and so on – during questioning of witnesses, the defense attorney also draws on and reproduces a redoubtable mode of domination. For the most part, only the defense attorney engages in the moment-to-moment enactment of patriarchal logic. This creates a powerful advantage for the defense and illustrates the power of what I refer to as socially structured talk: the tight interweaving of sequential, legal-institutional, and ideological mechanisms driving courtroom talk. If rape is routinely transformed into consensual sex, and that transformation occurs during adversarial cross-examination of the victim, then a stucturational form of analysis centered around asymmetrical relations and processes of power must displace members' categorizations for tracking the enactment or local production of patriarchal logic in use (see P. Hall 1985; Clegg 1989).

To recapitulate a prior discussion, while the defense attorney raises the topical relevance of age categorization, I believe that the topic of age is more of a diversionary tactic, a strategy diverting attention and possible attacks from less to more defensible positions. To demonstrate the subtle interaction between patriarchy and age categorization, consider a previous data extract. In the data extract considered earlier (on p. 61), the defense attorney describes the defendant and victim as co-incumbents belonging to the category "young people." Contemporaneously, the attendant category-bound activity "necking" is embedded within this categorization process, and operates in conjunction with the local sexual geography: a place location, "uh common PARKing area," where young people go to engage in various types of sexual activity. Yet, is the categorization work being conducted in this formulation just about age or place location? Are the categories selected for this description just relevant to what young people do at a certain geographical area? I think much more is going on here. I emphasize that patriarchal ideology underlies these surface categories and categorizations, interacting with them in complex ways, and, in the above instance, it operates in practice through a thoroughly unveiled allusion that when a woman agrees to go "necking" or "parking" she automatically consents to male standards for sexual activity.

Thus because co-incumbent age categorization masks an underlying patriarchal logic, only a structural approach to ideological practice can track the enactment of such powerful logic systems. But although patriarchy depicts an abstract organizing structure, members always and inevitably locally produce, negotiate, and assemble it into a normatively constraining structure. Patriarchy denotes not just an abstract mode of domination – a social structure – but also and simultaneously a cognitive, emotional, and linguistic organizing mechanism which both males and females mobilize during the performance of practical consciousness. I describe patriarchy as a logic in use to emphasize the point that it must be enacted and performed to reproduce the local and constraining facticity of moral inferences.

A NOTE ON THEORY AND EXPLANATION IN THE PRESENT STUDY

As mentioned above, although I draw heavily on conversation analytic methodology, this study is much broader in scope than the mere description and explication of conversational structures embedded in courtroom talk. I am interested in much more than the local technology of courtroom discourse. Much more theoretically, I am preoccupied with discovering the structured practices and social relations which generate both courtroom disciplinary regimes and patriarchal modes of domination. Much more generally, I am interested in explicating the structural generative mechanisms found in courtroom talk as fundamental constituents of social order.

To repeat and re-emphasize some issues discussed in chapter 2, sociology is ultimately concerned with the problem not just of action but of order, of how a plurality of actions are systematically ordered, patterned, and interconnected across space and time. Throughout history two distinct strands of intellectual thought have dominated the theoretical battleground regarding this question: individualism on the one hand, and collectivism on the other. The first solution locates the basis for social order in the negotiated outcomes of individual actors and actions without reference to prior collective circumstances; the second locates that order in an autonomous *sui generis* realm of collective social properties without reference to the contextual and negotiated activities of social actors (Alexander 1982: 90–112). Despite the considerable conceptual pull these dichotomous positions exercise on our theoretical imaginations, they ignore a third possibility, a position which simultaneously captures the properties of both collective social arrangements and the actions of contextually situated actors. The duality of structure circumvents this fierce insistence on a polarized conception of social order and concentrates instead on transcontextual structural practices and relationships as the dynamic structurational site for pursuing the question of order in social theory (Giddens 1982: 8, 1984; Cohen 1989). Such transcontextual properties and mechanisms are inherited from the past through memory traces, reinstantiated in the present performance of action, and thereby preserved for the future reproduction of performances. As structural properties, their continuity is preserved and their form maintained through historical periods and particular contexts, even through successive cohorts of new individuals. According to Giddens, social systems or nonrandom social patterns and relationships are constituted or reproduced via the institutional (structural) properties embodied in social activities.

The structural properties embodied in social activities generate the ordered patterns of social systems. I will return to Giddens's work in quite some detail in the final chapter of this study. For now I turn to how structured practices function as generative mechanisms in the rape trial.

Such an interest in the "how" or the generating mechanisms of social life lies at the heart of the realist scientific enterprise. According to Outhwaite (1987b: 175): "Realists play down the regularity in laws, in favor of their grounding in real operative mechanisms which may or may not produce observable results" (also see Outhwaite 1987a; Keat and Urry 1982; Issac 1987; Bhaskar 1989). These operative mechanisms contribute to the production of patterned and systematic surface interactions over the course of space and time, but the relationship between underlying mechanisms and surface outcomes is not deterministic. Because social reality represents an open system in which a multiplexity of mechanisms and structures interact during any given historical moment, outcomes exist only as tendencies: contingent possibilities which may or may not be realized during the course of interactions (Outhwaite 1987b: 175; see also Connell 1987: 116–17). When combined with particulars of context, other social structures like class and race, and the right historical circumstances, these structural mechanisms produce observable surface outcomes. The advantage of realism is that structural devices represent models of reality that can be analyzed independently of the effects or outcomes they generate.

In the rape trial context, legal-institutional rules, sequential devices, and patriarchal ideologies constitute structural mechanisms drawn on during the course of courtroom performance to reproduce the constraining and enabling facticity of rape and the legal system. The relatively enduring facticity of these systems is reproduced through the tight interweaving of structurational mechanisms. I refer to this dynamic process as the reproduction or discovery of rape. By the term "discovery" I make no commitment to particular trial case outcomes at any particular time, such as conviction, acquittal, or mistrial, since numerous other factors may be present, but to the structuring mechanisms that members wield during the course of system reproduction – sustaining and transforming the social facticity of rape and institutional systems of law. As a matter of fact, when employing the terms reproduce, produce, constitute, or generate, I explicitly refer to a mechanisms's *contribution* to reproduction. I make no claim that the devices described in this study characterize all or even the majority of reproduction practices. Yet even though I place primary emphasis on structural practices and relations in the rape trial context, local interactional practices which contribute to the reproduction of courtroom outcomes, these mechanisms draw on larger social-cultural configurations during the course of system reproduction. I hold the systemic patterns of patriarchy and the criminal fact about rape (witnessed in chapter 1) as constant or given. In so doing, I am following the methodological (not ontological) bracketing advocated by Giddens when analyzing the fine-grained performance of structuration.

> In institutional analysis structural properties are treated as chronically reproduced features of social systems. In the analysis of strategic conduct the focus is placed upon modes in which actors draw upon structural properties in the constitution of social relations. . . . The analysis of strategic conduct means giving primacy to discursive and practical consciousness, and to strategies of control within defined contextual boundaries. Institutionalized properties of the settings of interaction are assumed methodologically to be "given." (Giddens 1984: 288).

A final issue merits parenthetical mention. How does this study of talk relate to realist philosophy of science, and in what sense could the position advocated here claim the status of theory? Compare the above discussion of realism with the methodological quote of Sacks: "The idea is to take simple sequences of conversation and tear them apart in such a way as to find rules, techniques, procedures, methods . . . that can be used to generate the orderly features we find in the conversations we examine . . ." (Sacks 1985: 413).

While Sacks's statement does not propose theory or explanation as a logically integrated system of lawlike propositions in a positivistic sense (as Turner 1986 recommends), there is precious little in sociology or even the natural sciences that conform to such strictures. By contrast, models in CA and realist versions of social science are designed to provide sensitizing conceptual schemes for understanding social reality and to establish a cumulatively expanding framework for relating various new types of research to basic models. As Giddens (1984) notes in his preface: "conceptual schemes that order and inform processes of inquiry into social life are in large part what 'theory' is and what it is for." And, similarly, two prominent ethnomethodologists note that the basic issue is: "not whether this is 'really' theory in terms of some proffered formal definition, but rather by proceeding in this way we gain a deeper understanding of social reality" (Wilson and Zimmerman 1980: 75).

The restructuring of forms of theory in current social science lends some purchase on explanatory precepts based on questions of "what" and "how", rather than just "why" and "when" – on descriptions of generative mechanisms instead of correlation of regularities and prediction, on depth of insight instead of gross coverage of data (see A. Garfinkel

1981; Lieberson 1985; Keat and Urry 1982; Giddens 1976, 1984). Following Sacks, Giddens, Chomsky, Bhaskar, and others, I employ a type of realist imagery as a theoretical model to conceptualize the underlying "machinery" which generates the sytematic facts of rape and the legal system and to discover how rape is transformed into consensual sex via courtroom talk – how rape as an enforcement of the social order is reproduced in trial talk.

In the following two chapters I turn first, in chapter 4, to illustrate the turn-taking apparatus of natural conversation, and second, in chapter 5, to explicate how the turn-taking apparatus of the courtroom departs significantly from this natural system model and constitutes a disciplinary system of power, a system contributing to the reproduction of both rape and the legal system.

4

The Turn-taking Model for Natural Conversation

According to Sacks (1987: 54), a problem confronting members in social interaction involves the fine-grained, collaborative coordination of social action. More specifically, the smooth coordination, precision timing, and recursive transfer – the rhythmic synchronization – of speaker and listener roles in talk must be addressed as the normatively oriented to interactionally achieved object of analytic investigation. According to Sacks (in Sacks, Schegloff and Jefferson (SSJ) 1978: 10–11), for any model to merit serious attention it must account for a number of grossly apparent facts about conversational interaction.

1   Speaker change recurs, or, at least, occurs.
2   Overwhelmingly, one party talks at a time.
3   Occurrences of more than one speaker at a time are common, but brief.
4   Transitions from one turn to a next with no gap and no overlap between them are common. Together with transitions characterized by slight gap or slight overlap, they make up the vast majority of transitions.
5   Turn order is not fixed, but varies.
6   Turn size is not fixed, but varies.
7   Length of conversation is not fixed, specified in advance.
8   What parties say is not fixed, specified in advance.
9   Relative distribution of turns is not fixed, specified in advance.
10   Number of parties can change.
11   Turn-allocation techniques are obviously used. A current speaker may select a next speaker (as when a current speaker addresses question to another party); parties may self-select, in starting to talk.
12   Various "turn-constructional units" are employed. Turns can be

projectedly "one word long," or, for example, they can be sentential in length.

13 Repair mechanisms for dealing with turn-taking errors and violations obviously are available for use. For example, if two parties find themselves talking at the same time, one of them will stop prematurely, thus repairing the trouble.

If talk is a form of social action, and the social order is empirically organized around these concerted actions, then some mechanism must exist for members to produce and reproduce conversational social facts. The turn-taking system for natural conversation is the generating mechanism for making such social facts happen.

Before turning directly to elaborate the SSJ model, a technical point is in order. Talk is a generic term for a range of speech exchange systems. Trials, conversations, classroom sessions, debates, organizational and faculty meetings, presidential press conferences, and news interviews, to mention only a few, are all different types of speech exchange systems (SSJ 1978: 45). The systems of talk-in-interaction are organized along a linear array of types from complete preallocation of turns, such as debates, in which such properties as the order of speakership and length of turns are pre-specified, to local distribution of turns, such as natural conversation, in which there is no pre-specification of turn order, turn type or turn size. Medial exchange systems are sandwiched between these polar extremes. For example, in the rape trial, a medial system, who gets to talk, what they get to talk about, and when they get to say it are differentially distributed across social positions; attorneys ask questions, select witnesses to answer them in next turn, and then self-select themselves following answer completion (Atkinson and Drew 1979: 63).

But courtroom trials are not completely preallocated systems, since turn size and turn content are locally managed on a turn-by-turn basis. Nor is rape trial talk restricted to attorneys and witnesses on the stand. On the other hand, in debate systems the order, length, and to some extent, content of turns are all fixed in advance, as are the participants.

Natural conversation, in stark contrast to both debate and trial systems, implements turn order, turn size and turn type on a turn-by-turn or local basis. That is, turn allocation, turn size and turn type are implemented during the production of each new turn and not beforehand. Thus the local management nature of conversation marks it as a distinct form of talk from the other speech exchange systems. This distinction will be dealt with more extensively later on in the chapter and in chapter 5.

With these points in mind, Sacks, Schegloff, and Jefferson propose that the turn-taking system operates like an economy, which distributes a scarce resource – turns at talking – across participants in systematically achieved and normatively oriented to transactions (1978: 12). More formally, the turn-taking model consists of two components and a set of rules: the turn-constructional component, which specifies the unit types for constructing turns, and the turn allocation component, which operates as a set of rules for distributing turns between participants.

Turns are constructed out of discretely bound unit types, consisting of words, phrases, clauses, and sentences. The terminal boundary of a unit type is a transition relevant place (TRP), a structural environment where possible transition to another speaker becomes relevant. These surface syntactic constructions are monitored by conversationalists to predict or project a TRP, and that projection capacity provides a systematic basis for a clustering of otherwise deviant interactional activities and occurrences in or near these transition environments (SSJ 1978: 12–14).

According to Sacks, Schegloff and Jefferson, the turn allocation component specifies an ordered and recursive cycling set of options for speaker transfer. These are the following: Rule 1 states that at any TRP 1(a) current speaker may select next speaker; 1(b) next speaker may self-select; and 1(c) current speaker may, but need not, continue talking if other speaker(s) do not self-select. Rule 2 recycles the rule set: following the provision in 1(c) if a current speaker continues into a new turn unit, then on completion of that unit options 1(a)–(c) recursively cycle in that order and at each TRP until transfer occurs. The following examples serve to illustrate the rules.

(4.1)   Rule 1(a) (Sacks, Schegloff, and Jefferson 1978: 29)

   S: Oscar did you work for somebody before you worked for Zappa
   O: Yeh, many many.

(4.2)   Rule 1(b) (Sacks, Schegloff, and Jefferson 1978: 52)

   Jim: Any a' you guys read that story about Walter Mitty?
   Ken: I did,
   Roger: Mm hmmm

(4.3)   Rule 1(c) (Davidson 1984: 106)

   A: C'<u>m</u>on down <u>he</u>:re,=it's oka:y,
              (0.2)
   A: I got lotta stuff, <u>I</u> got <u>be</u>:er en stuff 'n,
   B: Mm hheh heh ...

Illustratively, when rule 1(b) is exercised the entire rule set reapplies for the self-selecting speaker, since that speaker is now current speaker, and, as current, may select next, or – following a noncurrent speaker's failure to exercise rule 1(b) and given the provision in rule 1(c) – may but need not continue talking. Put formally and theoretically, the turn-taking rules governing conversation are modeled as a hierarchically ordered and recursive cycling set of options operating at each TRP. Put simply, the system operates as a set of traffic rules governing conversational interaction.

RULE ORDERING AND RULE INTERACTION

Although turn-taking rules are hierarchically ordered to ensure that higher priority options constrain lower priority rules, reciprocal rule interaction is also built into the system, for lower order rules constitute secondary and derivative constraints on the use of higher order options. The higher ordered options constrain lower priority ones since the former become available before the latter. These ordered and weighted "traffic" rules are evident since rule 1(a) is available prior to rule 1(b): current speakers, employing pre-positioned or embedded positioned address terms, gaze, or first pair parts of adjacency pairs can select next speaker prior to next's potential self-selection.[1]

But in order to operate, rule 1(a) must be exercised before the initial unit's TRP in order to suspend operation of rule 1(b). Hence rule 1(b)'s presence in the rule set constrains the use of 1(a), whether or not 1(b) is invoked. Furthermore, although self-selection 1(b) is available prior to current speaker continuing into a new turn-unit 1(c), self-selectors must start up before current speaker continues into a fresh turn-unit, since the whole rule set will recycle again at that point. If a potential next, following failure of current to invoke 1(a), fails to self-select, then his/her opportunity to talk may well fade into the onset of another self-selector's turn, following exercise of 1(b), or current's continuance of a turn, following exercise of 1(c).

The option cycle relationship between 1(b) and 1(c) which makes the former available prior to the latter involves a differential silence duration metric: reaction time latency has a shorter duration than initiative time latency. That is to say, the onset duration interval between a current and self-selecting next is shorter than the lagged onset delay between a current reaching a TRP and then continuing into a new unit type. Subrules (b) and (c) are therefore distinct, not redundant (SSJ 1978: 54 n30; Levinson 1983: 298).

And if 1(c) is employed, rule 2 will apply derivately, with the entire rule set 1(a)–(c) recycling and hence rule 1(a)'s option taking application dominance over rule 1(b). In sum then, just as rule 1(a) is constrained by the presence of 1(b), rule 1(b) is constrained by rule 1(c)'s presence in the set (SSJ 1978).

Even though the turn-taking system provides for speaker transfer, this is not necessary or invariant because at each TRP rule options 1(a)–(b) may be withheld. Moreover, if these two rule options are suspended while 1(c) is exercised, then as long as this rule combination recycles at each forthcoming TRP a multiunit turn will be produced by the same speaker. For when a current speaker fails to select a next and nonspeakers fail to self-select, then current speaker has the option to continue into a new unit type and thereby recycle the entire rule set via rule 2. Thus the turn-taking system provides for the fact that turn size is mutable or emergent, not static, and that any piece of talk from a sound to an extended story may comprise a turn (Goodwin 1981). And when none of the options are invoked, the system shuts down (for example, informal family settings), a lapse which terminates when rule 1(b) is activated.

Still, multiunit turns involve a collaborative suspension of the turn-taking machinery. Failure of current speaker to select next, and failure of nonspeakers to self-select are therefore locally managed and interactionally achieved at each and every TRP. This is remarkable since the underlying structure of turn organization exerts pressure towards a minimization of turn size to a single unit type. The source of this constraint on turn size is motivated by the fact that current nonspeakers monitor a possible upcoming TRP as a place to start talking, that current speakers orient to this possibility of reasonable turn incursion as an organizational contingency of the turn system, and that current speakers therefore pack their talk into a single unit (Schegloff 1982). Since the turn-taking options are activated at each TRP, the achievement of turn size variation depends on the collaborative suspension of rule 1(b): potential next speakers must withhold talk for any multiunit turn-in-progress.

Several conversational devices are available for accomplishing this task. In order to suspend rule 1(b), story prefaces, list initiating markers, and preliminaries to preliminaries (Schegloff 1982; Houtkoop 1987) represent systematic mechanisms for requesting next speakers to withold talk. Likewise, potential next speakers can honor this request by witholding 1(b), and by employing back channel utterances, such as "uh huh," a device for allowing a multiunit turn in progress to continue (Schegloff 1982, 1988a: 115).

Story prefaces were first proposed by Sacks and operate with the sequential structure of, first, an offer to tell: Ken: "You wanna hear muh -eh my sister told me a story last night"; followed by, second, acceptance or rejection of the offer: Roger: "I don't wanna hear it. But if you must"; and, third, the ensuing telling sequence: Ken: "No. To stun me she says . . ." (Sacks 1974: 337–53).

Alternatively, list initiating markers announce a definite or indefinite number of forthcoming utterances, such as "let me mention three points" or "let me give you some examples," respectively (Schegloff 1982). A similar type of action projection, preliminaries to preliminaries (for example, "Can I ask you a question?"), can be invoked to project a multiunit turn (Schegloff 1980). Although these devices project a multiunit turn by a current speaker, the interactional contingency of turn-taking depicts a system where for such a turn-in-progress to succeed, recipients must honor the projection and withhold the self-selection option.

A further feature of this system involves the treatment of silence. Because the hierarchically layered turn options can be activated at each and every TRP and because the cycling of options is a time-bound process, silence is generated collaboratively by current and next speaker during the option cycle (Wilson and Zimmerman 1986).[2] When speakers fail to exercise options 1(a)–(c) various types of silence are generated. A gap or inter-turn silence occurs when a noncurrent speaker fails to exercise rule 1(b) or, following 1(a), fails to answer immediately; a pause or intra-turn silence is generated when, following failure of current to invoke 1(a) and failure of next to implement 1(b), a current speaker witholds option 1(c) or stops the turn-in-progress within a unit type; and a lapse is produced when rules 1(a)–(c) are suspended, producing an extended silence or state of disengagement. Alternatively, these silences are terminated when one of the options is enacted (Wilson and Zimmerman 1986).

Still more generally, silence is generated collaboratively by the cycling of options and is not attributable to mere response latency. The lagged onset gap between a current and a next employing self-selection, and the lagged onset pause when a current continues into a new constructional unit are both built into the system's real-time cycling process. Hence the turn-taking system not only accounts for the ordering of turn transfer but also depicts how silences of various sorts emerge interactionally. Notice in particular how the turn-taking system is finely sensitive to context. In informal contexts, for example, a family setting, a lapse in talk results from a failure to exercise one of the options. So the system accounts for rather long moments when members do not talk – when the system is closed down (see Schegloff and Sacks 1974; Davidson 1975). And conversation resumes when one of the participants activates the turn-taking machinery.

RULE ORIENTATION

Although turn transition occurs with a minimization of gap and overlap, such features of talk are quite obviously not eliminated. Due to the projective capacity of an upcoming TRP, potential next speakers possess the technical capacity to monitor those environments in order to gear into a turn, thus providing for the systematic occurrence of overlapping or simultaneous talk. Such overlaps may misproject the trajectory of a current turn-in-progress, but nonetheless occur in or near TRP as reasonable turn incursions. Since turn boundaries are emergent and not fixed, recipients might project the end of a turn unit, analyze the terminal boundary of a turn unit as a complete turn, and begin talking at an initial TRP, but that projection turns out to be inaccurate so that overlap results. As Jefferson (1973) has noted, tag-positioned address terms are routinely and systematically overlapped.

(4.4)   (Jefferson 1973: 48)

    Desk: Is it a stretcher patient Ma'am,

                                 [

    Caller: It's- Uh yes he is,

    Moreover, given the competitiveness built into the rule system and given the projection capacity of turn constructional units, two or more conversationalists can monitor TRP environments as possible starting points. In such instances, joint synchronization of turn entry by two or more self-selecting nexts will result in those nexts talking simultaneously even when turn completion projection is accurate. Thus rule 1(b) accounts for overlaps between current and next as well as between two or more potential next speakers. Because of the organizational and systematic motivation for potential next speakers to start at the first opportunity – a constraint imposed due to the scarce economy of turns – overlaps arise from both multiple self-selection and projection trouble.

    However, although overlaps and simultaneous talk are not infrequent and are precision placed at or near TRP, members still methodically attend to the "one at a time" rule in and through the resolution of overlap.

(4.5)   (Atkinson and Drew 1979: 42)

> D: Mmhm. Didju do any exercises in your trance?
>   (0.2) Er didju jus-
>   [
> P: .hhh Yes yes the heaviness n'lightness with my arm

Overlap may be resolved by: (1) one speaker dropping out during overlap; (2) speakers repeating or repairing overlapped segment; (3) one or both speakers stopping in mid-turn; or (4) one speaker topicalizing or formulating the overlap, as in "wait a minute let me finish" (Jefferson and Schegloff 1975; SSJ 1978; Schegloff et al. 1977). What might therefore appear as conversational deviance or rule violation in other approaches to talk, especially stochastic models of statistical probability (see Roger and Bull 1989), turns out to be rule orientation from a CA perspective: rules are conventional structures for actors' orientations.

To sum up the points that have been made thus far. The turn-taking system accounts for the grossly apparent facts of natural conversation in a parsimonious, cogent, and coherent manner. It provides for the overwhelming fact that conversation consists of single speaker turns with regular and orderly transition between speakers – that is, transition with a minimum of gap and overlap. And it captures the fine-grained structural details of conversation in a powerfully comprehensive model that is sensitive not only to the empirical regularities of social actions but also to the normatively accountable deviant occurrences which might otherwise escape analytic observation. Most relevant for the present context, we will see in chapter 5 how this culturally neutral turn-taking system and its associated properties are systematically transformed and exploited to manage the powerful interests and interactional contingencies of legal disciplinary regimes.

CONTEXT-FREE AND LOCAL MANAGEMENT

The turn-taking rules are locally and interactionally managed by speakers on a turn-by-turn basis. The order or transfer, content, and size of turns are interactionally contingent real-time processes which are negotiated at each new transition relevant place. The exercise or suspension of a particular option in the rule set is implemented through the design of each fresh turn. The production, recognition, projection, and misprojection of TRP are all handled within each current turn-in-progress, not beforehand. Consequently, the configuration of turn synchronization occurs in this dynamic interplay of mutual monitoring, adjustment, and coordination between current and next speakers.

At the same time, turn-taking rules are not only locally managed but also context-free or formal since the recursive cycling series of options operates across and independent of contexts/settings, participant identities, and topics. The rule system depicts a form of social organization that activates at each and every TRP without discriminating the indexical particulars of context. Yet the system still incorporates extreme sensitivity to the local interactional tasks at hand (SSJ 1978; Schenkein 1978). As a formal structural mechanism, the rule set applies recursively at each and every TRP, but what constitutes a TRP and what current and next speakers do there – what options are exercised or withheld – are context sensitive or contingent on the particular interactional tasks confronting participants. For example, the management of turn size – the achievement, or conversely, nonachievement, of a multiunit turn – is particularized at each TRP. In sum, then, the turn-taking system furnishes the structural parameters of talk-in-interaction, and constitutes an abstract/formal resource for particularizing – recipient designing – some here-and-now spate of talk.

ADJACENCY PAIRS

The exercise of rule 1(a) not only selects next speaker, but also prescribes the relevance of a particular social action that next speaker should warrantably engage in (SSJ 1978: 21). The basic type of conversational organization for relating utterances across adjacent speaker turns, hence *the major type of current selects next device*, is what Sacks referred to as the adjacency pair (Sacks 1972; SSJ 1978; Schegloff and Sacks 1974).[3] Canonically, adjacency pairs are structural units of conversation consisting of two adjacently placed utterances, a first pair part followed by a second pair part, produced by alternate speakers in alternating speaker turns. Moreover, there is a methodic relationship between the component utterances of the pair beyond that of mere adjacency: the occurrence of a first pair part selects some subclass of discriminately related second pair parts as a conditionally relevant next action – that is, a next action whose nonoccurrence may be noticeable, normatively accountable, or otherwise vulnerable to inferences that may be drawn from its absence. Put in illustrative terms, given a question, for instance, some type of answer is conditionally relevant for that question, such that whatever utterance occurs in the next speaker's response slot there will be a predisposition of expectation on the part of the prior speaker to hear that utterance as an answer; and if that answer is absent, then it is officially absent – it meaningfully belongs to next speaker. The constraints imposed by conditional relevance are thus normatively accountable. That is to say, those constraints are oriented to by members as external and coercive, as Schegloff notes with regard to summons/answer sequences: "A further inferential structure attached to the conditional relevance of A on S can lead us to see that this property has the status of what Durkheim intended by the term 'social fact'; i.e. the property is both 'external' and 'constraining'" (Schegloff 1972: 367; also see Suchman 1987: 79).

The adjacency pair concept underscores the idea of structure as a normatively oriented to and tightly constraining framework for generating interlocking social actions and shaping the local interpretations of members. Although adjacency pairs are interrelated to the turn-taking system via rule 1(a), possessing enough coercive power to allocate next turn, and to the overall organization of conversation, organizing closings and openings, they operate still more generally as a local or turn-by-turn organization, as a structural template for the organization of actions, and as an organization that controls or shapes the coherence, intelligibility, expectations – the sense – of social action.

Like other conversation analytic rules and structures, the adjacency pair concept is not designed to refer to statistical regularities of sequential action: the relative frequency of second pair parts following first pair parts. It refers instead to a structural framework which shapes the expectations and interpretations about the organization of social action. It depicts structure as an interactionally oriented to and normatively accountable framework for producing and recognizing social action. It describes a normatively institutionalized and tightly integrated sequence of action. And it detects structure not only from empirical frequency or regularity, but also – much more importantly – from those deviant cases where some normal form has been breached (Heritage 1984; Wootton 1989; Bilmes 1988).

These breaches, insofar as they are oriented to by members, bolster the credibility – indeed illuminate the reality – of structure. In extracts 4.6 through 4.8 below, consider first the absence of an answer, and second the presence of an insertion sequence, both of which *prima facie* appear to undermine the twin requirements of conditional relevance on the one hand, and strict adjacency between pair parts, on the other.

(4.6)   (Atkinson and Drew 1979: 52)

    A: Is there something bothering you or not?
          (1.0)

→**A:**   Yes or no

          (1.5)

→**A:**   Eh?

  B: No.

(4.7)   (Merritt 1976: 333)

  A: May I have a bottle of Mich?

  B: Are you twenty one?

  A: No

  B: No

(4.8)   (Goffman 1981: 7)

  A₁: Have you got the time?

  B₂: Standard or Daylight Saving?

  A₃: What are you running on?

  B₃: Standard.

  A₂: Standard then.

  B₁: It's five o'clock.

(4.9)   (Houtkoop 1987: 42)

  B: Why don't you come and see me sometimes

                                    [

  A: I would like to.

  B: I would like you to.

(4.10)   (Levinson 1983: 359)

  C: Hullo I was just ringing up to ask if you were going to Bertrand's party

  R: Yes I thought you might be

  C: Heh heh

  R: Yes would you like a lift?

  C: Oh I'd love one

Several observations are worth drawing from the above segments.

1   Insertion sequences – 4.7 and 4.8 – although violating the principle of strict adjacency, nevertheless preserve pair structure across multiple embeddings. Sequential constraints are thus powerful enough to bind actions across a sequence of positions. In these instances, conditional relevance is not removed, merely suspended or delayed until internal expansions, which are themselves nested adjacency pairs, conclude.

Insertion sequences depict a systematically variant configuration of talk woven into the design of sequential structure.

2   A first pair part interactionally projects and normatively constrains a second pair part as an institutionalized next action. As a normatively accountable structure for action, the adjacency pair concept not only describes the regularity with which second pair parts follow first pair parts but also the orientations of conversationalists to such conventions when they are breached. This orientation to structure is displayed by repeating or partially repeating the first pair part, by complaining or making inferences about its absence (either to that speaker or reporting such occurrences to others), or by employing misplacement markers, such as "Oh by the way" or "Let me tell you about X before I forget," which mark a disjunctive/unrelated contribution, as in 4.6.

3   The interactional cement that binds adjacency pairs is not adjacency, but conventional/cultural expectations about the organization and design of social actions. The concept refers to a structural organization for producing coherence and interpreting social action. Failure to recognize this property leads to the misinterpretation of the concept as a statement about empirical invariance or as a generalization describing how first pair parts will be followed by second pair parts.

4   Following Harold Garfinkel, a central tenet of CA revolves around the insight that conversationalists design their actions to be recognizable/mutually intelligible for each other, and that these design features provide participants with institutionalized resources and constraints for interacting with each other (Wootton 1989). Given that these design features are oriented to by members, stochastic modeling of paired actions omits the structural significance that rules and constraints possess for participants. As Wootton notes, the structural significance of adjacency pairs is independent of and bears an unknown relationship to frequency counts or other statements of empirical regularity. Nor would knowing mere empirical frequency permit analytic inferences regarding members' orientation to adjacency structures. From stochastic modeling of action, the above violations/structural variations – departures from the normal forms – would incorrectly appear to undermine that structural organization (Wootton 1989).

5   Deviant, nonoccurring, and infrequent actions or other rule violations are rule oriented and therefore within the realm of the model. Clearly then, the adjacency pair concept is best conceived as a structural organization: a current turn is sequentially implicative – that is, it projects a normatively required and inferentially expected next action – for a fitted/complementary second action in next turn by next speaker. It

constitutes a morally constraining, Durkheimian, social fact (Schegloff 1972; Suchman 1987).

6 Although adjacency pairs canonically operate over two turns – as strictly local systems – they more accurately represent flexed structures since internal and external expansions occur as systematic transformational options. More sharply put, adjacency pairs permit systematic transformations both on internal grounds, because of insertion sequences and embedded expansions, as in 4.7 and 4.8, and on external grounds, because of pre-sequences, as in 4.10, and third-turn comment options, as in 4.9 – pre-expansions and post-expansions respectively. In a more provocative vein, since a second pair part may constitute both a first pair and second pair part, as in 2.5 (see p. 43) – a simultaneous dual pair part, that is, three part sequences occurring as

1 Complaint;
2 Complaint about complaint (second pair part response to 1 and first pair part for 3);
3 Response.

portray sequential modulations on canonical structure which serve as evidence for a "deeper" organization of adjacency triplets (Houtkoop 1987: 38–51).

I need to temper and elucidate these observations in one very important respect. Even though adjacency pairs are pervasive structures, conversation is not a seamless stretch of these sharply constraining and tightly organized structures. More generally, if not more accurately, a current and next utterance are, to varying degrees of tightness, interlocked, as Heritage notes.

> conversation is not an endless series of interlocking adjacency pairs in which sharply constrained options confront next speaker. Rather conversation is informed by the general assumption – common to both speakers and hearers – that utterances which are placed immediately next to some prior are to be understood as produced in response to or, more loosely, in relation to that prior. This assumption provides a framework in which speakers can rely on the positioning of what they say to contribute to the sense of what they say as an action. (1984: 261)

According to Schegloff (1988a: 109–18), adjacency relationships, as a component of the turn-taking organization, operate backwards and represent a weaker form of sequential organization than adjacency pairs: "Next turns show understanding of prior turns . . . *independently of whether they are components of adjacency pairs or not*" (emphasis in the original). By contrast, adjacency pairs, as units of sequence organization, endow mere temporal succession with a structurally constraining and morally inferential set of paired actions. In addition to operating backwards, displaying some appreciation, some understanding of the prior utterance, adjacency pairs possess a powerful projection capacity. Adjacency pairs superimpose powerful forward and backward looking operations on mere serial occurrence, bequeathing on turns-at-talk a conventional binding power beyond that of simple adjacency.

In sum: adjacency pair structure is exhibited from (1) regularity of resoponse, (2) deviant cases in which some regular form is expected but breached, (3) insertion sequences and other transformations on canonical structure, and (4) misplacement markers. This dual evidence of structure – adherence to and departure from regular form – provides a powerful and comprehensive methodological framework for the analysis of interlocking social actions. Deviant cases, empirical regularity, and sequential variations are *indicia* of structure. As we discussed previously, that sequential operations are autonomous, self-organizing, not justified by reference to exogenous reality is a deep leitmotiv of conversation analysis. That adjacency pairs are endogenous, internal organizations is merely an aspect of this general thesis. When looking at courtroom micro-modes of domination, we will see how this structural template for action functions through institutionally endowed power arrangements.

PREFERENCE ORGANIZATION

Although the occurrence of a first pair part conventionally projects and interactionally requires a complementary next action, adjacency pair structure is complicated by the fact that dual and often multiple options exist from which to fulfill these second pair part obligations. Additionally, these relevant next options represent nonequivalent and institutionally ranked alternatives, a ranking exhibited in the differential design of sequences and turns, not in the psychological disposition of conversationalists.

In conversational analytic terms, this differential design reveals a preference system: the loading of turn components which inhabit turns in a systematic and institutionalized order. The structural design properties for preferred actions reveals that they are linguistically unmarked and compressed through simple turn formats: through (1) no delay, (2) inhabiting a whole turn, and (3) conveying directly. Conversely, dispreferred actions are linguistically marked and expanded through complex turn formats: through (1) delays, (2) qualifications, (3) accounts, and (4) indirection (Pomerantz 1975, 1978, 1984; Levinson 1983; Heritage 1984; Atkinson and Heritage 1984; Sacks 1987).

(4.11)   (Atkinson and Drew 1979: 58)

> **B:**   Uh if you'd care to come over and visit a little while this morning I'll give you a cup of coffee.
>
> →**A:**   hehh Well that's awfully sweet of you, I don't think I can make it this morning .hh uhm I'm running an ad in the paper and-and uh I have to stay near the phone.

(4.12)   (Sacks 1987: 58)

> **A:**   Yuh comin down early?
>
> →**B:**   Well, I got a lot of things to do before gettin cleared up tomorrow. I don't know. I w- probably won't be too early.

(4.13)   (Atkinson and Drew 1979: 58)

> **A:**   Why don't you come up and <u>see</u> me sometimes
>
>   [
>
> →**B:**   I would like to

(4.14)   (Levinson 1983: 308)

> **C:**   Um I wondered if there's any chance of seeing you tomorrow sometime (0.5) morning or before the seminar
>
> →   (1.0)
>
> →**R:**   Ah um (.) I doubt it
>
> **C:**   Uhm huh
>
> →**R:**   The reason is I'm seeing Elisabeth

In extracts 4.11, 4.12 and 4.13 above, notice that invitations can be either accepted or rejected. The acceptance of the invitation in 4.13 occurs directly with no delay and inhabits the entire turn. The rejection in 4.11, however, exhibits the following turn shape: (1) a delayed preface [hehh Well]; (2) an appreciation component [that's awfully sweet of you]+a mitigated or indirect rejection [I don't think I can make it this morning]; and (3) an account [I'm running an ad in the paper and- and uh I have to stay near the phone]. Similarly in extract 4.14 a request projects either an acceptance or rejection as a relevant second pair part. Notice here that the rejection is performed in the dispreferred format: delay [1.0 gap]+preface [ah um]+pause [(.)]+indirect/mitigated rejection [I doubt it]+account [The reason is I'm seeing Elisabeth]. In each of these cases, the differential design of dispreferred and preferred actions is displayed through the ordering of turn components and turn shape construction. In sum: rejections and disagreements are "pushed down" into the turn, or otherwise delayed, mitigated, accounted for, and softened, as in 4.12.

On the other hand, preferred actions are governed by a quite different logic of social action: they occur immediately with little or no gap, and are direct. Notice in example 4.13 above that the acceptance of the invitation occurs immediately, without mitigation, and inhabits the entire turn. This focus on the ordering of second pair part components is referred to as practice-based preference (Schegloff 1988b: 453–5).

Alternatively, structure-based preference (or what linguists call conductivity) involves first pair parts projection of a second pair part as a preferred response. For example, "'You're going, aren't you?' prefers a yes answer, while 'you're not going are you?' is built to prefer a no answer, and 'Yuh comin down early' is designed to prefer agreement" (Sacks 1987: 57; Schegloff 1988b: 453). According to Schegloff, if a first pair part is designed to project a particular preference, for example, through tag and leading questions or other forms of presupposition built into a turn, then preference is built into sequence structure and not in the design of the response, unless that preference is revised with a subsequent preference. These operate as follows.

(4.15)   (Pomerantz 1984: 61)

> →J: It's really a clear lake, isn't it?
> R: It's wonderful.

(4.16)   (Sacks 1987: 57)

> →A: Well is this really whatchu wanted?
> B: Uh ... not originally? <u>No</u>. But it's uh ... promotion?
>   en it's <u>very</u> interesting, I've been doing this onna part
>   time <u>basis</u> fer a number of <u>years</u>.

Conversationalists also possess the delicate technical capacities not only to project a preferred response, but too even revise such preferences in light of anticipated or potential rejections. In order to forestall or preempt a dispreferred response, speakers may revise, re-project, or reformulate a current turn-in-progress in the direction of a more favorable response (Davidson 1984).

(4.17)   (Sacks 1987: 64)

> A: They have a good cook there?
>   ((pause))

→   Nothing special?
    B: No ...

(4.18)   (Davidson 1984: 11)

    P: Oh I mean uh: you wanna go t' the store
→   er anything
→   over et the Market Basket er anything?
    A: [   ]
                °hhhhhhhhhhhhhhhh h=
    Well ...

In the above cases, preference systems interact with turn design and turn-taking rules in significant and complex fashion. First, given that preferred actions should occur immediately post (or even prior to completion of) first turn, speakers possess the fine-tuned, split-second capacity to monitor micro-delays as foreshadowing an upcoming rejection or disagreement. Second, given the technical capacity of speakers to monitor TRP for recipient activities, a short micro-pause or delay components of various types can be interpreted as rejection/ disagreement implicative, and may indeed augur poorly for the preferred projection. Finally, given the organizational mechanics of turn-taking, in particular rule 1(c), speakers possess the technical capacity to build additional components into the turn to preempt or forestall rejections and disagreements, and simultaneously produce a subsequent version more acceptable to recipient. So in face of a potential nonpreferred response, speaker can abort the projected preference, product a modified version, and, in so doing, invite the recipient to respond to the subsequent version. In the fluid micro-movements of alignment and realignment, we can observe the dynamic interaction between next speaker's withheld/ nonoccurring turn and current speaker's turn-in-progress.

The above examples illustrate this process in vivid detail. Because of rule 1(c) speakers can expand turn design through post-positioned "monitor spaces," such as "er anything," to examine the rejection/ acceptance implicativeness of recipient's response and to produce a subsequent revision of the invitation, such as "over et the Market Basket," moving in the direction of anticipated acceptance of her invitation (Davidson 1984).

The synchronized coordination and collaborative interweaving of mutual adjustment and readjustment observable in preference system operation is motivated by and intimately related to the logic of face considerations. Preference systems demonstrate the interlacing of conversational mechanics and face work. They describe the management of face threatening actions through modulations of conversational structure. And they illustrate how threats to face, support or destruction of social solidarity, and the nature of our social relationships are interactionally managed and communicated through the institutionalized design of turns and sequences (see Goffman 1967; Levinson 1983; Heritage 1984).

That preservation of participant's self-esteem is deeply interwoven with preference systems as face-preserving strategies applies in the following sense. On the one hand, the preferred properties of turns and sequences embody institutionalized structures which support social solidarity. On the other hand, since dispreferred actions threaten social solidarity, they are managed with dispreferred design features, structural modulations which preserve face and social relationships. For instance, a quick, unmitigated, and unaccounted for rejection of an invitation would be seen as culturally rude, if not hostile, and would most likely create a rift between participants. The packaging design for dispreferred actions – delays, indirection, and accounts – provides institutionalized solutions to the interactional problems of preserving face and maintaining social solidarity. Such design features also illustrate the interactional and ongoing achievement of the social fabric; they illuminate how the precarious yet resilient texture of our social relationships is achieved through the differential design and modulation of conversational structure. Once again, preference systems refer not to the psychological dispositions of speakers, but to the structural ordering of internal and between turn properties, to structural aspects of turn design. As a statement and extension of Durkheimian sociology, I agree with the most appropriate remarks by Collins:

> I would theorize this pattern by saying that turn-taking is very Durkheimian. It is an interaction ritual characterized by mutual focus of attention, which builds up its own "collective conscience" and its own constraints. These constraints are manifested, in typical Durkheimian fashion, when they are violated . . . The theory of the conversational turn-taking mechanism is thus part of a broader micro theory, about how solidarity is produced, and broken down, in micro-interactions. (1988b: 248)

Most importantly, we will see how these politeness rituals undergo striking transformations during the adversarial combativeness of cross-examination.

REPAIR SYSTEMS AND UNDERSTANDING

A major environment for preference system operation includes the organization of repair, conversation's central social control mechanism. Since virtually anything can emerge as a "repairable" or "trouble source" (Schegloff, Jefferson, and Sacks 1977), repair does not refer to error and correction, but to problems involving misunderstanding, mishearing, non-hearing, and other interactional dilemmas. As Schegloff (1987: 211) notes, "Repair is a major resource in maintaining and restoring intersubjective or mutual understanding in interaction. . . ."

In their classic study on repair, Schegloff, Jefferson, and Sacks (1977) propose a taxonomy that discriminates between self/other initiation of repair on the one hand, and self/other outcome on the other. The matrix distinguishes the following options: (1) self-initiated/self-repair, (2) other-initiated/self-repair, (3) other-initiated/other repair, and (4) self-initiated/other repair. The trajectory from repair initiation to repair outcome is governed by, first, the differential positioning of repair initiation/solution opportunity relative to the trouble source, and second, the self/other distinction between initiation and repair. More sharply put, self/other initiations and self/other repair opportunities are differentially placed relative to the trouble source, and that differential placement and opportunity corresponds to structural preferences for (1) over (2) and (2) over (3).

(4.19)   (Schegloff, Jefferson, and Sacks 1977: 366)

→ **A:**   but c'd we- c'd I stay up? [self-initiated/self-repair]

(4.20)   (Schegloff, Jefferson, and Sacks 1977: 364)

A: She was givin me all the people that were go:ne this yea:r
→   I mean this quarter. [self-initiated/self-repair]

(4.21)   (Schegloff, Jefferson, and Sacks 1977: 366)

H: And he's goin to make his own paintings
B: Mm hm,
→ **H:**   And- or I mean his own frames [self-initiated/self-repair]

(4.22)   (Schegloff, Jefferson, and Sacks 1977: 377)

Ken: 'E likes that waider over there,
→ **Al:**   Wait-er? [other-initiated]
Ken: Waitress, sorry [self-repair]

(4.23)   (Schegloff, Jefferson, and Sacks 1977: 378)

   L: But y'know single beds 'r awfully thin tuh sleep on

                          .

                          .

→ E: Y'mean narrow? [other-initiated/other-repair]

The repair initiation opportunity space operates over four positions across three turns, including the trouble source, transition space in same turn, next turn, and third turn, with preference corresponding to each opportunity space (Schegloff et al. 1977). Still more technically, second speakers may delay next turn, thereby providing an extended opportunity space after speaker's first turn for an extra opportunity at self-initiation/self repair.

Notice that examples 4.19, a trouble source repair, and 4.20, a transition space repair, are each self-initiated and self-repaired. In both these cases, the structural opportunity for self-initiation/self-repair comes first: first opportunity immediately post trouble; second opportunity at end of turn or in the transition space.

The third opportunity for repair initiation and repair solution occurs in next turn relative to the trouble source. In 4.22, recipient produces a next turn repair initiator (NTRI), withholds the repair option, and thereby invites speaker to self-repair in third turn, which he/she subsequently accomplishes. Of course, recipient may pass an opportunity to repair, in which case the fourth repair initiation space may yield both self-initiation/self-repair, as in 4.21 above. And finally, example 4.23 illustrates other initiation/other repair in second turn. Put most succinctly, first turn provides two opportunities for speaker to self-initiate/self-repair: once in the trouble source, and once in the transition space; second turn provides the opportunity for other-initiation using a NTRI, and other-initiation/other-repair; and third turn provides the opportunity for self-repair from either other-initiation (given a NTRI in second turn) or self-initiation.

According to Schegloff et al. (1977), the evidence for the preference of self-repair over other-repair can be summarized as follows:

1   The empirical frequency of self-initiation/self-repair over other-initiation/other-repair.
2   The structural opportunity for self-initiation/self-repair comes first.
3   Next speaker's other-initiations overwhelmingly yield self-repair.
4   Delay by second speaker after first two opportunity spaces.
5   Other repair consists of modulated downgrades, as in "Y'Mean" or "I think."

In summary, repair practices are organized in such a way that self-initiations yield self-repair, while other initiations also result in self-repair, both of which provide evidence for the differential and nonequivalent status of repair alternatives. Following the previous discussion of preference and face considerations, the preference for self-initiation/self-repair over other-initiation/other-repair is motivated by and deeply interwoven with face and self-esteem preservation: other correction, would *inter alia*, imply incompetence. Notice here the interweaving of sequential and face-preserving organizations: opportunities to initiate and implement repair are "differentially distributed between self and other" (Schegloff 1987: 210). This point is of considerable importance, especially in the rape trial, and we will return to it later.

All that remains now is to say something about the interrelationship between repair organization, on the one hand, and understanding in conversation, on the other. As we have seen, conversation is a real live, interactionally driven and context anchored performance. Conversational utterances unfurl on a moment-by-moment basis as contingently enacted and improvisationally managed achievements. As we have seen, the sequential organization of natural conversation blends together an endless or recursive seam of current and next speakers. Generating this system requires conversationalists to continuously monitor each other's contribution in order to secure sequential valency: to produce relevant and coherent responses in relation to some prior utterance, to recognize transition relevant places, and to address failures of understanding. The point is well put by Suchman: "Our communication succeeds in the face of such disturbance not because we predict reliably what will happen and thereby avoid problems, or even because we encounter problems that we have anticipated in advance, but because we work, moment by moment, to identify and remedy the inevitable troubles that arise" (Suchman 1987: 83).

Next speakers display that understanding or lack of understanding of a prior turn in next turn; and prior speaker, in third turn, displays his/her analysis of the previous turn (Heritage 1984: 258). This third turn option is a structurally designated position for speakers of first pair parts to confirm or disconfirm the adequacy of the second pair part. If the former, then some "normal trajectory" of the sequence will occur, as a covert confirmation of the displayed understanding thus far. If the latter, then the projected trajectory of the sequence will be derailed, and will continue with a different sequential implicativeness.

According to Heritage, such paired actions represent the building blocks of intersubjectivity:

conversational interaction is structured by an organization of action which is implemented on a turn-by-turn basis. By means of this organization, *a context of publicly displayed and continuously up-dated intersubjective understandings is systematically sustained*. It is through this "turn-by-turn" character of talk that the participants display their understandings of "the state of the talk" for one another. It is important to note that, because these displayed understandings arise as a kind of by-product or indirect outcome of the sequentially organized activities of the participants, the issue of understanding *per se* is only rarely topicalized at the conversational surface. Through this procedure the participants are thus released from the task of explicitly confirming and reconfirming their understandings of one another's actions. (1984: 259; emphasis in the original)

This is much too strong a claim, for – as Heritage goes on to recognize – numerous understandings remain covert in talk, strategically hidden. More narrowly but more accurately, only overt surface understandings are displayed in talk. Conversationalists leave numerous meanings and understandings undisplayed, or perhaps even better, underdisplayed in talk. But I will deal with that along with other problems in CA later on. Suffice it for now to note that since second pair parts display some type of understanding of the first pair part, producers of first pair parts have the option of remedying any misunderstanding in third turn. Additionally, insofar as participants display their understanding and recognition of social action for each other, they also provide professional analysts with a proof procedure (SSJ 1978; Heritage 1984) for the description of conversational materials – a methodological procedure which is varyingly transparent in the following examples.

(4.24) Radio call-in show

   A: I'd- I- I'd like to uh::::: I don't know if you know or not (0.5) but to me it seems uh wast- you know Rodchester Union Electric and Rodchester Telephone Company (.) now I know their pouring money into the radios and TVs in their area (0.4) but why do they have to advertise they got uh monopoly here.

   B: ... You know how many people (.) you know people call this program and they always scream about the utilities and phone companies and I- I'm just kind of curious how many people (0.5) right now in their homes if your listening to this program (.) how many have about four different lights on, how many of you got the radio on ... burning all this useless electricity ..

 → **A:**   Uh I- I- was just wondering uh you know <u>Why:::</u> (.) they have to advertise.

(4.25)   (Terasaki 1976: 45)

     M: Do you know who's going to that meeting?
     K: Who.
→ **M:**   I don't know!
     K: Ouh:: prob'ly: Mr Murphy an' Dad ...

(4.26)   (Heritage 1984: 258)

     A: Why don't you come and <u>see</u> me sometimes
                                        [
     B: I would like to
     A: I would like you to

In extract 4.24, aside from the interactional tasks that A's question might be accomplishing, such as being deliberately ambiguous (Weiser 1974), an interesting yet complex topic in its own right, notice that A can hear B's response as a complaint about his complaint, can locate a complaint as a prior social action that would have elicited a complaint about his prior complaint as a proper sequel, and can see how his first pair part, while (ostensibly) not produced to be a complaint, could be so analyzed. For A, the third turn option is taken up to deal with B's misunderstanding: to retroactively reformulate his previous action.

Mutatis mutandis extract 4.25 is a practically identical process. Here K treats M's first utterance as a pre-announcement, which would have yielded the puzzle answer in M's third turn. K's analysis turn out to be incorrect, however, since M was actually asking a question. In fact, K's answer is not forthcoming until M recycles her question, coming up with a reformulated input (i.e. I don't know!), which allows K to come up with a different or "correct" output (i.e. Ouh:: prob'ly: Mr Murphy an' Dad).

Since these understandings and misunderstandings are publicly produced, they are available as a resource for analysts as well; members' analyses provide a proof procedure: a methodological resource for both participants and analysts. For example, in extract 4.26 second speaker analyzes first speaker's action as an invitation, not as a complaint, an action which might have elicited an excuse, apology, or account as a complementary next action. For participants and analysts, the adequacy of A's analysis is displayed incarnately in B's third turn option. And, in just this way, the local, intersubjective definition of the situation emerges incrementally and processually through the dynamic moments of real time. As Moerman and Sacks (1988) note, conversation possesses a built-in mechanism for understanding.

That the sequential organization of natural conversation provides a critical interpretative resource for displaying understanding was put forth in an early statement by Schegloff and Sacks.

> By an adjacently positioned second, a speaker can show that he understood what a prior aimed at, and that he is willing to go along with that. Also, by virtue of the occurrence of an adjacently produced second, the doer of a first can see what he intended was indeed understood, and that it was or was not accepted. Also, of course, a second can assert his failure to understand, or disagreement, and, inspection of a second by a first can allow the first speaker to see that while the second thought he understood, indeed he misunderstood. It is through the use of adjacent positioning that appreciations, failure, correctings, et cetera can be themselves understandably attempted. (1974: 240)

There is also considerable evidence that conversationalists draw on sequential positioning as a resource in the production and comprehension – for interpreting the meaning – of talk (Schegloff 1984; Schegloff and Sacks 1974). Following Heritage (1984), we noted that conversation is managed on a turn-by-turn basis. Each turn is both "context shaped" and "context renewing." Each action is generated and comprehended via the prior turn and the larger sequential organization in which it is embedded. Simultaneously, because each action furnishes the environment for producing a next conversational activity, conversationalists must draw on these twin contextual properties of sequential organization as resources for designing their respective turns. Conversationalists orient to sequential positioning as a primary interpretive resource for making sense of one another's contributions.

These backward and forward "looking" properties of context possess a major corollary: an utterance in isolation might be seen, analytically, as doing a particular action, while in real live sequential context it, in reality, turns out to be doing something completely different. As Schegloff and Sacks note, the syntactic, semantic, or pragmatic grounds (or any other grounds for that matter) for interpreting action, when taken out of sequential context, might well yield incorrect results.

(4.27)   (Schegloff and Sacks 1974: 240)

    B: Yeah. Well get on your clothes and get out and collect some of that free food and we'll make it some other time Judy then.

    C: Okay then Jack

    B: Bye bye

    C: Bye bye.

Commenting on extract 4.27, they write:

> While B's initial utterance . . . might be grammatically characterized as an imperative or a command, and C's O.K. as a submission or accession to it, in no sense but a technical syntactic one would those be anything but whimsical characterizations. While B's utterance has certain imperative aspects in its language form, those are not the ones that count; his utterance is a closing initiation; and C's utterance agrees not to a command to get dressed . . . but to an invitation to close the conversation. The point is that no analysis, grammatical, semantic, pragmatic, etc., of these utterances taken singly and out of sequence, will yield their import in use, will show what coparticipants might make of them and do about them. That B's utterance here accomplishes a form of closing initiation, and C's accepts the closing form and not what seems to be proposed in it, turns on the placement of these utterances in the conversation. Investigations which fail to attend to such considerations are bound to be misled. (Schegloff and Sacks 1974: 253)

Any conversational activity – answers, insults, and as we have seen closings – involves a complex interaction between sequential location on the one hand and topical coherence on the other (Levinson 1983: 293). To use a final example, consider the following:

(*4.28*)   (Moerman and Sacks 1988: 185)

> **Roger:**   Ken face it you're a poor little rich kid.
> **Ken:**   Yes, Mommy. thank you.

Viewed in isolation, Ken's utterance might be an answer, agreement to some command, or whatever, by a child to his mother. Viewed sequentially, it does not engage in any of those tasks. Nor is Ken talking to his mother. For Ken's utterance follows Roger's: "Ken face it you're a poor little rich kid," which summons up the fact that, both conventionally and empirically, insults are sequentially implicative for return insults as possible next actions (Moerman and Sacks 1988: 185).

In this chapter and the previous two, I have traced through the theoretical background and importance of the sociology of talk as it pertains to the question of social order, to the production and reproduction of modes of domination, in general, and to the analysis of sequential organization, in particular. I have illustrated how the fine-tuned rhythmic texture and systematic order of talk are generated through conversational procedures, or, as Sacks (1984a: 26–7) puts it, by and through a machinery. And I have argued that CA does not attempt to statistically describe aspects of talk, nor does it attempt to just descriptively mirror what participants routinely do, but attempts to account for the structural resources and constraints that conversationalists provide for each other to shape the trajectory of talk-in-interaction – to co-organize and coordinate the temporal succession of unfolding and mutually intelligible social actions. In the next chapter I move far beyond conventional CA's concern with both conventional *a priori* and empirical structures of conversational competence, to sketch how conversational procedures are asymmetrically distributed in the rape trial context, and thereby represent sophisticated and multiplex processes of power, processes drawing on and reproducing both legal disciplinary regimes and patriarchal modes of domination.

NOTES

1 Post-positioned tags operate as second cycle options, which activate rule 1(c) to initiate turn transfer (SSJ 1978).
2 Goodwin (1981: 18) has illustrated how current and next may assign different and divergent meanings to silence, a situation that creates misprojections for turn transition due to expansions of turn size.

John: Well I, I took this course
            (0.5)
Ann: In how to quit?
            [
John: which I really recommend

As Goodwin notes, designations of silence as a gap or pause do not stand independently of the interpretations of partcipants. In the above fragment, John produces a unit type "Well, I, I took this course" which is followed by a 0.5 second silence. Now from Ann's point of view John has completed a turn unit, and the 0.5 second silence represents a gap, or inter-turn silence, a transition relevant place, and thus she starts to talk. John, however, continues into a new unit type via rule 1(c) and hence, retroactively transforms the 0.5 second silence into an intra-turn pause.

The above fragment also illustrates the notion of the turn as a mutable, time-bound process. Turns are expandable, not fixed, and reveal the interaction between rule set members 1(a)–(c). Failure to exercise 1(a) and 1(b), and withholding option 1(c), even for 0.5 second, leads to a silence which is terminated when Ann employs 1(b) and John employs 1(c). Although Ann begins to talk, her analysis of John's turn-in-progress turns out to be a misprojection which turns her utterance into a warrantable violation, a failure of turn synchronization (see Goodwin 1981).

3 When a first pair part is exercised, the option cycle 1(a)–(c) is activated on completion of the second pair part. In some adjacency pairs, questions for example, there appears to be some turn transfer skewing in the direction of the first pair part speaker.

5
Talk and Power in the Rape Trial

In the foregoing sections, I described the formal mechanics of social organization: the turn-taking system as an institutionalized and structural mechanism for distributing a scarce resource among conversationalists. I presented the sequential machinery of conversation as an analytically isolated system, an interactional order *sui generis*. And I discussed the turn-taking, adjacency pair, and repair systems as organizational domains consisting of social actions, systems of enablements for and constraints against enacting those actions, independently of macro social structures, social identities, or any other qualities of particular conversational incumbents and contexts.

This concept of talk as an interactionally autonomous domain has proved to be a powerful working premise for the naturalistic description of sequential relationships between social actions (Zimmerman 1988). As a working premise, however, it does not necessarily translate into empirical reality in all contexts. Further questions remain to be addressed. Does CA provide a coherent analytical framework with which to pursue studies of talk and power in organizational contexts? How do conversational structures and devices interact with social structures, with modes of domination? What analytic tools are necessary to reveal such relationships in processual and fine-grained detail? When, specifically, does social structure impinge on talk, affecting its organization and trajectory? Put most succinctly, when is social structure "procedurally consequential" for the talk which it encapsulates and when is it not (Schegloff 1987)?

When observing trial talk, for example, the scope of opportunity to talk is both differentially and asymmetrically distributed across social structure. Although the locus of conversation organization consists of action constraints and enablements, nonconversational speech exchange systems preallocate – to varying degrees – the opportunities for action. Differential access to the procedures of talk is prestructured or built into the social organization of particular speech exchange systems, constituting a major resource of power and constraining the form of the interaction. Moreover, if language is the symbolic embodiment of social values, then the meanings and ideology of domination that are necessarily transmitted through and interwoven with conversational procedures – the normative sexual scripts governing male/female interaction – furnish powerful interpretative resources for categorizing social actions, for ascribing meaning, and for making sense (Henley 1977; Schur 1984, 1988; Goffman 1987; Herman 1989).[1]

I referred to this interpenetration of talk, social structure, and power as socially structured talk – the substantive mechanics of social organization. In this section I will discuss how CA and cognate linguistic approaches analyze the interaction between talk and social structure through variation in a particular speech exchange system, and describe how the concept of socially structured talk – at least in the rape trial but doubtless more generally – can forge a more cogent and coherent conception of the duality of structure.

ORGANIZATIONAL TALK

Even though CA considers natural conversation as the primordial form of talk-in-interaction (Heritage 1985, 1989; Schegloff 1987, 1988a), a type of base structure from which other forms of talk are transformationally linked, Sacks and others recognized early on the differential import of talk in other contexts. As I mentioned previously, talk-in-interaction is arranged along a linear array of speech exchange systems. The polar extremes along this continuum consist of debate systems on the one hand and natural conversation on the other. The variation in these different systems reveals that preallocation of turn order, turn or sequence type, and, to a lesser extent, turn size is built into organizational forms of talk (Sacks et al. 1978; Schegloff 1982, 1987). Unlike natural conversation, which is locally managed on a turn-by-turn basis, organizational talk prestructures conversational enablements and constraints for participants – asymmetrically allocating opportunities to participate in talk, and constraining the length and type of those opportunities. This pre-existedness of social structure represents a differential social organization: *the differential power that derives from structural location in the social organization of particular speech exchange systems.* Even the classic study of repair organization (Schegloff et al. 1977), a study in pure CA, contains the hypothesis that "other-repair" is finely sensitive to the structural location of participants; adults "other-correct" children, and more powerful "other-correct" less powerful conversational participants.

Bearing these points in mind, conversation analysts have studied a range of different speech exchange systems exhibiting differential participation rights based on the structural location and therefore power of participants. These different contexts include classrooms (McHoul 1978; Mehan 1979), news interviews (Clayman 1988; Greatbatch 1986, 1988; Heritage 1985; Heritage et al. 1988), plea bargains (Maynard 1984), doctor/patient consultations (West 1984; Heath 1986; Frankel 1983, 1984, 1990; Treichler et al. 1984; Fisher 1988; Todd 1989; Fisher and Todd 1983), police/citizen calls (Sharrock and Turner 1978; M. Whalen and Zimmerman 1987; J. Whalen et al. 1988), helpline calls (Watson 1978, 1987), murder interrogations (Watson 1990), trial talk (Atkinson and Drew 1979; Drew 1985, 1990, 1992; Brannigan and Lynch 1987), political oratory (Atkinson, 1984, 1985; Heritage and Greatbatch 1986), labor negotiations (Francis 1986), and counselor/student interaction (Erickson and Shultz 1982).

In these organizational contexts, access to sequential structure is asymmetrically distributed across social position, thereby constituting a major resource for accomplishing domination in talk (Molotch and Boden 1985: 285; Kollock et al. 1985; Scheff 1984: 127–42). One participant has the power to allocate turns, to frame the topic or agenda, and to manage the sequence type. In the rape trial, for example, defense attorneys allocate each next turn to the victim, frame the topic to be addressed in her turn, and restrict that topic through the syntactic manipulation of question and answer sequences.

Within a much broader framework, encompassing gendered modes of domination, conversation analysts have discovered that turns and topics of talk are asymmetrically distributed across gender (Zimmerman and West 1975; West and Zimmerman 1977, 1983, 1985; West 1979; West and Garcia 1988; Fishman 1978). Males interrupt females to a much greater extent than females interrupt males, and although females initiate most of the topics in conversation, their chances for topic "success" are much less than for males. While females produce the interactional work to sustain male topics, male work is designed to undermine female topics; males curtail development of female topics, fail to pursue them, and initiate unilaterial topic changes (see West and Garcia 1988).

Consequently, the categorial identities of male and female interact with and are grafted on the situated identities of speaker and listener discourse roles to create the dynamic processual relevance of gender for talk-in-interaction – creating, sustaining, and negotiating these interactionally emergent identities through the succession of moments in real time and within the exigencies of communicative performance. Put another way, gender categories are relevant, at precision placed moments, for the talk-in-interaction, so that males and females produce and reproduce patriarchal domination through conversational forms of power.

But the production and reproduction of social structure involves more than access to the formal procedures of talk. Even though access to sequential structure constitutes a major resource for accomplishing power in social interaction, the substantive ideology of domination – the topic and content of social organization – interlocks with and is mapped on to formal procedures to create an institutionally anchored system of male hegemony: a two-tiered system of courtroom disciplinary regimes and patriarchal domination. The ideology and moral order of patriarchy are processually assembled, concealed, and enacted through the categorization work embedded in courtroom talk. As suggested earlier, social structure is produced and reproduced by the repetition and routinization of actions across time and space. Yet paradoxically and irremediably, because each social action is unique, actors must engage in categorization work to assemble unique actors, actions, and events into cognitively similar if not identical for-all-practical-purposes categories. Every "another first time" is fitted to a pre-existing category, creating a seamless stretch of "same" for-all-practical-purposes social actions and actors, and searing the comfortable, oppressing, and even inevitable facticity of social structure deep into consciousness (Garfinkel 1967; Shibutani 1986: 52, 150; Turner 1988: 151–3).

Most relevant to the present study, discovering the category "rape victim" relies on moral ascription and assessment of category-bound rights, obligations, and activities, but the criteria for assessing category performance, dividing women into "rapable" and "unrapable" categories (MacKinnon 1989: 175), are patriarchally – and hence power – driven. The moral order involves power. *Sequential-institutional power* captures the observation that some actors possess the organizational resources to manipulate the structures of conversation and other procedures of talk in order to make their accounts count. *Patriarchal power* functions as a system of ideological categorizations and sense production conventions linking actions to actors (or vice versa), a system that conceals male sexual reality as nonsectarian or universal and that interprets reality and experience according to male norms while simultaneously disqualifying the female's experience of sexual terror (see MacKinnon 1987, 1989; Walby 1989; Smart 1989). Both forms of power coalesce in the rape trial to create, sustain, and reproduce the sense and intelligibility of patriarchal hegemony. The concept of *socially structured talk* builds off these studies of institutional and dominational talk, yet still expands beyond them to encompass the complex interweaving of ideological categorizations, formal structures, and institutional power.

In sum, then, some CA research addresses formal sequential analysis; other work analyzes sequencing in institutional contexts; and still other studies examine the relationship between sequential structure and statistical analysis of interruptions and topic change based on the social variables of gender and status – social domination accomplished through mechanical manipulation of sequential structure. Yet none of these approaches focus on multiplex systems of domination, like courtroom talk and patriarchy, nor do they attempt to map ideological categorizations on to sequential structures to capture the intersecting parameters of social structure and talk. In order to probe the duality of talk and social structure in the rape trial context – how the structural properties of institutional and patriarchal modes of domination are drawn on in strategic interaction and reproduced as an outcome of this process – the collapse of meaning into sequential-structural location must be augmented to include patriarchal categorizations.

This steadfast reluctance to address the intersection of talk and social structure is not a critique of CA, however. Nor is it a claim against the autonomy of the interaction order. It is instead a delimitation of CA's field of inquiry and its preoccupation with the sequential organization of social actions. It is a claim that substantive ideologies of domination – the content of social organization – are centrally implicated in the production and reproduction of social structure. While patriarchy may not necessarily affect sequential structure in the rape trial, and I make no claim that it does (though courtroom organization does), the interactional work of ascribing blame and allocating responsibility for the incident relies on patriarchy as an interpretative resource for assessing and understanding action.

I am addressing two hypotheses here, both of which are inextricably intertwined, but may be distinguished for ease of exposition and analytic purposes: one is that the patriarchal categorizations governing male/female interaction are demonstrably relevant to meaning and interpretation; and the other is that courtroom context is procedurally consequential for sequential structure.

As we will see in detail later on, contrast sets, three-part lists, and puzzle sequences – occurring singly or in variant combinatorial formats – are employed not only in adversarial cross-examination, but also in political speeches and doubtless in an array of situations where persuasive power is being employed, irrespective of the topics or contents involved (Atkinson 1984; Drew 1990, 1992; Heritage and Greatbatch 1986). Because they operate in a wide range of contexts, accomplish an array of interactional tasks, and are employed by participants of various social identities, the devices constitute formal conversational procedures. In courtroom cross-examination, however, the opportunity to implement such powerful persuasive resources is asymmetrically distributed. As illustrated below, the rhythmic, rhetorical, and grammatical organization of the devices reveals not only a remarkably fine-tuned system of temporal regulation between defense attorney and victim, but also a differential ability to participate in talk: only attorneys can manipulate sequential structure to produce the persuasive charisma of legal discourse.

(5.1)   Trial 1

0490→	**DA:**	How did'ju wind up in his automobe::l?
0491		(1.8)
0492	**V:**	I got in.
0493		(1.3)
0494→	**DA:**	<u>WHY</u>::::.
0495		(1.6)
0496	**V:**	Because he said we were goin to uh <u>party</u> at uh friend
0497		of his house
0498		(2.7)
0499→	**DA:**	But'chu didn't kno::w (.) his <u>last name</u> (.) <u>where he</u>
0500		<u>worked</u> (.) or <u>where he was from</u> correct?
0501		(1.0)
0502	**V:**	°Yes.
0503→	**DA:**	You didn't know uh <u>thing about him</u> did'ju?
0504		(1.0)
0505	**V:**	°No.

Looked at sequentially, the courtroom speech exchange system is procedurally consequential for the talk which it encapsulates, first because the structural distribution of discourse options permits only attorneys to ask questions and direct the trajectory of talk, and second because the form or structure of sequential organization, the trajectory of the interaction, is transformed in distinct ways.

But substantively, what is accomplished, what is achieved interactionally in fine-grained context, and what form of domination is being produced and reproduced depends on content, not just form. If that is indeed the case, and I think it is, then membership categorizations must be mapped on to those structures. Otherwise the DA's *contrast with an embedded three-part list* or *contrast list*, "But'chu didn't know his last name, where he worked, or where he was from, correct?" (lines 0499–0500) despite being the second part of a formal structure (following the victim's *puzzle solution* "because he said we were going to a party at uh friend of his house") could refer to virtually anything – representing any social action from a question of idle curiosity to an accusation against the victim. When we analyze this utterance in courtroom cross-examination and its repeated application in closing argument, however, the device generates a finely crafted and selectively designed piece of categorization work; it invokes a blame inferential assertion that the relevant category for assessing this action and the actors involved is consensual sex, not a crime of rape. In strategically enacted performance, it possesses accusatory and blame-implicative power of considerable scope. It therefore exhibits much more than sequential power. Inescapably, patriarchal power is crucial to the interpretation of this social action, to its sense, and to the interactional work being accomplished.

Patriarchal power, more formally, is being produced and reproduced in this exchange between the V and DA. Patriarchal power, more precisely, shapes interpretations about particular sexual encounters so that they look more like consensual sex than rape (MacKinnon 1989, 1983). Patriarchal power conceals male normative standards of sexuality as the standard, stabilizing its hegemony through covert objectifications grounded in members' categorization work – structured through, organized around, and driven by socially organized methods of talk.

Looked at in this light, contrast sets and lists indicate an inconsistency or disjuncture between normatively appropriate and structurally required category-bound activities, knowledge, and obligations a *bona fide* V needs to possess on the one hand, and the moral inferences generated from the V's violation of those requirements on the other (Smith 1978). They possess an "if A then B" logic, but where, it turns out, B is disjunctive with or does not follow A. The mutual intelligibility and meaning of inequality are socially structured and interactionally accomplished in structurational performance. Inequality is assembled and performed through puzzle/solution and contrast list devices. Knowledge of the accused's last name, place of employment, and residence – category-bound knowledge and obligations – interactionally emerges as a source of structural constraint for incumbency in the category "victim." The social construction of moral character and therefore the interpretation of the act as consensual sex or rape emerge from an inferential logic built into the very fabric of conversational procedures; for example, the V's credibility is cast strongly into doubt because her actions and inactions during the incident were inconsistent. Most importantly, however, since categorization work involves power, inconsistency is only inconsistency from a male, not female perspective. Even though the sequential procedures of talk may well be, in conversational speech exchange systems, autonomous from and impervious to externally constraining social facts, since they are transcontextual, the substantive ideologies mapped or grafted on to these autogenic procedures are indeed socially structured. The fact that a woman consented to sexual intercourse because of absent category-bound requirements is an interpretation based on patriarchal standards of sexuality and sexual access – what I call patriarchal logic-in-action – a standard which legitimates and objectifies ony the male experience of reality as a legal social fact (MacKinnon 1989).

By way of contrast, to illustrate the processual relevance of categorization work on sequential structure, consider my earlier example of complaining about complaining. In the complaint about complaining both the organization and logic of sequential structure are affected by categorizing the prior speaker as a chronic complainant or one of the other species of the device. The CAC deletes the relevance of the prior topic, designates the hierarchical supremacy of a new topic, and continues the sequence not just with a different topical agenda but with a different projected trajectory and inferential implicativeness as well. The mechanism has organizational consequences for talk-in-interaction. This categorial relevance for sequential structure still does not address what I mean by a substantive mechanics of social organization, and the present study fails to broach the interaction between formal and substantive mechanics in this very strict sense.

Because of the focus on formal structure, even studies of institutional talk stop short of a substantive mechanics of social organization. The formal mechanics of social organization address the fact that access to the procedures of talk is organizationally anchored and asymmetrically distributed across social position. Although organizational domination is processually enacted and thereby reproduced through manipulation of sequential mechanisms, the production and reproduction of modes of domination like patriarchy require a substantial departure from CA precepts, to a more orthodox conception of social structure, because it is unclear how class, gender, and racial modes of domination are procedurally consequential or categorially relevant for sequential operations (if they are at all) – at least in the trial talk under consideration here.

Once again and more forcefully, this is not a critique of CA but a limitation of its focal problematics; I find little utility in criticizing a realm of inquiry for failing to address interpretative and macro structural phenomena because it seeks to discover and describe sequential structures instead. In contrast, I attempt to explicate both formal and substantive mechanics of social organization to unveil the production and reproduction of legal disciplinary regimes and gendered modes of domination in the rape trial. In the following sections of this chapter, I will first describe the sequential structure of courtroom talk, and describe how this speech exchange system is procedurally consequential for the talk which it encapsulates. Secondly, I will describe how the substantive mechanics of social organization – membership categorizations, ideology, and normative frameworks (patriarchal logic in action) – are mapped on to and grafted on these sequential mechanisms, and how male hegemony interpenetrates with talk as a strategically enacted performance to produce and reproduce social structure. If coercive sexuality bears a close connection to approved schemas of male/female interaction, if the way men and women are talked about represents one way that language is the symbolic embodiment of social values and power (Schur 1984: 143; Ervin-Tripp 1987: 19), then courtroom talk will display the unfolding of these norms in processual and dynamic – actually lived time – detail. The intersecting parameters of sequential, legal organizational, and patriarchal structures capture what I mean by socially structured talk and embody the instantiated moment of structuration – a structurational totality (see Burawoy 1985: 59)

COURTROOM TALK

According to Benson, "organizations constitute important instruments of domination in the advanced industrial societies" (1981: 279; see also R. Hall 1987; Pfeffer 1982; Scott 1987; Galbraith 1983: 6–7). On an interactional level, a mere glimpse of trial talk reveals such domination quite dramatically and transparently.

(5.2)   Trial 2 (vol. 1, page 119, lines 10–16)

>   DA: So you were aware of the meaning of this song, "Going to go
>   Downtown", and in the colloquial, and used in the street
>   language, "Gonna go Downtown and get me some ass", is that
>   correct?
> → V: Yes; but I didn't know she was buying that album.
>   Can I ask you a question? Can I?
> → J: No ...

(5.3)   Trial 2 (vol. 1, page 138, lines 4–15)

>   DA: Didn't you in fact leave Stratman Park out of that statement
>   because you thought it might be detrimental to you in the
>   prosecution?
>   V: No. No.

DA: Did you mention in that statement going to the Mobil Station twice?

→ PA: Your Honor, if he's going to continue this line of questioning about everything that might have been left out, could he offer her a chance to explain the discrepancies, if any?

→ J: No ...

(5.4)   (vol. 2, page 837, lines 12–17)

DA: Did you report to him, Ma'am, or did you give him a statement?

V: I remember telling him that the tampon I was wearing was//

→ DA: Ma'am, would you answer that yes or no, did you give him a statement?

V: Yes, I did.

(5.5)   (vol. 3, page 109, lines 13–24)

DA: Your testimony is that up until the time you came into court here today, you never sat down with your attorney and discussed what your testimony here would be.

V: I don't think it matters, because I am only telling the truth

J: Just a moment, now.

V: I never told her what I was going to say.

→ J: That's fine. Just let me say this to you. Just listen to the questions and answer the questions ...

The institutionalized power (Lenski 1984: 52–8; Galbraith 1983: 54–71) found in trial cross-examination illustrates the procedural consequentiality or relevance of context on the talk that it encapsulates. The procedural connection between social structure and talk or the way that courtroom context affects the organization and trajectory of talk exhibits the following features.

1 Turn allocation techniques, turn order, turn type, and distribution of turn type are relatively fixed (Atkinson and Drew 1979).
2 Talk is restricted to judges, witnesses, and attorneys, and is designed for an overhearing, co-present but nonspeaking audience – the jury (Atkinson and Drew 1979).
3 Talk unfolds according to global activity structures and procedural/ evidential strictures. Global structures designate the linear ordering and internal organization of courtroom talk, partitioning it into discretely bound and sequentially occurring activity segments such as opening statements, direct and cross-examination of witnesses, redirect and recross examination of witnesses, closing arguments,

judicial instructions and so on. There are local activity types within global contexts, such as objection and question/answer sequences, some of which transform both the participation structure and sequential organization of courtroom activity. Procedural and evidential strictures refer to formal legal rules regulating the nature of testimony, evidence, and questioning.

TURN-TAKING IN COURTROOM EXAMINATION

I want to unpack these observations in turn and in some detail. First, unlike natural conversation, in which turn-taking techniques are locally managed, courtroom talk exhibits a relatively restricted system of turn selection: attorneys control the selection of next speaker, controlling that selection through current selects next technique. And, on completion of witnesses' turn, attorneys then self-select themselves as next speaker (Atkinson and Drew 1979). This unequal access to the turn-taking system is clearly revealed in the segment 5.2 above, where the victim attempts first to self-select herself and second to employ a current selects next technique. But the attempt to subvert the courtroom format – to wrest control – is resolutely and quickly quashed; the projected question is preempted in its preliminary stage, suffering the fate of other *overt subversions* and therefore contributing to the reproduction of courtroom domination.

Still more technically, the above extracts raise a number of points for consideration. First, the focal courtroom format reveals a fixed or *preallocation of turn order*: attorneys speak first, and witnesses second (Atkinson and Drew 1979). Second, the *type of turn* produced is restricted to surface syntactic question and answer adjacency pairs (Atkinson and Drew 1979). Third, turn or sequence types are *differentially distributed* among courtroom participants: attorneys produce question first pair parts, and witnesses respond with answer second pair parts. And last, because the opportunity to ask questions belongs only to attorneys, *turn selection techniques* are preallocated systemically, so that only attorneys allocate next turns and thus control, manage, and constrain – in any improvisational fashion – the turn taking system. As the examples illustrate, courtroom context is procedurally relevant to sequential organization, first because of turn preallocation, by prestructuring the order of speakership, and second because of turn-type preallocation, by prestructuring the turn type that a particular speaker produces. As the examples demonstrate, these facts about sequential organization in trial talk are secured not only from their regular occurrence or empirical frequency, but also from the normative sanctions imposed on participants when the rules are breached.

I will discuss in more detail how courtroom preallocation impinges on the internal organization of turns and sequences and, derivatively, on the organization of topics, but first I want to address two major exceptions to this (for now) focal format.

REPAIR SEQUENCES

There are exceptions to the focal format: attorney/questioner and witness/answerer. First, the victim can transform or realign the focal discourse identities by initiating a repair sequence, so that turn order, turn type, and turn allocation become temporarily inverted. In such instances, the victim speaks first and the DA second; the victim asks a question and the DA answers; and the victim exercises a current-selects-next device.

(5.6)   Trial 1

    DA: The first time you became concerned was when.
               (4.5)
→ **V:**   Concerned for my safety?
               (1.1)
→ **DA:**   Sure.

(5.7)   Trial 1

    DA: There are <u>SCRATCHES</u> on yer back here. Didn't that
              come (.) from from having yer back exposed on the <u>field</u>.
              (4.0)
              Didn't that come when you were moving around by
              yourself in the field?
              (1.5)
→ **V:**   When I was struggling?
               (0.4)
→ **DA:**   <u>NO</u>:::

These extracts, especially 5.7, introduce and underscore a theoretical point of considerable importance. The concept of socially structured talk envisions power as a socially structured, contingently enacted, and chronically negotiated resource mobilized within the exigencies of communicative performance and within a range of opportunities and constraints operating from moment to moment across real time. Even though the balance between autonomy and constraint is differentially distributed across courtroom position practices, such that judges and attorneys possess more options and resources than witnesses, the dialectic of control (Giddens 1979; Issac 1987) or the dialectic of autonomy and constraint (Hall 1985) must be explicated, not taken as given. How attorneys and witnesses maximize and expand their autonomy over the resistance of each other, opposing attorneys, and judges requires unprecedented scrutiny of courtroom performance, to the processes and achievement of power in actually lived moments (P. Hall 1985, 1987; Luckenbill 1980).

With these points in mind, the victim's repair initiation in 5.7 is one method for turning the tables, as it were, on the defense attorney. From the DA's emphatic "NO:::" it is rather apparent that the "opening" created through the victim's footing shift (Goffman 1981) has exposed a vulnerability which can be exploited on future occasions; repair initiations can function as victim's devices for neutralizing, transforming, and derailing both topical and sequential implicativeness and, more generally, for puncturing, contesting, and usurping – if only for a short time – the DA's control over the testimony and questioning. I will discuss similar instances of power negotiation as they arise throughout this chapter.

OBJECTION SEQUENCES: STRUCTURE I

Nor is the victim the only participant who can transform the focal format. Secondly, but much more pervasively, the PA and judge can self-select and simultaneously select next speakers through objections, requests for clarification, and, infrequently, warnings. While the victim transforms courtroom discourse structure through next turn repair initiations, an internal expansion of sequential structure, the prosecuting attorney's objections transform not only the discourse structure but also the participation structure of the court – creating an external expansion of sequential structure (Schenkein 1980: 41).

(5.8)   Trial 1

> **DA:**   So thit essenchely what yer testifying to here in <u>court</u> (.)
> is the statement that you gave to detective Kuba is that
> correct?
>
> **PA:**   <u>Objecshun</u> °yer honor
> ────────
> (1.3)

DA: °It's cross examinashun °yer honor.
              (3.7)
J: Overru::led.
              ((Cough))   (1.0)
DA: Essenchuly yer testifying to what waz in the statement
              >izint that correct<?

(5.9)   Trial 1

DA:= It implies (7.4) tuh many people that implies sexual activity
              dozen it?=
PA:= Objecshun yer honor
              (2.5)
J: ((Clearing throat)) (2.3) Overru::led.

Thus simple characterizations of courtroom format as involving just two participants, the DA and the V, where the former asks questions and the latter answers them, are fraught with a host of difficulties because they fail to capture the complexity of discourse design on at least two grounds. I have already demonstrated that victims frequently ask questions in particular sequential environments. From the above examples, notice also that the prosecuting attorney may object to the DA's question on procedural or evidential grounds or both, objecting to the form or to the procedural propriety of the question. And, once initiated, objections transform both the *participation structure*, the particular configuration of discourse identities and the relevant activities they may engage in (see Erickson and Schultz 1982: 17), and the sequential organization of courtroom discourse. The projected trajectory of the question/answer sequence is thereby derailed, preempted, or delayed, and continues not only with a different sequential implicativeness and discourse structure, but also with a transformed participation structure. The objection preempts the victim's answer, selects the judge as next speaker, and requires the judge, most formally, to either overrule or sustain the objection. If the latter, then the DA must rephrase the question, or initiate a completely different line of inquiry; if the former, then the DA may repeat or reformulate the question previously put forth to the victim. Once again, these sequential observations are available not only from empirical regularity, but also from the normative accountability of violations like the following.

(5.10)   Trial 3 (page 115, lines 15–24; page 116, lines 1–7)

DA: And how much did you make an hour at the department store?
V: Three ten an hour.

PA: Your Honor, this entire line of questioning is not relevant to the proceeding.

J: Well, I think we have let him wander pretty far. I suggest that unless you have some foundation to offer you proceed with other//

V: I didn't accept any money from Mr Matlock

DA: Three ten an hour?

PA: Your Honor, again//

V: I live very cheaply, sir. I don't buy things that most people do.

→ J: It isn't going to do me much good to say you don't have to answer a question if you insist on answering it.

V: I am sorry

(5.11) (Atkinson and Drew 1979: 214)

Counsel: How old's Mr (Chaplin)?
                      (0.5)
Opposition counsel: Objection
Witness: I don't know
                      (4.5)
→ Judge: The answer may stand she doesn't know.
                      (13.0)
                     Uh (0.5) Miss Le Brette (0.5) uh when you
                     hear the District Attorney object don't make
                     any answer until I tell you you've to answer
                     the question or not=
Witness: =Okay

Much less frequently but much more accurately, the judge may also mediate the objection sequence, first by interpreting the victim's testimony when it has become a matter of some dispute, and second by other-initiating and other-repairing the question that was objected to, with both mediations occurring in the sequential location of post-objection.

(5.12) Trial 1

DA: (hhh) (1.0) Are you telling me that you don't know what you remember without the statement n you n you don't know what you(::r) Are you tellin me you don't know (.) what items you remember without reading the statement=

PA: =Objection yer honor she has <u>testified</u> that (.) she stated (0.5) <u>what she remembered</u>? (0.7) She testified as to what she remembered as to <u>WHAT HAPPENED</u>!

→ J: I think what she has testified to thet sez- (.) her testimony
          toda::y (.) wuz re<u>freshed</u>(.) some what (.) on certain items
          (:by) the statement she read Friday.

(5.13)   Trial 1

DA: How often have you been to the Grainary?
                (5.3)
V: °We::: (.) ( )
                [
PA: Objection yer honor that has nothing to do:: (.)
          with the (evidence in this case).
→ J: You mean prior to this incident.
DA: Prior to this incident.

(5.14)   Trial 2

DA: Isn't it a fact that you smoked marijuana and drank beer
          on Chouteau Island?
PA: Objection. Objection, your honor.
→ J: On this date?
DA: On August the 7th and August the 6th ...

(5.15)   Trial 1

DA: That might be from a sideways movement?
                (1.3)
          Back and forth?=
PA:=   That calls for a conclusion your honor.
J: Yeah that's susta::ined.

When PAs self-select through an objection, they not only self-select
themselves to talk, but also and simultaneously select the judge as next
speaker and select the particular action for next turn: overrule or sustain
the objection. Yet still, the PA's objection often provides a *post-objection
option space* for the DA to self-select and provide the basis for the
objected-to question or to withdraw it prior to the judge's ruling. By
withdrawing the question, the DA attempts to neutralize an impending
objection and thereby preempt the judge's ruling.

(5.16)   Trial 1

DA: So thit essenchely what yer testifying to here in <u>court</u> (.) is
          the statement that you gave to detective Kuba is that correct?

PA:	Objecshun °yer honor.

(1.3)

→ DA: °It's cross examinashun °yer honor.

(3.7)

J: Overru::led.

(5.17) Trial 1

DA: Linda isn't it tru::e (.) that you wanted to have sex with Brian n' he wouldn't let you (0.5) >I mean he couldn't<

PA: Objection yer honor that's been asked and answered (already).

(1.0)

→ DA: Let me be more specific your honor I'll re-fraze the question (.) Isn't it true ...

(5.18) Trial 1

DA: Did you have any marijuana?

(.)

V: No.

(.)

DA: You have used marijuana have you not?

(.)

V: Yes I have.

(1.8)

DA: You enjoy its use do you not?

PA: Objection yer honor (that isn't relevant)

[[

V: ( )

→ DA: I'll withdraw that (   ) yer honor

[   ]

J: Sustained

(1.6)

J: Now- (.) in regards (.) to that (.) come forward please.

As the above examples illustrate, DAs produce "withdrawals" immediately post-objections, prior to the judge's "ruling." Yet as seen in 5.18, the attempt to foreclose that ruling does not necessarily yield the preferred outcome. If successful, *pre-ruling withdrawals* and rephrasing withdrawals not only yield three-part structures, so that the minimal sequential format remains intact, they also limit or contract the participation structure within the objection sequence: DA and PA.

DA: I   Question
PA: II   Objection/grounds
DA: III   Withdrawal

Let me summarize the sequential structures of the objection sequences just looked at and then briefly consider two theoretical issues posed by the data. Following that I will turn to a more speculative excursion into the interactional functions conducted through objection sequences.

(1) The minimal or contracted objection sequence exhibits one of the following structures: a contraction of discourse structure on the one hand, or a contraction of both discourse and participation structure on the other. The former occurs much more frequently and prototypically; the latter operates as an attempt to delete the ruling part of the sequence and hence preempt the judge's participation in the objection sequence.

(in 5.9 and 5.15)

DA: I   Question
PA: II   Objection/grounds
J: III   Ruling

(in 5.17 and 5.18)

DA: I   Question
PA: II   Objection
DA: III   Offer to withdraw (rephrasing and pre-ruling withdrawals)

Or, much less frequently, we find the PA's objection post V's answer.

(in 5.10)

DA: I   Question
V: II   Answer
PA: III   Grounds
J: IV   Ruling

Similar to the structure portrayed in 5.9 but still distinct are cases when the objection component is elided and therefore automatically absorbed into the grounds objection component, as in examples 5.10 and 5.15.

(2) Expansions on this minimal three-part structure are systematically fashioned intrasequentially on the one hand, and sequentially on the other, the former occurring when the appended grounds component

expands internal turn structure, the latter when the component expands sequential structure. The intra-turn expansion occurs in 5.13, while sequential expansions are displayed in 5.8 and in 5.19 below.

(in 5.13)

DA:	I	Question
PA:	II	Objection+grounds
J:	III	Ruling (elided)

(in 5.8)

DA:	I	Question
PA:	II	Objection
DA:	III	Grounds for question
J:	IV	Ruling

(in 5.19)

DA:	I	Question
PA:	II	Objection
J:	III	Ruling$_1$
PA:	IV	Grounds for objection
J:	V	Ruling$_2$

A legal point is worth emphasizing concerning 5.19 below. When the PA objects, the legal basis for the objection implicates another option that affects the internal design of the objection turn: expanding the PA's turn to [objection+grounds]. Or the objection may exhibit an [objection+pause+grounds] turn shape. The procedural connection between courtroom context and objections is this. If the PA produces the ground for the objection, but not the correct one, the judge can overrule it, even though other legal grounds for objecting exist (Mauet 1988). So the option to expand internal turn-shape by producing the grounds for the objection constitutes a hazard for the objecting party. Because providing the legal basis for objections is required only if it is not apparent from the context of the question, activating the option might unnecessarily jeopardize the success of the objection (ibid.). As a second-best strategy, PAs may initiate objections, pause before providing the grounds, and in so doing establish the sequential environment for a quick favorable ruling which would preempt the grounds component altogether. Of course, this type of delay also creates the DA's grounds option space. If the PA invokes the post-objection pause, then the DA may self-select and exercise the grounds option, although this latter option space may be deleted or elided by a quick ruling. And as a third-best strategy, which rarely succeeds, PAs often initiate objections, withhold the basis, and then, given the judge's overrule, provide the previously elided basis.

(5.19)   Trial 2 (page 111, lines 10–15)

> DA: Have you seen any other driver's licenses in connection with this case?
> PA: Objection, your honor.
> J: Overruled.
> → PA: Beyond the scope of direct.
> J: Overruled.

(3) Of course, both internal turn-shape and sequential structure may be expanded within the same objection sequence, as in the following.

(5.20)   Trial 2 (page 123, lines 20–4; page 124, lines 1–8)

> DA: Would you explain to me why you now think they didn't?
> V: I just do.
> DA: Do you know what that feels like?
> V: Yes.
> DA: To have somebody climax inside of you?
> PA: Objection, your honor.
> J: Objection sustained.
> DA: Your Honor, I'm not delving into this woman's past sexual history.
> PA: Objection to the speech, your Honor.
> J: The Court understands your reason, Counsel, and objection sustained.

(5.21)   Trial 2 (page 150, lines 2–9)

> DA: Didn't you make the statement that five or six people had intercourse with you twice? I believe it was.
> V: Yes.
> PA: Objection, your Honor, unless he establishes when these statements were made.
> DA: She just admitted making the statement, your Honor.
> J: Objection sustained.

(5.22)   Trial 2 (page 234, lines 16–24)

> DA: And what was interfering with your free choice?
> PA: I'll object, your Honor. That's been asked and answered already. The other people present.

DA: I object to his putting words in the witness' mouth.
J: Yes. This would be improper. Objection overruled.
DA: Thank you ...

(5.23) Trial 2 (page 809, lines 12–17)

DA: Well, were these people close friends of yours?
PA: Objection to the relevancy.
DA: It is relevant.
PA: With respect to the issues.
J: Objection sustained and the//

Although objection sequences might appear *prima facie* structurally unstable, given the possible variational formats displayed in the foregoing fragments, they more accurately represent an improvisational set of options and combinations of options based on an inner logic of sequential and legal action. The objection activates the contextual resources for the smooth, forward moving and closely coordinated trajectory from contracted to variant expanded structures, with participants modulating the progression of their own and each others' sequential movements as talk unfurls from moment to moment. More elaborate and expanded structures are constructed out of basic three-part components – primarily through grounds components built into the internal design of turns and sequences – creating rhythmically interlaced inter- or intra-turn expansions or combinatorial sets of both. The structural formats of 5.20 through 5.23, which exhibit these multiplex expansions, are sketched below.

(in 5.20)

DA:	I	Question
PA:	II	$Objection_1$
J:	III	$Ruling_1$
DA:	IV	Grounds
PA:	V	$Objection_2$+grounds
J:	VI	$Ruling_2$

(in 5.21)

DA:	I	Question
V:	II	Answer
PA:	III	Objection+grounds
DA:	IV	Grounds
J:	V	Ruling

(in 5.22)

DA:	I	Question
PA:	II	Objection+grounds
DA:	III	Objection to objection+grounds
J:	IV	Ruling

(in 5.23)

DA:	I	Question
PA:	II	Objection+grounds$_1$
DA:	III	Grounds
PA:	IV	Grounds$_2$
J:	V	Ruling

Because the objection produces a post-objection option space, appended grounds components may be produced in the objection turn by the PA, or in the next turn by the DA, or both. But, crucially, the judge wields the power to compress or delete the option space for both DA and PA. In the case of clearcut violations, the objection sustain may be implemented immediately – latched on to, occurring simultaneously with, or even overlapping the PA's objection. This is dramatically illustrated in the following example.

(5.24) Trial 1: Recross

> **DA:** Have you been instructed to remain (.) ca::lm (.) and collected
> on this stand (1.0) by anybody (.) that that's the best way to get
> uh rape conviction=
> **PA:** Objection your honor
> =[[
> **J:** No- <u>SUSTAINED</u> AND THE (uh) JURY'S ORDERED
> TO DISREGARD THE LAST STATEMENT!
>   (1.4)
> No::w Mr:: (.) Wasserman you know better n' that ...

And *mutatis mutandis* the same process may occur with overruled objections. In both cases, the grounds components often wind up occurring in the sequential location of post-ruling, an "unhappy" if not futile environment for invoking grounds for either the DA or the PA, since the recycled ruling inevitably repeats the prior. I am saying here that post-ruling components are quickly killed by the J.

Moreover, since various blame allocation work is conducted through objection sequences, a matter taken up in the interactional functions section, and since appended grounds components are the specific mechanisms for engaging in such work, the possibility exists that an [objection+grounds] component will inherit another [objection+grounds] component as a mirror image sequel in next turn, as in example 5.22. But, much more frequently, yet less spectacularly, grounds components produced by one attorney are often sequentially implicative for a grounds component in the next turn by opposition attorney, as displayed in examples 5.20 to 5.23.

To summarize the structure of these sequences. We have considered a number of objection sequences engaging one to three participants, occurring over three to six turns, composed of variant clusters of sequential and intrasequential combinatorial options. We have seen how the choice of options creates variations in sequential, discourse activity and participation structures, some of which expand these structures, others of which contract them. And we have observed participants' delicate maneuvering over these sequences to create, negotiate, and constrain the sequential environments, contexts, and resources for each others' movements.

Far from being ritualistic routines, objection sequences are structurally multiplex and interactionally dense discourse strategies. Looked at within the trial framework as a whole, these sequences possess a distinct organization and logic. I mentioned that the rape trial constitutes a particular speech exchange system which is broken down into and occurs as a progression of global activities: jury selection, opening statements, direct and cross examination, redirect and recross, closing statements, etc. Each global activity type, such as cross-examination, reveals a distinctive participation structure, a particular configuration of discourse participants at a given time, and a local discourse activity structure: the type of utterances or talk discourse participants may warrantably produce. Objection sequences, with their distinct component utterances – objections, grounds, rulings – with their sequential variations, and with their distinct participant structure – PA, DA, and J – weave in and out of question/answer sequences to help fashion the complex interactional texture of courtroom talk. Put more forcefully and radically, objection sequences constitute a variable yet omnirelevant form of question/answer sequence peculiarly exploitable in adversarial courtroom speech exchange systems.

OBJECTION SEQUENCES: STRUCTURE II

I mentioned previously that I would raise two theoretical points about objection sequences, and it's now time to turn to these. Although the study of objection sequences takes up a good portion of legal texts concerning trial practice (Mauet 1988; Tanford 1983; Bailey 1985), they have been relatively neglected or mentioned only parenthetically in the literature on trial discourse (see O'Barr 1982; Atkinson and Drew 1979).[2] My concern here will be to review some of the considerations of Atkinson and Drew and of O'Barr, and ask how the preceding discussion and data of objection sequences stand with respect to this earlier work on trial discourse. But first, why bother with objection sequences? Why would objection sequences matter anyway to the structure of question and answer sequences, the focal format of courtroom discourse, other than tangentially at best?

One way they matter is the following. According to Atkinson and Drew (1979), O'Barr (1982), Brannigan and Lynch (1987) and others, courtroom testimony involves the production of credibility from witnesses. The format of courtroom discourse, as we have seen, allocates turns between two participants along a strict linear – from DA to V – turn trajectory (see Atkinson and Drew 1979: 68). If this is the case, then, given the recognizable completion of a question, the ensuing silence belongs to the witness, so that delays in answering a question provide inferentially rich resources for ascribing blame and allocating responsibility. Since the next turn belongs to the victim, conventional moral imputations about her credibility revolve around first, the normative constraints of conditional relevance, especially the time-lag or duration interval between question completion and answer onset, and second, the timing and length of intra-turn pauses.

If, however, the participation structure of the court is organized around DA, V, PA, and J, with the subproperty – subgroup – of PA, DA, and J, then the post-question gap does not belong to the victim, but instead represents what I have referred to as the post-question objection option space: the option position for doing objections. And that option space, as we have seen, belongs to the PA, not the victim, in which case the relevant sequence is not

DA: Question
V: Answer

but is instead the built-in, omnipresent, and omnirelevant

    DA: Question
    PA: [objection option space]
    V: Answer

   As I noted, when the objection option is exercised, a participation and sequential transformation is rapidly thrust into prominence, which takes precedence over the prior question/answer sequence. More explicitly, while the DA may indeed control the current-selects-next option, there is evidence on several counts that the PA's right to self-select represents a priority turn selection option over the V's answer. First, consider four objection environments: (1) pre-answer objections, as in example 5.8; (2) immediately "latched" pre-answer objections, as in 5.9, 5.12, and 5.15; (3) *turn interruptive objections*, such as 5.13; and (4) post-answer objections, such as 5.21. Overwhelming objections occur in the first three turn positions: turn environments that are structurally prior to the V's turn position. Second, turn interruptive objections serve as further evidence for priority of the PA's self-selection turn option. Even though the DA may exercise the current-selects-next option, and have the V start up her turn, the PA possesses the power, through the self-section option, to warrantably interrupt and then strand the V's current turn-in-progress. Turn interruptive objections demonstrate that the PA's self-selection option takes precedence *even retroactively* over V's answer. And third, the J's admonishment of the V in example 5.10 and W in 5.11 illustrate how violations of normative structure are quickly sanctioned and courtroom order thereby reproduced.

   This being the case, the turn-taking system for courtroom cross-examination is much more complex, much more negotiable, than O'Barr, Atkinson and Drew, and others have envisaged. In fact, when the objection option is activated, a realm of other activities become automatically operable: grounds components, side bar conferences, recesses, trial motions, overrules, sustains, judge/attorney conferences, grounds components, to mention but a few. In some of these cases, not only is the question/answer sequence displaced or suspended, but the trial itself is suspended, as J, DA, and PA attend to evidential and procedural issues.

   Another theoretical issue raised by Atkinson and Drew merits consideration also. They claim that objection sequences are a special type of interruptive remedial insertion sequence, which is more or less tangential to the focal question/answer format between attorney and witness (Atkinson and Drew 1979: 64).

   There are major problems with this formulation. Since the adversarial contexts under analysis here (that is, cross-examination) bristle with objection sequences throughout the course of the trial, and since they are systemic or built into the structure of courtroom discourse, it's difficult to conceive of them as interruptive. Moreover, such sequences behave much differently from insertion sequences. First, unlike the *bona fide* insertion sequences discussed previously in this chapter and chapter 4, objection sequences involve participants different from those doing the question/answer inserts. Second, the culmination of the insertion sequence in natural conversation maintains the integrity of the adjacency pair sequence; conditional relevance is preserved across the expansion inserts, even across multiple embeddings. In contrast, objection sequences, when a judicial sustain gets issued, ostensibly delete the relevance of the answer altogether. Last and most importantly, even when the objection is overruled, an answer is rarely forthcoming. Overwhelmingly, when the objection is overruled the question is repeated, rephrased, or otherwise reformulated, creating a completely new or fresh adjacency pair – often for good reason. Consider the DA's first – pre-objection – question below compared with the second, following the judge's overrule. Concerning the meaning of the word "pardying," notice that the DA's first question defines the term with the phrase "implies sexual activity," whereas the second question both transforms and upgrades that description to "means sexual activity."

(5.25) Trial 1

  → **DA:**   =It implies (7.4) tuh many people that implies sexual
              activity dozen it?=

     PA: =Objecshun yer honor
              (2.5)

     J: ((Clearing throat)) (2.3) Overru::led.
              (1.0)

  → **DA:**   To many people yer age (.) that means sexual activity does
              it not?
              (2.6)

     V: Tuh so::me yes (.) I guess.

Thus question/answer sequences are bounded by and interwoven with, most frequently, a post-question objection space on the one hand, and, much less frequently, a post-answer objection space on the other. Together these two facts about courtroom discourse reveal that question/answer pairs are endemically, irremediably, and systemically vulnerable to radical transformations, and that objection sequences constitute an omnipresent set of constraints exerted on these focal pairs. Still more radically, I claim here that objection sequences together with question/

answer pairs are what question/answer sequences look like in adversarial cross-examination. That is, they *are constitutive of such pairs*.

What about those cases in which the PA does not object in the post-question position, but instead activates the option in the post-answer position? Keep in mind, when referring to a post-question or post-answer objection option space, I am formulating a realm of deep or underlying structural phenomena: structural positions that may or may not be realized during any given moment in some spate of talk. For structural positions to be realized, the PA must first exercise the option post-question but pre-answer, and the V must then withhold or delay the answer option post-question. If the question/answer sequence goes through, then the PA may invoke the option post-answer, though implementing the objection in this less preferred – second – position is most frequently suppressed. So the underlying sequential structure of [question + objection option + answer + objection option] sequence results in surface realization from the interactional achieved coordination of objection exercise, on the one hand, and of answer delay on the other.

Let me specify this underlying structure more formally. If the DA's turn is constructed with a current-selects-next device, then the right and obligation to talk belongs to the victim, unless the PA self-selects prior to V's answer; the PA's option takes precedence over the V's. The PA's self-selection should be precision-timed to coincide with DA's question completion, but prior to onset of V's turn. And if the PA self-selects, participation, discourse, and sequential structure are automatically transformed into the objection sequence, preempting V's participation until objection sequence completion and participation structure reverts back to DA and V. And most importantly, objections *strand* the DA's question, potentially and retroactively deleting it, but leave a *recoverable trace* should the objection be overruled. The same process operates recursively – at each and every post-question (and post-answer) environment.

A final point is worth emphasizing. I am not disputing in any sense here that conventional/moral inferential work operates in and through question/answer sequences, but ascribing blame and allocating responsibility for the incident are also fundamentally tied to issues of silence for generating impressions of credibility. But the theoretical points I am addressing questions whether much analytic leverage can be gained by subsuming turn or discourse organizational properties under an intentionalist vocabulary of meaning driven by conventional moral inferences. If the derivation and production of moral credibility, assessment, culpability, and the like are discourse driven, if they are organized around the recursive cycling series of turn options, then we need to specify the turn organizational – the structural – properties of such production, including objection sequences (though keeping in mind the deep interaction between moral inferences and turn organization).

Moreover, on a methodological level, I have sought to incorporate objection sequences within the turn-organizational system of adversarial cross-examination. Rather than viewing such sequences as remedial or interruptive insertion sequences, as tangential aberrations on some focal sequence, I have attempted to build them into the underlying structure of question/answer sequences. I have posited an underlying framework to encompass and generate these flexed option structures. While the adequacy of this analysis may require further and serious refinements, much beyond the scope of the current study, the machinery I have presented here proposes to deal with such sequences both parsimoniously and nonarbitrarily, providing a formal basis for generating them.

OBJECTION SEQUENCES: FUNCTIONS

Having stipulated the structural/sequential properties of objection sequences in some detail, I want to spend some time on a more speculative excursion to designate their interactional functions, the interactional work that may be conducted in and through them.

First, and most obviously, post-question objections may be designed to "freeze" the sequence in progress, "stranding" the DA's question, and to have the relevance of the victim's answer suppressed or suspended. But because, as we will see shortly, many questions are loaded, that is, because they presuppose the factual status of the statements embedded in them, objections may not mitigate the blame-ascriptive work and the moral inferences conveyed in just the question part, even if the objection is sustained and the answer preempted. When looking back at some of the above sequences, especially (5.24), notice that DAs produce numerous questions even when an objection and a sustain of it are practically guaranteed, demonstrating that the impressions being produced for the jury are frequently produced in the question alone.

On the other hand and less obviously, post-answer objections may be designed not so much for quashing the immediately prior question/answer sequence, but instead for smothering a move in a projected sequence. Once the DA tips his/her hand, as it were, toward an upcoming line of questioning, the PA's objection may place the projected trajectory and completion of some forthcoming sequence in jeopardy. So just as DAs design much of their talk as pre-sequences or preliminaries, with an eye to a projected sequence, the PA may similarly interpret a given utterance as foreshadowing some forthcoming action, and therefore object not so much to affect the immediately preceding activity but to suppress what that activity is a preliminary for – what it is leading up to (see Atkinson and Drew 1979). And, the same process may occur in post-question objections as well. The objection in example 5.10, a hitch-hiking case, emerges as the PA's tactic to curtail testimony which – eventually as it turns out – strongly alludes to the V engaging in prostitution with the defendant. Similarly, the turn-interruptive objection in 5.13 indicates the PA's sensitivity to the fact that the DA's discussion of the "Grainary", a bar across the state line with a lower drinking age than the V's home state, is selectively and specifically designed for a forthcoming action, a credibility assessment concerning V's moral character: that she is under age in her state, so she crosses the state line regularly to drink and "party." And PA's objection reveals the pre-sequence or preliminary tracking of the DA's sequential movements to subvert a potentially damaging line of upcoming testimony. In short, post-answer and turn-interruptive objections most frequently, and post-question objections less frequently, may operate with an eye toward where the sequence, where a given line of testimony, is going, rather than attempting to thwart or undermine immediately local activities.

Second, objection sequences provide interactional resources for avoiding and allocating blame by both prosecution and defense. In 5.20, the DA is conducting a line of testimony which exposes the victim's prior sexual history. Even though circuitous, the moral inferences available through descriptions of ordinary events, such as "knowing what it feels like to have somebody climax inside you" secures the impression for the jury that the victim is sexually experienced. Despite rape shield laws and other procedural/evidentiary restrictions, the victim's sexual history or purity is still vulnerable to discrediting, is still an interactionally emergent issue in court, and is still conducted through mundane characterizations of social action. And even though the moral inferences embedded and exposed within the question/answer sequences alone appear sufficient to foster an impression of the V's sexual history, the DA's further move overtly marks and highlights the inferential connection in the post-objection grounds: "I'm not delving into this woman's past sexual history." If there was once an inferential puzzle for the jury, however slight, the DA has converted those "covert" inferences into an "exposed" connection. Once again, the appended grounds component is conducting significant interactional and impression management work.

Furthermore, just as the DA elaborates blame implications in objection sequences, the PA can also provide various cues and blame avoidance devices for the V. In 5.22, an instance where the DA objects to the PA's objection, the latter's grounds component contains a possible answer the V might employ. Much less overtly, the PA's objections may suggest answers to the V, and may signal a caution that the current line of questioning contains hazards. Yet that process creates a severe dilemma for the PA. The PA's objection dilemma involves, on the one hand, straddling a thin line between cuing the V and preempting a possible line of questioning; but on the other hand, and quite ironically, attempting to suppress such testimony actually amplifies, and overtly marks that very same objectionable material. In the jurists' minds, attempts to suppress testimony represent attempts to conceal testimony, regardless of the procedural and evidentiary propriety of the objection.

Another interactional resource found in objection sequences has been alluded to previously. Just as a sustain of the objection may suspend or alter a given line of questioning, curtailing testimony on a particular topic, the overrule of an objection may (1) open the floodgates, as it were, for pursuing a particular topic, and (2) serve as a warrant for upgrading the blame-attributional descriptors in a rephrased version of the question. As I noted, when objections are overruled, the V's answer is rarely forthcoming, nor does the DA simply repeat the question on the recycle. Instead, the question or the descriptors embedded in it are often rephrased, reformulated, and revised to upgrade blame implicativeness. Once again, notice how the question in 5.25 regarding the definition of the term "pardying" is recovered – "implies sexual activity" versus "means sexual activity" – in the post-ruling position.

> Trial 1

→ **DA:** =It implies (7.4) tuh many people that implies sexual
            activity dozen it?=

PA: =Objecshun yer honor
           (2.5)

J: ((Clearing throat)) (2.3) Overru::led.
           (1.0)

→ **DA:** To many people yer age (.) that means sexual activity does
           it not?
           (2.6)

V: Tuh so::me yes (.) I guess.

Third and last, objection sequences impose constraints that affect both the internal design of turns and the organization of sequences. They affect internal turn structure because of courtroom procedural restrictions governing the form of questioning, in particular, by exerting pressure on repetitious testimony. Hence a puzzle confronting the DA concerns the

repetition of key testimony, of key points in their defense argument.
How do DAs circumvent potential objections based on repetition
grounds, neutralizing impending objections before they get off the
ground, to continue a given line of questioning and to repeat key topics?
What devices do they employ to maneuver around such restrictions, and
how can they do so warrantably, avoiding an objection and sustain such
as those on lines 0730 and 0731 in the following?

(5.26)   Trial 1

```
0700   DA:   D'you know what- (.) road you turned right off to?
0701          (1.0)
0702   V:    No.
0703          (1.3)
0704   DA:   Somewhere around Maryville?
0705          (0.5)
0706   V:    Yes.
0707          (2.9)
0708   DA:   Were you concerned for your safety at that point in time?
0709          (1.5)
0710   V:    Yeah.
0711          (2.0)
0712   DA:   When you turned right?
0713          (1.0)
0714   DA:   WHY:::
0715          (4.4)
0716   V:    We'll I didn't know (.) where I was going, I didn't know
0717         if that was a short cut or not.
0718          (.)
0719   DA:   When you left the Grainary you had no idea who you
0720         were going with did'ju.
0721          (2.2)
0722   V:    No:
0723          (.)
0724   DA:   You had no idea what kind of people they were, did'ju?
0725          (.)
0726   V:    No.
0727   DA:   When you left the Grainary your only concern was
0728         that the man was attractive, isn't that true?
0729          (1.7)
0730→ PA:   Objection your honor she's already testified to that.
0731→ J:    Yeah- (.) Sustained (.) it's repetitious.
0732          (3.2)
0733   DA:   So:: your concern when you turned right was only
```

```
0734              that you weren't sure where you were going?
0735                 (1.5)
0736  V:          Yes.
0737                 (1.2)
0738  DA:         The first time you became concerned was when.
0739                 (4.5)
0740  V:          Concerned for my safety?
0741                 (1.1)
0742  DA:         Sure.
0743                 (1.0)
0744  V:          When he parked the car.
0745                 (1.6)
0746  DA:         But you weren't concerned for your safety when you
0747              left the parking lot?
0748                 (2.2)
0749  V:          °No
0750                 (1.3)
0751  DA:         N'you weren't concerned for your sa::fety (.) when
0752              your girlfriend drives across somebody's else's lawn?
0753                 (2.9)
0754  V:          No.
0755                 (.)
0756  DA:         N'you weren't concerned when Brian follows the wild lady
0757              (.) wh- just driven across somebody else's lawn
0758                                                    [
0759→                                           Objection your honor=
0760→ J:         =Sustained.
0761                 (17.1)
0762  DA:         You said you didn't know where your purse was...
```

On line 0730 the PA objects to the previous testimony on the grounds of being repetitious, and the J sustains the objection (even though, interesting enough, the questions immediately prior to this were just as repetitive). However, throughout the trial, spatiotemporal deictics routinely and warrantably circumvent repetition restrictions. I refer to these as temporal repetition markers, and they fall into two classes: time markers like "at that point in time," and temporal locators like "when" which introduce a subordinate clause. In both cases, temporal repetition devices mark previously elicited testimony, but that testimony is syntactically "new" and hence procedurally proper because technically new information is being conveyed. As the progression of descriptions about the incident unfold during questioning, temporal repetition devices continuously update old information, positioning that information at new locational points, repeating it with "at that point in time" as in line 0708 (or "when you left the parking lot," etc. on lines 0746–57).

So throughout cross-examination the victim's knowledge about the defendant's last name, about where he worked, about where he was from, and her concern or lack of concern about her safety – evidence which is potentially damaging to her version of the incident – emerge repetitively and cumulatively through "that point in time," "the first time," "when X, Y, and Z" and so on. Put most succinctly, the DA manipulates temporal repetition devices to proleptically neutralize an impending objection through the following steps: (1) produce a question that is organized around category-bound knowledge the V should possess (0708 and 0738); (2) append a time marker or temporal locator or both to the question (0708–12 and 0738); (3) elicit the V's confirmation that she possessed certain category-bound states (0710 and 0744); and (4) post V's answer employ a contrast with an embedded three-part list that is generated by or fed from prior violations of that same category performance (0719–28 and 0746–57).

A particularly powerful and expanded variation of this format happens on line 0714. Here the DA exercises a puzzle/solution sequence option and builds the ensuing contrast list off of the puzzle solution, not the temporal locator or the time marker. I say this is a powerful strategy because the puzzle sequence, when this option is activated, bleeds or removes the conditions governing one contrast list, the DA's "concern for safety" theme on line 0708, "feeds" the conditions which govern the application of its own distinct sequential list, the V's "I didn't know theme" on line 0716, yet still preserves the withheld list for a disjunctive (following the objection sequence on line 0738) repeating action sequence (Shenkein 1980: 43). This second sequence, in short, duplicates its mirror image predecessor, both structurally and blame inferentially: the V must possess category-bound knowledge and concerns at some interactionally emergent and temporally relevant moment in history, a moment, of course, constructed by the DA and not the V.

Moreover, because objection sequences constrain the output of questioning, leaving the question temporarily stranded without an answer and absorbing the sequence into a new participation and discourse activity framework, DAs may relax such restrictions by packing multiple blame components into a compressed intra-turn designed format. Given the property of turn preservation – that deep intrusions into internal turn structure (i.e. interruptions) are routinely withheld even in the case of the most overexposed procedural and evidentiary violations – intra-turn blame lists are not structurally vulnerable to objections, in stark contrast to inter-turn or sequential blame lists. But even though the question is immune from objection intrusion, the answer is, as we have seen, quite vulnerable. This multiple list compressed turn design resolves the problem of ascribing blame and repeating blame components without exposing the rhythm of the list to objections, repairs, or unexpected answers, disruptions that are likely with expanded sequential (inter-turn) lists.

Illustratively, contemplate and contrast the two three-part sequential contrast lists in example 5.26 above (lines 0719–28 and 0746–57) with the following.

(5.27) Trial 1

0450	DA:	When you left the parking lot that night did'ju know (.)
0451		this- mister Windwood's first name at that point?
0452		(0.8)
0453	V:	Yes.
0454		(2.8)
0455	DA:	Did'ju know his last <u>name</u>? when you left the parking lot
0456		that night?
0457		(0.5)
0458	V?	°No.
0459		(0.5)
0460	DA:	Did'ju know Brian's last <u>name</u>? when you left the
0461		parking lot tha- that night?
0462		(0.5)
0463	V:	°No.
0464		(.)
0465	DA:	Did'ju know where Brian was <u>from</u>? when you left
0466		the parking lot- (.) that night?
0467		(1.0)
0468	V:	°From Illinois.
0469		(1.1)
0470	DA:	Did'ju know where Winwood was <u>from</u>? when you left
0471		the parking lot that night?
0472		(0.7)
0473	V:	°No.
0474		(1.1)
0475	DA:	Did'ju know where Winwood as <u>work</u>? when you left
0476		the parking lot that night?
0477		(0.7)
0478	V:	°No.
0479		(.)
0480	DA:	Did'ju know where Brian <u>worked</u>? when you left

0481		the parking lot that night?
0482		(0.9)
0483	V:	°No.
0484		(4.2)
0485	DA:	Did he force you to get in- to his automobe::l in
0486		the parking lot?
0487		(0.8)
0488	V:	°No.
0489		(3.9)
0490 →	DA:	How did'ju wind up in his automobe::l?
0491		(1.8)
0492	V:	I got in.
0493		(1.3)
0494 →	DA:	WHY::::.
0495		(1.6)
0496	V:	Because he said we were goin to uh party at
0497		uh friend of his house.
0498		(2.7)
0499 →	DA:	But'chu didn't kno::w (.) his last name (.) where he worked
0500		(.) or where he was from correct?
0501		(1.0)
0502	V:	°Yes.
0503 →	DA:	You didn't know uh thing about him did'ju?
0504		(1.0)
0505	V:	°No.

The compressed intra-turn list occurring on lines 0499–500 appears finely tailored to exploit turn preservation and to circumvent possible objections based on repetition grounds, since the three blame components represent reformulations of immediately prior testimony (see 0460–80). If we compare the *compressed intra-turn contrast list* with the *expanded inter-turn contrast list* in 5.26, the latter reveals much more exposure to an objection than the former. And keep in mind that since the question is already loaded, it appears much more crucial for the question to make it through in the clear than for the answer: intra-turn lists offer a built-in safeguard against objections, while single question/answer or sequential lists yield a built-in liability.

To summarize. There may be strategic, as well as interactional and stylistic, motivations for intra-turn blame lists – the multiple packing of intra-turn blame components – which interact with both objection sequences and turn preservation properties. In contrast to sequential blame lists, they are not structurally vulnerable to objections or to other disruptions. Because the question will go through, though perhaps not the answer, the differential design of these inter- and intra-turn components appears sensitive to the severe disruptions – both sequential and stylistic/rhythmic – objection sequences may pose. Quite clearly, adversary cross-examination is not just a war of words (Danet and Bogach 1980; Danet 1980), but a war of turns – even a war of sequential maneuvering.

This is a skeletal characterization of objection sequences, one that barely captures their delicate and complex organization. Much more needs to be analyzed. Even though they are suffused throughout courtroom talk, objection sequences have not been analyzed in previous studies. In this discussion and analysis of objection and repair sequences, suffice it to state here that adversarial cross-examination talk departs from the focal question/answer format in two ways: first, the victim's repair initiation subverts turn order and turn-type distribution, but preserves the participation structure of DA and V; and second, the PA's objection preempts turn order, creates a range of variational options for the objection sequence, and transforms the participation structure from DA and V to PA, DA, and J. The former case displays an internal expansion and transformation of sequential structure on the one hand, while the latter depicts an external expansion and transformation of both sequential and participation structure on the other. Together, they reveal the contingent, fluid, and dynamic processes of mutual alignment and flexed coordination not only between questioner and answerer but among multiple participation structures as well. Together they reveal how courtroom preallocation affects who gets to talk, when they get to talk, and what they get to talk about.

MULTIUNIT TURNS AND SILENCE

As Atkinson and Drew (1979) have noted, another difference turn preallocation makes in courtroom contexts involves (1) the construction of multiunit turns, and (2) the duration and distribution of silence. Just as cross-examinationn weaves in and out of multiple participation frameworks, threading different forms of social action into prominence and partitioning those actions into different sets of participants, it also impinges on sequential organization within its focal framework of DA and V. The preallocation system generates variations in the organization of multiunit turns and gaps/pauses because conversational constraints are, to varying degrees, systematically relaxed.

For natural conversation, as witnessed earlier, the competition over turns produces a constraint toward minimization of turn size. Multiunit turns are locally accomplished and contingently coordinated on a turn-unit by turn-unit basis. At each transition relevant place, potential next speakers must withhold the self-selection option to allow the current speaker to construct a multiunit turn. But this competition over a scarce resource is systemically relaxed between DA and V. Since only the DA exercises the current-selects-next and self-select options, and since the V only answers after the recognizable production of a question and not before, multiunit turns emerge as a product of courtroom preallocation: free from the contingent and productional vulnerabilities characteristic of conversation.

(5.28)   Trial 1

```
0217   DA:   When were you on yer ba::ck in the fie::ld?
0218   V:    When he first (1.9) pulled me outa the car? (1.0) and (0.8)
0219         uh (.) knocked me down (0.5) >when he wuz< (.) hit me
0220         a couple of times n he attempted to:: (.) force me to (   )
0221                                                            [
0222   DA:                                                        Were
0223         you bein dragged at that point?
0224   V:    No.
0225               (4.5)
0226   DA:   Didn't you have (6.5) JUS TALKING ABOUT the fie::ld
0227         the second time (.) >that's it< (0.7) restricting these
0228         questions to that point n time (4.3) didn'ju tell (1.8) Brian
0229         you wanted to have intercourse with him out in that field?
0230               (0.9)
0231   V:    No sir I did not=
0232   DA:   =Didn't you do that b'cuz you couldn't ha::ve intercourse
0233         with him inside the car?
0234               (0.9)
0235   V:    No I did not.
0236               (.)
0237   DA:   N wernchu angry out in the field b'cuz he- wuz (.) not
0238         particularly interested in it all?
0239               (0.9)
0240   V:    No sir.
```

As 5.28 shows, first the victim, in line 0218, and then the DA, in line 0226, produce multiunit turns. Yet although both possess the power to produce such turns, the victim's ability to construct long turns can be restricted by the DA and the J (which I will show later). Even so, the lack of competition among courtroom participants ensures a degree of freedom that is built into or systemic in court, a freedom that is absent in natural conversation.

But as discussed in detail above, they are not totally free. For as I mentioned, multiunit turns, like other turns, often inherit objections. If the PA demurs, a question composed of multiple turn units can be derailed, delayed, or displaced. Although this option indeed confronts participants, objections are routinely withheld until completion (or near completion) of the current turn in progress. They are rarely exercised "in route," as it were, and although turns containing even transparent evidentiary and procedural violations are recognizable prior to completion, so that sustainable objections could be produced at recognition point, a clear preference exists for the preservation of turn completion and therefore the "one at a time rule." Even so, while the DA may indeed produce a turn in the clear, the fate of the sequence is rarely so fortunate; the PA typically raises objections post DA's question, but prior to victim's answer.

Nor is the victim's ability to construct multiunit turns so fortunate. That attorneys appear reluctant to interrupt each other's current turn-in-progress, that they withhold or suppress objections until turn completion, expresses a resigned concession not necessarily extended to the victim and other witnesses on the stand. The asymmetry exhibited through turn preservation on the one hand and turn usurpation, interruption, and deletion on the other represents a major power device and plays a prominent role in the asymmetric relationship between DA and V. In this regard, notice how the V's turn in line 0220 is interrupted well before the unit's projected completion point.

This interlacing of sequential structure and strategic legal maneuvering – the procedural consequentiality of courtroom context on sequential organization – confronts participants not only in the construction of multiunit turns but in the organization of silence also. Just as the constraint governing minimization of turn size is relaxed in cross-examination in contrast to conversation, because the pressures of competitive overlap and simultaneous talk are systemically foreclosed, so the constraint on minimization of silence – gaps, pauses, and lapses – is similarly mitigated. The lack of turn competition not only opens up the likelihood of turn maximization but also creates the conditions for gap and pause maximization. Inter-turn gaps, intra-turn pauses, and pre-topic shift lapses punctuate the rhythm and pace of courtroom testimony.

More importantly, the control and manipulation of silence constitutes a critical power resource in courtroom talk. Because it embodies the inferential basis for assessing the credibility of testimony and the character of witnesses, silence is continually being negotiated, mediated, and contested in cross-examination. The definition of the situation is constructed in the fine-grained and detailed density of gaps and pauses of varying durations. The rich inferential implicativeness occurring in the midst of these moments reveals an interpretative device of considerable power. If that is indeed the case, the crucial issues then become: Who wields this resource? Who controls it? How can silence be manipulated, and negotiated? How does it serve as a stylistic and persuasive mechanism to animate the texture of testimony, and how does it interact with turn maximization to produce an interactional advantage for one participant but not the other? Let's start to answer these questions by adding some more data to example 5.28.

(5.29) Trial 1

> DA: Aren't you saying (.) that the first time
>   (1.5)
>   you didn't resist
>   (3.0)
>   I'm not asking you what was in your mind I'm asking
>   you if in fact you didn't
>   (1.0)
>   you did not <u>resist</u>?

(5.30) Trial 1

0348	DA:	You say- that (.) Brian's car led the way over to::: (.)
0349		this Glen Carbon area.
0350		(.)
0351	V:	Mmhmm=
0352	DA:=	>How do you know that was Glen Carbon<?
0353		(.)
0354	V:	There's uh:: (1.5) water tank? Maybe? Uh big silver bubble=
0355		[ ]
0356	DA:	(what)
0357	V:	=thing (1.0) that says- Glen Carb- Glen Carbon
0358		(3.6)
0359	DA:	(OK) but you don't actually know whether or not you
0360		were in Glen Carbon (1.6) or had you been told you were
0361		in Glen Carbon at that point in time?
0362		(1.3)
0363	V:	I was told that was (2.0) uh part of Glen Carbon.
0364		(0.5)
0365	DA:	By the police officers?
0366	V:	°Mmhmm
0367		(1.2)

0368	DA:	(OK) so you don't actually know it was Glen Carbon
0369		(2.8) of your own personal knowledge
0370		(0.7)
0371	V:	No I assumed it when I'd seen (that big)
0372		[
0373	DA:	And when the police officers
0374		<u>told</u> <u>you.</u>
0375		(25.0)

(*5.31*)   Trial 1

0134	DA:	Those items that you've already sho::wn (to be) people's
0135		exhibit one two three ARE ACTUALLY in substantially
0136		the same condition they were that night aren't they?
0137		(3.2)
0138	DA:	Was your sweater this wrinkled?
0139		(0.4)
0140	V:	No.
0141		(.)
0142	DA:	Were your pants that wrinkled?
0143	V:	No
0144		(1.0)
0145	DA:	Was this jacket that wrinkled?
0146	V:	°No.
0147	DA:	Then they're not in substantially the same <u>condition</u> are
0148		they?
0149		(2.5)
0150		<u>ARE</u> <u>THEY</u>?
0151	PA:	Objection your honor=
0152	J:	=No just uh minute (.)hhh let her answer (.) your fire'in
0153		about three questions (.) before she has uh.

(*5.32*)   Trial 1

	DA:	Now- this was ranked and pulled is that correct.
		(1.5)
	DA:	Allegedly?
		[[
	V:	( )

(*5.33*)   Trial 1

	DA:	Linda isn't it tru::e (.) that you wanted to have sex with
		Brian n'he wouldn't let you (0.5) >I mean he <u>couldn't</u><

(*5.34*)   Trial 1

> **DA:**   Isn't it tru::e that Brian told you
>   (3.1)
>   that he had uh girlfriend and a child
>   (3.2)
>   and that he was very concerned (a)bout- them
>   (.)
>   and that's why he could not perform that night.
>   (1.0)
> **V:**   °No.

These extracts introduce three closely related points about the manipulation and interpretation of silence: (1) how it operates as a stylistic device for the production of speech clarity; (2) how it interacts with turn transfer and maximization of turn size; and (3) how it conveys impressions about testimony and credibility. I will take up each of these points in turn, but first let me review some conceptual distinctions I made earlier, in chapter 4.

Recall that intra-turn silence was defined as a pause, while between-turn silence was defined as a gap. The former occurs in the midst of a current speaker's turn, as in the first three pauses in 5.34 above; the latter occurs between the end of a current speaker's turn and the onset of a next speaker's turn, as in the 1 second pause between the DA's turn and the V's response in 5.34. When a current-selects-next option is employed, on completion of that speaker's turn the ensuing gap "belongs" to the selected next speaker. According to Atkinson and Drew (1979: 67–8), O'Barr (1982), and others, what this means for courtroom talk is that the silence following the DA's question is a gap that belongs to the V, and on completion of her answer, the following silence is a gap that belongs to the DA, because next turn automatically reverts back to him/her. Yet as I have pointed out, objection interludes may radically transform this simple assessment of response lag between a question and answer. Whether or not a gap belongs to the V depends on the interactional collaboration of other participants.

To make matters even more complex, assigning the status of gap or pause to any given stretch of silence cannot be achieved *a priori* because turn boundaries are irremediably mutable and emergent from the fine-tuned synchronization and continuously monitored, updated interpretations of current and next. It is frequent for a current speaker to interpret a moment of silence as a pause before continuing into a new turn unit, while next speaker treats it as a gap and begins to talk (see Goodwin 1981: 18; Suchman 1987: 76). In such cases, simultaneous talk emerges as current and next assign divergent interpretations to the silence. In example 5.32, the V treats the DA's 1.5 second silence as a gap and therefore begins to talk; the DA, on the other hand, treats the same silence as a pause before continuing into a fresh turn unit. Hence the output of both operations yields simultaneous talk, so that the DA's "allegedly" overlaps and winds up deleting the V's inaudible answer. As Goodwin (1981: 19) puts it: "Thus, the same silence yields alternative classifications at different moments in time and from the perspective of different participants." Consequently, the status of silence must be tracked and conceptualized as a time-bound and interactional process organized around the interpretations of participants. I would add, however, that in cross-examination these interpretations incorporate socially structured and contingently enacted processes of power to mold and uphold the asymmetrical relationship between DA and V. With these points in hand let's turn to the operation of and interaction between silence and power in cross-examination.

(1) Courtroom language exploits silence as a stylistic device for productional clarity and audibility. Most textbooks on trial procedure (Bailey 1985; Brown 1987; Tanford 1983; Mauet 1988) and texts on trial discourse (Atkinson and Drew 1979: 198–205; O'Barr 1982: 97–111) emphasize the management of style through silence, primarily as a "pin drop" effect for attributing blame (Brown 1987: 80). Atkinson and Drew, however, are the only authors to analyze silence as a mechanism of productional clarity: as recipient designed for comprehension by a co-present but nonspeaking audience, that is, the jury. According to them, courtroom testimony may be punctuated by relatively frequent and extended intra-turn pauses. That is, talk may be partitioned into temporally bounded segments to product a type of punctuated delivery style. In my data, this speech style is best illustrated in examples 5.29, 5.34, and line 0226 in 5.28.

In terms of production and comprehension, courtroom context is procedurally consequential for and motivated by this slow, rhythmic phrasing on at least two counts. First, because the jury cannot initiate repairs or request that an utterance be repeated, questions and answers possess a "nonrecoverable" property, a "one-shot affair" with no retakes, that makes enunciation clarity crucial. If the jury fails to comprehend an utterance because of audibility problems, then the utterance and the interactional work it was designed to accomplish may not be recovered. As Akinson and Drew (1979: 198–205) correctly note, such discretely bound segments are recipient designed or specifically tailored for the jury – designed especially for clarity of monitoring.

Second, the problems posed by and the necessity of productional clarity are not just limited to facilitate the jury's audibility requirements. DAs may load or build pauses into utterances to reduce the chances of embarrassing errors, disfluencies, or repairs which might spoil a competent performance or disrupt the rhythm of questioning or both. In this regard, errors like 5.33 above and 5.35 may thwart and undermine the DA's attempts to manage a credible performance for the jury.

(5.35)　Trial 1

> DA:　OK- I- <u>MAM</u> what items wuz (it) <u>were</u> (1.0) <u>WHAT WERE</u>
> 　　　　<u>THE ITEMS?</u>　　　(1.9)　　　　　　　　that you <u>didn't</u>=
> 　　　　　　[　　　　　　　　　　　　　　　　　]
> 　　　　　　((Slight audience laughter))
> DA:　=remember until las Friday?
> 　　　　(6.0)

As a statement concerning how intra-turn pauses operate as impression management devices for the selection and design of error-free utterances, and for facilitating greater clarity in production, I could not put it better than F. Lee Bailey.

> Once you are "on camera," there will be no chance to review and edit what you say to make it come out better the next time. There will be no chance to consult with others, looking for a better way to express a thought. There will be no retakes, such as actors enjoy and often need. There will be no erasure of the words and utterances you have committed to history. If you goof, so be it. You and your client will be stuck with what you have done at all times, for better or for worse. (Bailey 1985: 41)

(2) Silence interacts in complex ways with turn size and turn transfer. As we have seen, pauses provide time to design additional turn components and build them into turn structure. Since there is a relative lack of turn competition, because of turn preallocation, and since turn-type prealloca-tion and turn preservation ensure that turn transfer is not initiated until the recognizable production of a question first pair part, courtroom systems generate the twin properties of gap/pause maximization on the one hand and overlap minimization on the other. Together, both these properties interact to produce a third property: turn maximization. Consequently, since the V prospectively orients to a forthcoming utterance as a question, turn initiation is withheld for a multiunit turn in progress, until a clearcut question component occurs; a recognizable question must be produced before speaker transition and the V answers.

But such multiunit turns organized around pause clusters appear to pose considerable ambiguity for turn transfer, for they quite warrantably open up transition-relevant places where next speaker could start up a turn (Atkinson and Drew 1979: 198–205). Considerable ambiguity arises regarding turn transition, since additional turn components can be added progressively and recursively after a possible TRP, and the V may orient to this possibility. Looking back at 5.34 the V could have interpreted the end of "child" as a TRP and started a turn. But in 5.31 on line 0150, the DA treats a 2.5 second silence as a violation of conditional relevance, a gap that exceeds the tolerance interval or threshold for answering a question. As it turns out, the DA's prompt elicits a judicial mediation of conditional relevance.

In still other cases, response lags of considerable duration are retroactively transformed into pauses, as in the following.

(5.36) Trial 1

```
0065   DA:   Esssenchuly yer testifying to what waz in the statement
0066         >izint that correct<?
0067              (0.8)
0068   V:    I- (.) testified °as to what happened.
0069              (0.7)
0070   DA:   Well WHAT were the items that you hadn't
0071         remembe::red when you- remember as of Friday?
0072              (6.2)
0073   DA:   Or donchew remember that?
0074              (1.0)
0075   V:    I don't know.
```

Is the DA's utterance in line 0073 marking a violation of conditional relevance? Or is the 6.2 second silence a gap that winds up as an intra-turn pause? Or is it both? If the tolerance threshold for courtroom questioning – conditional relevance response time – is different than it is for natural conversation, or externally mediated, considerable ambiguity may arise about transition relevance. If the DA's turn is constructed out of multiturn units, which may be punctuated and partitioned through pausing, then any possible completion point may be followed by another unit and recursively until completion. Further, if the post-question turn environment constitutes the PA's objection option space, not the V's answer turn, then V's delay may be warranted and provided for systemically. And finally, if the V's onset delay following a question is a pause designed to provide error-free response, then she is merely employing the same slow, punctuated delivery found in the DA's repertoire of strategic options.

I think what is going on in these extracts is something entirely different however. The DA wields the power to maximize the size of his/her turn, to maximize intra-turn pauses and minimize overlaps in his/her utterance, in sum, to design turns for stylistic effectiveness, while attempting to minimize such stylistic and strategic options for the V. The DA can minimize the V's turn size overtly, by insisting on a strict yes/no answer to a polar interrogative or tag question (which we will look at shortly), that is, without allowing any elaboration in the answer. Or the DA can minimize the V's turn covertly, through interruptions and overlaps, as in extracts 5.30 (lines 0371–4), 5.28 (lines 0220–2), and 5.32. While turn preservation may hold for the DA's turn, the V's turn, as mentioned, is not so fortunate.

Similarly and most importantly, the DA may reach a potential transition point where a recognizable question has been produced, treat the V's gap as a delay and hence as a violation of some tolerance interval, and then proceed to load additional turn components into the turn – constructing a multiunit turn by transforming a gap between DA's question and V's answer into an intra-turn pause, with its general and particular perquisites. This negotation and juggling of silence permits the DA to win either way. The power capability of the DA to retain or relinquish the turn places the V in a serious double bind. If the DA reaches the terminal boundary of a turn constructional unit and the V delays, then he/she can pack additional – potentially damaging – segments into the turn. At the same time, if the V hesitates, delays, or pauses before answering, then negative attributions about her veracity may arise (Walker 1985: 55; O'Barr 1982; Atkinson and Drew 1979). And, of course, if the V answers immediately, she may not be able to search for a favorable or effective answer.

More generally, the DA juggles silence as a powerful interactional and interpretative resource to generate a credible performance for the defense, and to deprive the exercise of this strategic conversational option by the V. Insofar as maximization of gap and turn size constitute properties of courtroom talk, such properties represent two dynamic processes of power and reflect the asymmetrical relationship between DA and V – structured through, organized around, and driven by the differential distribution of conversational resources. Insofar as ambiguity about transition relevance and turn transfer represent properties of courtroom talk, such ambiguity reflects the fact that the frequency and duration of pauses/gaps is greater for – is under the control of – the DA than the V. Consequently, ambiguity is constructed as an interactional accomplishment based on what I have referred to as socially structured talk – a power resource that gives the DA considerable scope for manipulating silence and other discourse devices. Let's look at these properties in processual detail.

(*5.37*) Trial 1

> DA: Then they're not in substantially the same <u>condition</u> are they?
>   (2.5)
>   ARE THEY?

(*5.38*) Trial 1

> DA: Well <u>WHAT</u> were the items that you hadn't
>   remembe::<u>red</u> when you- remember as of <u>Friday</u>?
>   (6.2)
> DA: Or donchew remember <u>that</u>?

(*5.39*) Trial 1

> DA: Now- this was ranked and pulled is that correct.
>   (1.5)
> DA: Allegedly?
>   [[
> V: ( )

In these cases, which are segments from various data extracts displayed earlier, the DA builds additional turn components into turn structure, first, to prompt a response and, second, to mark the V's delay in answering as accountable. The DA, in extract 5.37, exposes the absent response through a *partial repeating prompt* "<u>ARE</u> <u>THEY</u>?", a type of overt violation marker, which not only marks the V's violation of conditional relevance but also creates the impression that she is reluctant to answer the question or being evasive. A much more common strategy, bcause it is less likely to inherit an objection, emerges in extract 5.38. In this case, the DA employs a *conjoined* or *disjunctive expansion prompt* "Or donchew remember <u>that</u>?", a type of covert violation marker, which not only marks a violation of conditional relevance and imputes blame by trying to impeach the V's credibility and raise suspicions about her memory, but also allows the DA to build additional components "off" of the gap. Another disjunct occurs in example 5.30 on line 0359, while a conjoined prompt is illustrated in example 5.29 "I'm not asking you . . .", though the distinction between disjuncts and conjuncts is fuzzy, to be sure. Prompts, in general, function to mark a threshold violation of conditional relevance, on the one hand, and to impeach the V's credibility and memory on the other.

Two other devices which build off of silence to generate turn expansions I refer to as first, *legalistic dubitative particles* and, second, as *evidential markers*. Dubitative particles, like "allegedly?" in 5.39, routinely function as "doubt markers." Like the other devices, this qualifying tag expands the DA's turn off of a gap. But unlike the other devices, it expands not with a new sentence or even with a clause but as an adverbial with a questioning intonation. Dubitative particles question or impugn the veracity of the V's statement.

Evidential markers – "(OK) so you don't actually know it was Glen Carbon (2.8) *of your own personal knowledge*" from example 5.30 on line 0368 – demonstrate the dynamics of courtroom epistemology: the basis or grounds for judging the legitimacy of accounts (see Molotch and Boden 1985). By repressing attempts to gloss the basis for a claim, by insisting on finer and finer discriminations of detail, the DA can destabilize and discredit virtually any account from the V. As we will see later in this study, discovering rape is organized around and assembled through *inter alia* such courtroom epistemology. Evidentials like "of your own personal knowledge" or "how did you know that was Glen Carbon?" are clearly designed to address the basis of the V's knowledge about some state of affairs, with the former well suited toward turn expansive work off of silence.

(3) Silence conveys impressions about testimony and credibility. Several authors have commented about the effects of a V's hesitancy on the jury's impressions (Walker 1985; O'Barr 1982; Atkinson and Drew 1979; Brannigan and Lynch 1987), especially the close correlation between pausing and inferences regarding concealment/lying. What I have demonstrated in the foregoing discussion and analysis has less to do with that correlation than with how this sort of impression management gets assembled through ordinary discourse mechanisms, in particular, how the DA possesses the socially structured power resources to manipulate turn size, turn transfer, and silence to manage these impression.

The DA, however, controls more than intra-turn silence. Since the next turn automatically reverts back and therefore belongs to the DA following the V's answer – provided for by turn preallocation – the ensuing response lag (between answer and question) provides considerable scope for delaying the start of next turn. And the DA may strategically design this environment for an unspoken or silent comment – a pin-drop effect – on the prior turn: the V's prior answer (see Brown 1987; Atkinson and Drew 1979). That is, the DA can withhold the start of next turn to display disbelief, convey blame attributions about or stress the significance of the V's answer, and therefore convey that same impression to the jury: allowing it to sink in, as it were.

Extracts 5.40 to 5.43 depict this tactical dimension of silence designed for effect.

(*5.40*) Trial 1

	DA:	Is it your testimony::::? (1.0) under swor::::n (.)
		>SWORN< oath (0.8) that in four hours at the Grainary (.)
		you only had two drinks?
		(1.2)
	V:	Yes
→	DA:	(45.0)
	DA:	Linda ...

(*5.41*) Trial 1

0628	DA:	Did she only have two drinks?
0629		(4.1)
0630	V:	Yes- I think- if she did drink it was uh few.
0631		(1.5)
0632	DA:	Not many?
0633		(0.8)
0634	V:	No=
0635	DA:	=But she drove right across some strange peoples
0636		lawn didn't she?
0637		(2.6)
0638	V:	°Yes.
0639		(2.0)
0640	DA:	She was in a pardying mood wasn't she.
0641		(2.1)
0642	V:	Yes.
0643	DA:	So were you wern't you.
0644		(2.0)
0645	V:	Yes.
0646 →		(25.5)

(*5.42*) Trial 1

	DA:	I:: assu::me (1.0) tell me if I'm correct? (0.9) uh
		thet- you could arrive
		home any time you wanted to without
		getting into trouble.
		(2.5)

V: There were limits.
               (4.3)
DA: Four or five in the morning would be O.K?
V: °Yes
→   (5.7)

(5.43) Trial 1

0618   DA: You were <u>attracted</u> to Brian weren't you.
0619   (5.9)
0620   V: I thought he was a nice (2.3) clean looking (.) man.
0621   DA: He was <u>attractive</u> looking <u>correct</u>.
0622   (1.5)
0623   V: °Yeah.
0624   DA: And <u>basically</u> when you left that parking lot all
0625   you <u>knew</u> about him was that he was a good lookin
0626   <u>man</u> (.8) isn't that true
0627   (2.9)
0628   V: °Yeah.
0629→   (12.5)
0630   DA: When you got over...

While most unspoken third turn comments are rarely so dramatic, these examples illustrate the type of interactional work that can be achieved within this structural environment. Because of turn preallocation, with its general and particular perquisites, this type of interactional work, this type of sequentially implicative power organized around silence, permits the DA to exploit sequential resources in particular structural environments. More technically, because turn-type preallocation permits questions only and because third turn comments are procedurally and evidentiarily impermissible, such that displays of skepticism frequently found in natural conversation like "sure" or "do you expect us to believe that?" or more general comments in third turn environments are ruled out in courtroom cross-examination, third turn silent comments resolve problems posed by legal constraints. More technically, since overt comments would be argumentative or assume facts not in evidence and therefore be objection vulnerable, the third turn unspoken comment resolves such problems through the silent imputation of meaning – the silent attribution of blame.

Given the multiple levels of talk-in-interaction (Cook-Gumperz 1981: 38), the silence occurring in these particular environments accomplishes other types of interactional tasks, such as constructing topic shift positions, marking the terminal boundary between topics, or preparing another question. But for now this sequential environment – [question–answer–gap] – appears structurally conducive for exploiting this silent effect, and for accomplishing blame implicative work: namely, for stressing the V's answer through silence (Atkinson and Drew 1979: 68; O'Barr 1982: 110; Bailey 1985: 162). Brown describes how this technique leaves the jury time to "absorb" the answer.

> When the opposition witness during your cross has finally been coaxed or coerced into making a material admission that is important to your case, it is often effective to stop asking questions for a moment and let the response sink in with the jury. A moment of quiet in the courtroom can be startling, and in some cases it wakes up a juror or two. I call this the pin-drop effect. (Brown 1987: 80)

This structural base of power, persuasive language resources through which participants influence one another's actions (Hall 1985; Van der Zanden 1987; Cook-Gumperz 1981), sets the stage for a performance that constrains the capabilities of one participant, the victim, while enabling those of another participant, the defense attorney. The dynamics of this asymmetrical relationship and its construction through processes of power exist in detailed, real live moments of fine-tuned rhythmic alignment and synchronization between courtroom participants. While access to these resources – for now, turn size and silence – is socially structured, the procedures of talk must be enacted and coordinated in performance to produce and reproduce advantages or disadvantages inherited from the past. Socially structured talk is the concept I employ to capture this delicate balance between structure and agency.

In courtroom cross-examination, the balance between autonomy and constraint – the dialectic of control – involves asymmetrical access to and manipulation of linguistic resources and strategies. These are, as I have shown, strongly biased in favor of the DA. I have shown how silence and multiunit turns constitute power resources in courtroom talk, and how the successful management of these devices involves the differential power that derives from structural location in courtroom social organization. More specifically, I have shown how the DA minimizes the V's conversational resources through silence and multiunit turns and how he/she suppresses the V's use of strategic discourse options and devices through socially structured talk.

This is not to suggest that the DA employs silence, intra-turn pauses, and a slow phrasing rhythm of questioning as the only or even basic normative style. To be sure, the DA may employ a rapid-fire staccato delivery style or what Tannen (1984: 64) calls a "machine-gun" questioning style, which translates into a powerful device because it pressures the V to answer quickly: without time to fashion a favorable answer. What I have emphasized here is that insofar as conversational style constitutes persuasive power, it thereby enhances and expands the DA's scope for action, for employing strategic conversational resources, while limiting and suppressing the V's discourse maneuvering field. What emerges from the extracts presented above is that the *third turn option space* constitutes a sequential-structural position for conducting such interactional work as initiating objections, composing unspoken comments on prior turn, binding topics and positioning for topic shifts.

Reproducing rape involves these dynamic yet opaque processes of manipulating talk and employing power. The DA attempts to maximize the effectiveness and persuasive power of talk for the jury, while minimizing those of the V. Having canvassed the more opaque mechanisms and tactics of courtroom power, let's move now to probe the more transparent yet perhaps most powerful techniques.

THE SYNTAX OF QUESTION AND ANSWER SEQUENCES

Another powerful mechanism for manipulating turn size in cross-examination is turn-type preallocation, which organizes turns into question/answer sequences and which governs the distribution of these types between DA and V: the DA asks question first-pair parts and the V responds with answer second-pair parts. Yet if we finely discriminate the logic of question/answer sequences, the notion of preallocation reveals considerable structural variability on at least two counts. First, the linguistic syntax governing questioning provides the DA with a range of strategic options. And second, the social activities pursued within these syntactic options display much more than syntactic question/answer pairs. Together, both these observations reveal considerable local management or structural variability within the constraints of turn-type preallocation.

I have adopted, refined, and reformulated the following taxonomic framework for the syntax of questioning from Quirk et al. (1985), Danet et al. (1980), Woodbury (1984), Harris (1984), Walker (1987), Philips (1984, 1987), and use it here to illustrate the questioning syntax employed in the rape trial. The following list is by no means exhaustive, but it does represent the most frequent strategic options exercised by the DA.

1   *WH interrogatives* (how, why, where, when, which, who, what)
     "How did'ju wind up in his automobe::l?" "Why::::"

2 *Polar interrogatives* (grammatical yes/no questions characterized by subject–operator inversion)
"Did'ju know where Bruce <u>worked</u> . . .?"

3 *Declaratives with pre-posed truth clause*
("In fact" "As a matter of fact") "In fact, the- the- the (.) hospital (.) found some dirt o:::n a:: portion of your body (.) didn't they?"

4 *Polar interrogative with truth clause in negative interrogative frame*
("Isn't it true" "Isn't it a fact that") "Is it not true (.) pardying (.) among people yer age (1.1) does not mean go to a pardy."

5 *Declarative with negative truth tag* (confirmatory tag)
("isn't that correct") "Essenchuly yer testifying to what was in the statement >isn't that correct<"

6 *Declarative with positive truth tag* (confirmatory tag)
("is that correct" or elided to "right"? and "correct"?) "So you don't know what you do and don't remember? is that accurate?"

7 *Reverse polarity tags* (checking tags "was she," "doesn't it." When the statement has no operator, dummy auxilary "do" is used. An enclitic negative particle 'nt forms the negative)
"tuh many people that implies sexual activity doesn't it" "She was in a pardying mood wasn't she." "When you left the Grainary you had no idea who you were going with did'ju."

8 *Pre-posed "didn't you"* (negative grammatical yes/no question) ("did you" "didn't you")
"Didn't you do that b'cuz . . ." ">Didn't you testify in direct examination that you knew how many times you were struck in the face and say it was <u>two</u>?<"

9 *Declarative or prosodic yes/no questions* (no subject–operator inversion thus identical to declarative except for final rising questioning intonation. Designed to invite hearer verification)
"So:: your <u>concern</u> when you turned right was only that you weren't sure where you were going?"

10 *Yes/no questions with embedded WH triggers* (even though these questions possess subject–operator inversion, they actually contain embedded WH questions)
"Can you show us where the marks are on your fa::ce? from having been slapped?"

11 *Disjunctive interrogatives*
"Were you lying when you gave the statement or are you lying in the courtroom?"

12 *Legalistic dubitative particle/qualifying tag* (doubt marker "Allegedly")
"Now- this was ranked and pulled is that correct (1.5) Allegedly?"

The taxonomy of question forms reveals that while turn type preallocation restricts first pair parts to questions only, the range of syntactic options allows considerable scope for choice and strategic maneuvering – for manipulation of question form (Woodbury 1984; Harris 1984; Walker 1987). Following Hall (1980), I defined the concept of *socially structured talk* to stress that who gets to talk, what they get to talk about, and how much they get to say are interactionally managed through the asymmetrical distribution of power among courtroom participants. And if power involves one actor possessing more options and resources than another or even the ability to expand one's options while severely restricting those of one's adversary (Hall 1985: 310), then the interaction between socially structured talk and question form translates into the differential control capacity and coerciveness of question form. The differential design of question types exhibits varying degrees of enablement and constraint on V's answer; the DA controls the sequential and syntactic capital to influence and restrict the V's choice of answer. Much like the physical act of rape, where the V is relatively powerless in the face of male aggression and brute strength, so she is similarly passive and limited in response to the DA's influence during questioning (see ibid.).

For instance, all yes/no questions attempt to restrict the size and choice of V's answer: limiting answers to yes or no; and, within this question class, tag questions, negative grammatical Y/N questions, pre- and post-posed interrogative frames not only restrict size and choice, but maximize conduciveness (or speaker-based preference): favoring, presupposing, suggesting – leading the V to one response over the other (Hudson 1975: 13). By contrast, WH questions are much less constraining, and enable the V to select and choose – within limits – both the size and phrasing of the answer. In between these constraining and enabling extremes are polar interrogatives or grammatical Y/N questions, which still narrow answer choice and size, but are not leading or conducive questions. Hence, on syntactic grounds alone, the DA's structurational power encompasses the resources for (1) restricting the V's choice of answer, (2) constraining the size of her answer, (3) leading her to the desired answer, and (4) selecting the underlying presuppositional framework encompassing her answer. Put simply, the differential design of question types operates to limit her ability to talk.

The DA's power to employ linguistic repertoire strategically penetrates far beyond just restricting answer size and type, and even beyond leading the V to the desired answer, even beyond eliciting favorable testimony. In addition to this syntactic repertoire of options, but building off it, the DA possesses the power to control the topic or agenda, to phrase evidence,

and to "load" questions in order to convey impressions about that
particular question's truth content. What is particularly compelling about
these observations is that such impression management techniques
attempt to manage not only the V's answers, but also the jury's
interpretation of evidence. In this sense, loaded or leading questions may
register strong impressions about evidence, regardless of the answer,
because they frame expectations about both the forthcoming answer and
the question's truth content (Wrightsman 1987: 106, 328; Brown and
Yule 1983: 30–1; Loftus 1975; Loftus and Zanni 1975). As a result of
manipulation of syntactic question form, the jury may register not just
the facts, but also the presuppositions and blame implicative imputations
the DA embeds within that question. More pointedly, the jury's
impressions can be significantly managed through presuppositions about
truth content embedded within leading questions (Loftus 1974; Brown
and Yule 1983: 30–1; Wrightsman 1987: 106, 328), which doubtless
accounts for their frequent use in cross-examination.

To illustrate these blame-implicative queries and to discriminate the
degree to which the DA can impose interpretations on evidence through
manipulation of question form, I want to contrast a WH question, the
least coercive and controlling form, with a tag question, the most coercive
and controlling.

(5.44) Trial 1

0520	**DA:**	So one of the objectives, when you lef that pardy
0521		at the parking lot wuz to go out n pardy, is that correct?

·
·

0527	**DA:**	What's meant by <u>PARD</u>ying (2.2) yer- yer- what?
0528		nineteen? (0.6) <u>We</u>re you nineteen at that time?
0529		(1.5)
0530	**V:**	°Yes.
0531		(2.5)
0532	**DA:**	What's mean among- (1.2) youthful people (.)
0533		people yer age (.) Brian's age by <u>pardying</u>?
0534		(3.0)
0535	**V:**	Some take it jis to go en (1.3) with some frens,
0536		people en (.) have uh few drinks (1.3) en some do
0537		smoke (0.7) some do take th- pills.
0538		(2.6)
0539	**DA:**	[[Pardying
0540	**V:**	(Drugs)

```
0541                    (1.2)
0542    DA:    Is it not true (.) pardying (.) among people yer age,
0543           (1.1) does not mean go to a pardy.
0544                  (1.6)
0545    V:     That's true=
0546    DA:=   It implies (7.4) tuh many people that
0547           implies sexual activity dozen it?=
0548    PA:=   Objecshun yer honor
0549                    (2.5)
0550    J:     ((Clearing throat)) (2.3) Overru::led.
0551                    (1.0)
0552    DA:    To many people yer age (.) that means
0553           sexual activity does is not?
0554                    (2.6)
0555    V:     Tuh so::me yes (.) I guess.
0556                    (1.3)
0557    DA:    En- at the very le::ast it means the use (.) of intoxikints.
0558                    (1.1)
0559    V:     Yes.
0560                    (2.1)
0561    DA:    So:: when- (.) they suggested- (0.3) who
0562           suggested that you go pardying?
0563                    (5.0)
0564    V:     I don't know who- first brought it up (.) they did (0.7) mention
0565                                                 [        ]
0566    DA:                                              (then did)
0567                    (1.0)
0568    V:     Did mention that (.) uh (0.5) there would be frens who
0569           had the apartment (0.4) who'd be having uh pardy.
0570                    (1.9)
0571    DA:    (So) the word pardying (.) les go pardy, something
0572           like that ( ) correct? not just go to uh pardy=
0573                           [                      ]
0574    V:                          °mmhmm
0575    DA:=   correct?
0576    V:     °mmhmm
0577                    (.)
0578    DA:    We're talking about pardying (.) as it's defined by::
0579           (.) people yer age? correct?
0580                    (0.5)
0581    V:     °Mmhmm (.) yeah.
```

Note the difference between the DA's WH question and the V's response occurring on lines 0532–9, and the DA's yes/no tag questions and the V's responses on lines 0546–55. In the former, the V exercises a degree of autonomy in the phrasing of her response. In the latter, her response is severely constrained by the DA's choice of syntactic form and phrasing of evidence. An almost identical instance unfurls on lines 0561–81. The DA's first question is a WH-Q, soliciting a response phrased and selected by the V; but quite clearly her response was not the response the DA had hoped to elicit, for the V employs the response latitude afforded by WH-Q answer frame to radically subvert the meaning of "pardying," from a sexual/drug using activity to a place/activity formulation. As a result, the DA is forced to pursue the solicited response through Y/N tag questions – abandoning the previous pursuit through WH-Q forms – with their strategic advantages, and exposing a vulnerability in the DA's definition that could imperil the blame implicativeness of the term "pardying." Here the DA attempts to have the V employ the term "pardying" as previously defined, abandons the attempt when she shifts its meaning, and pursues the preferred response with a transformation and manipulation of syntactic form. Thus, while the WH question can possibly "hang" the V in her own words, it may also expand her autonomy in the response frame. But even though the WH-Q response frame represents an opening for the V, that autonomy is contingent on and granted by the DA through his/her choice of syntactic options.

Not only are the syntactic constraints and enablements on response size and type visible in this extract, the presuppositions embedded in the different question types are also more or less transparent. That is, while some of these question types signal the DA's presuppositions about a given question's truth content, and display such presuppositions to the jury, others are much more neutral. Although WH-Q, like "What's meant . . . by pardying" in line 0532 and "Who suggested . . ." in line 0561, presuppose the question's propositional content, the first question presupposing the term "partying" but not the meaning, the second question presupposing both the term and the meaning, the question's truth content is contingent on the V's answer. On the other hand, the Y/N tag questions and pre-posed truth tags occurring in lines 0542, 0546, 0552, 0571, and 0578 contain maximum conduciveness, signaling the DA's attitudes or belief with regard to the question's truth content. They are much more controlling than WH questions because they presuppose the answer, and derivatively the question's truth content, as well as limiting it to Y/N. Ironically, given the differing degrees of enablement and constraint exhibited through question form, the V is compelled to collaborate in her own undoing, as it were, through DA's choice of topics, phrasing of evidence, and manipulation of syntax – through the process of soliciting a response.

Yet the DA's position of superordination and repertoire of syntactic options does not automatically convert into linguistic domination. While the DA may attempt to limit the size and type of answer through question form, answers are not automatically copied or mirrored in the V's response frame, even though Phillips (1984) found that only 20 percent of WH questions yielded non-copy compared to 10 percent of yes/no questions. Although a Y/N question may be designed to solicit a Y/N answer, the V may elaborate the answer, and may even delete the question's relevance entirely through a category or topic shift. Consider the following extracts.

(*5.45*)   Trial 1

0618	**DA:**	You were <u>attracted</u> to Brian weren't you.
0619		(5.9)
0620	**V:**	I thought he was a nice (2.3) clean looking (.) man.
0621	**DA:**	He was <u>attractive</u> looking <u>correct</u>.
0622		(1.5)
0623	**V:**	°Yeah.
0624	**DA:**	And <u>basically</u> when you left that parking lot all you
0625		knew about him was that he was a good lookin <u>man</u> (.8)
0626		isn't that true
0627		(2.9)
0628	**V:**	°Yeah.
0629		(12.5)
0630	**DA:**	When you got over...

(*5.46*)   Trial 1

DA:	Can you drink over at Saint Louis?
	(0.9)
V:	No.
	(1.0)
DA:	So you come over here so you c'n git some <u>alcohol</u> is that correct?
	(1.0)
V:	That's not the sole purpose (.) no.
DA:	<u>That's</u> <u>one</u> of the purposes is it not?
	(1.4)
V:	Yeah.

In example 5.45 the DA initiates a topic about the V's feelings about her assailant "You were attracted to Brian weren't you", and raises the relevant category-bound attribute of "feelings" toward one's partner in an intimate, personal relationship. But relationships may also be impersonal or cordial and thus also involve the category relevance of perception toward the relational incumbent. So categorial attributes include, minimally, perceptions and feeling. And it is the former category that the V asserts the supremacy and relevance of, not the latter. The V employs the more neutral categorial attribute of "perception about looks" to delete and transform the category frame of "intimate relationship" provided by the DA's question.

Undaunted, the DA in next turn not only pursues or takes up the V's topic but also repeats the syntactic form of the previous question – a tag question – in suggestive metonymic association that serves his purpose better than her nonsexual response about Brian's appearance. The DA not only repeats the V's topic but also upgrades the question form from a reverse polarity tag to a positive truth tag, eliciting confirmation while pursuing a Yes or No response. In so doing, the DA asserts the supremacy of and sustains the relevance for responsiveness to syntactic form, self-explicating the accountable relevance of question copy to question form while simultaneously honoring the V's topic shift.

Put another way, one's perception about another's looks may conventionally and routinely involve categorial gradation of the description and the descriptors embedded in it. By insisting on a yes/no copy to the question, the DA does not allow for gradational movements, for slippage, in category membership, like "nice clean looking" and so on. Still more covertly, the V's answer elaboration constitutes a footing shift or realignment of identities and hence the use of power. To assert the relevance of and supremacy for the prior footing, the DA not only pursues the V's topic, allowing a transformation to a term often associated with her wording/phrasing, but quashes the shift from a strict yes/no answer to a more elaborate one: a covert solicit or elicit of yes/no. One last point: the realignment of the realignment can be accomplished either overtly, by requesting a response that copies question form and marks the violation as in example 5.4, or covertly, by repeating the question or a reformulation of it, as in examples 5.45 and 5.46. Pollner (1979, 1987) refers to this form of contextualized socialization as a self-explicating transaction.

But the DA's attempt to coerce the V's response overtly poses a serious dilemma, because overt restrictions reveal rather transparent attempts to not just restrict testimony but to suppress it as well. And such "exposed" strategies leave the jury in the position of inferring or interpreting what it is the DA is attempting to conceal. Clearly then, just as we saw that objections create a dilemma for the PA because he/she can be seen as attempting to suppress testimony, so do similar attempts to restrict testimony create liabilities and dilemmas for the DA.

Another lack of responsiveness or failure to copy consists of the V's frame elaboration in example 5.46. In this case, the V elaborates the answer frame with a negative or downgraded inclusion "that's not the sole purpose" of the DA's exclusive or maximum description, "so you come over here to get some alcohol." The DA not only pursues that topic with a positive inclusive upgrade "that's one of the purposes", but also pursues a yes/no answer to the question. So among the multiple levels of relevance discourse operates on, two in evidence here consist of topic and question copy or deletion, with one or both being abandoned, pursued, or negotiated.

In summary, through posing a question, the DA provides and presupposes the answer frame in V's next turn, even if question form is not automatically copied or mirrored. The balance between autonomy and constraint or the dialectic of control, while strongly biased in favor of the DA, is still contingent, because the V may elaborate, shift, or delete the topic. While manipulation of question form constrains the V's ability to build on DA's turn, such constraint is a chronic, moment-to-moment achievement. It's something the DA has to work for.

More generally, in this section on the syntax of question and answer sequences, I have described several dimensions of the DA's power: the power to control topics, to phrase evidence, and to restrict the size and type of answer. Derivatively, I have explored the DA's power to manage impressions on both the V and, more importantly, the jury, through leading questions and conductivity, both of which constitute nothing less than the power to define the situation, to define what counts as reality, in sum, the power to make one's account count.

When discovering rape, the presentation of testimony and interpretation of evidence involve the symbolic mobilization of linguistic support to persuade the jury to accept the DA's definition of the situation (see Hall 1980). Such control over testimony and manipulation of question form exhibits how the repertoire of syntactic options embodies a strategic interlacing of both syntactic and sequential organizational impression management.

Still more theoretically, if we consider that the reciprocal interaction between autonomy and constraint is differentially distributed in particular forms of social organization, with some actors possessing more options and resources than others, then the ability to limit the victim's choice and size of answer through linguistic manipulation of syntax and conductivity embodies power in action: power as a social process (Hall 1985: 310–11). If we consider that the dialectic of control involves asymmetrical access to and manipulation of this maximal range of linguistic resources, then clearly the ability to sift through and select among these devices represents how participants influence one another's behavior in blow-by-blow, syntactic-sequential detail. Syntax is indeed a powerful disciplinary device in courtroom cross-examination, and is deeply enmeshed in sequential and interactional organization.

But there is much more to talk than syntax. Linguistic syntax can only take us so far. To fully appreciate the density and multiplexity of courtroom talk we must turn away from linguistic syntax and turn to the syntax of social action: the sequential-organizational relationships between social activities.

SOCIAL ACTIVITIES AND POWER

Although courtroom speech exchange systems preallocate conversational resources, trial talk still preserves many of the local management features of natural conversation (Atkinson and Drew 1979: 66): syntactic options become available and must be exercised from moment to moment; the size and content of turns must be locally managed; turn transfer must be temporally co-organized to achieve the one-at-a-time rule; the fine-grained timing and rhythmic alignment of speaker transitions must be accomplished; and turn types, including expansive structures of varying degrees of complexity, other than syntactic question/answer sequences must be accomplished nonetheless within question/answer adjacency pairs. That is to say, although turn types are syntactically restricted to question/answer pairs, this is only a surface linguistic description which glosses a wide range of interactional activities conducted through question/answer formats. Just as the syntactic options for questioning are multiplex, the social activities and discourse options operating through syntax are similarly multiplex and must be locally managed.

Yet while social activities must be locally managed, the concept of socially structured talk captures the observation that the scope for managing them, for securing and reproducing the strategic autonomy over the actions of other participants, rests in the DA's favor not the V's. It reflects how the asymmetrical distribution of discourse devices and procedures of talk organize, stabilize, and reproduce the hierarchical power relations embedded in the courtroom. It illuminates in processual detail how the DA controls potent resources to make his/her account count.

Why does that matter? As we have seen, one way it matters is that position practice options available as authoritative resources allow the

DA to control the size and content of turns through manipulation of syntactic form. Furthermore and more importantly, since the DA is doing the questioning, transition from and initiation, pursuit, or abandonment of a given topic are largely under his/her control. Since the DA is doing the questioning, the ability to phrase and present evidence, to summarize what has been said, and to selectively combine various strands of previous testimony is largely under his/her control. And finally, since the DA is doing the questioning, the ability to weave expansive and emergent sequential structures out of the fabric of base question and answer pairs is under his/her control. Put most succinctly, as long as the DA is doing the questioning, he/she controls the flow of talk, leaving the V little opportunity for orchestrating its trajectory.

Two questions seem unavoidable when addressing question/answer sequences and social activities. First, what are the types of social activities and discourse devices designed through question and answer format? And second, what is the relationship (if any) between syntax and social action?

Can syntax be distinguished from conversational resources? Put differently, is it possible to finely discriminate between syntax on the one hand and conversational activities on the other? Where does one end and the other begin or vice versa? Is one more relevant for trial talk than the other or are both equally enmeshed in the rape trial, so deeply intertwined as to make them empirically non-isolable?

These are issues worth raising if we are to analyze the social organization among and between social actions. Yet if we recognize that talk exists – or perhaps better coexists – on multiple levels, such as syntax, pragmatics, discourse, that these levels are complementary, and that they interact with each other in complex and multiplex ways, the above questions can be dispensed with for the tasks at hand, though certainly not dissolved.

Nor are these questions irrelevant. I am merely stating that one level, the organization of social activities, can be analyzed without making reference to and invidious contrasts between other levels of discourse, and can be analyzed as a distinct and relatively autonomous domain.

As I discussed at the outset of this chapter, that the syntactic, semantic, and pragmatic functions of utterances, words, and sentences should be accounted for in terms of the sequentially organized activities they perform represents a deep leitmotif in both conversation analysis and ethnomethodology, and has been proposed, independently, by Garfinkel, Sacks, Schegloff and others; and it is this preeminently sociological proposal which is refered to as the sequential organization of talk-in-interaction: the social activities being performed via the organizational positioning of talk within a sequential context. By social activities I am referring not only to speech acts, like accusing, requesting information, questioning, apologizing, complaining, nor merely to more abstract conversational functions, like challenging, impeaching, formulating, metalinguistic framing, innuendos, signaling surprise and displaying disbelief, repeating, summarizing, ascribing blame and allocating responsibility, but also to discourse devices, like topic changing, topic shifting, pursuing or abandoning a response, relevance binding, puzzles, lists, contrast structures and pre-sequences – devices occurring singly or in combinations of various sorts. Thus conversational activities encompass a much broader and more complex domain of action than the syntax of question/answer pairs looked at earlier.

Given such multiplexity, there is no simple one-to-one mapping or isomorphism between linguistic form and social functions/activities (Levinson 1980). There is, for instance, no automatic algorithm for mapping accusations or similar blame-implicative queries on to question form (that is, syntactic questions might be *doing* complaining, requesting, accusing or any number of social activities). Even though an utterance is syntactically constructed as a question, syntactic form alone does not permit the derivation of social actions designed through question form. While mapping unit acts on to utterance units or specifying the relationship between social activities and syntactic form spawns a welter of problems and issues – perhaps best left untouched – several remarks are in point here.

When speaking of social activities, CA attempts to uncover the types of social actions that are produced and oriented to by members. While syntactically we would say, for example, that a question solicits information and inherits an answer as a normatively binding sequel to it, conversation analytically, we would observe that, for the same utterance unit, an accusation is sequentially implicative for a rejection/excuse/justification or similar defense component as a relevant and preferred next action. Sequential organization and logic possess a distinct dimension of language use, separate from syntax, because discourse activities make sense only in a conventionalized context with other activities, in fine-tuned and coordinated performances. And these can be specified or located because they constitute social facts: external, general, and constraining phenomena, not with a mechanical existence, but with a cultural life achieved in moment-to-moment transactions among members. (In fact from a CA perspective, syntax and social activities bear an unknown relationship to each other.)

With these points in mind, consider the following extract.

(5.47)   Trial 1

> DA: You testified that when you arri::ved in this (0.5) second (4.4)
>   area (1.5) uh:::m (.) you said- (1.0) <u>you</u> <u>weren't</u> <u>giving</u> <u>in</u> <u>again</u>
>   (1.0) that was the?? (1.4) exact testimony is it not=
>
> V: =Yes=
>
> DA: =<u>you</u> <u>weren't</u> <u>giving</u> <u>in</u> <u>again</u> (1.4) does that mean the first time
>   you gave in.
>   (1.7)
>
> → V: That's because he <u>threatened</u> me.

The arrowed utterance in 5.47, the V's justification/excuse, illustrates
how the methodology of CA operates. According to the conventional
structure of sequential logic, accusations inherit excuses, denials, and
justifications as sequentially relevant and preferred next actions, of which
the V's "That's because he threatened me" is a classic instance.

But since not only accusations but also questions and other speech acts
may be followed by a "no" for instance, a question arises regarding
analytic specification of an answer to a question on the one hand, and a
rejection/denial to an accusation on the other, the former organized
around syntax, the latter organized around sequential activities. In 5.47
the mapping problem is indeed solved through conventionalized sequential functions, because an excuse is employed – locking in the sequential
pair.

Often, however, accusations and other social actions fail to meet pair
part requirements so transparently, because of objections and because
numerous second pair parts are not only tied to accusations but fulfill pair
part obligations to other speech actions as well. The V's "No" on lines
0439 and 0446 in 5.48 below are rather clearcut instances.

(5.48)   Trial 1

```
0397   DA:   You met him at (.) one-fifteen or so in the morning?
0398              (.)
0399   V:    Mmhmm
0400   DA:   When the place was closing up?
0401              (.)
0402   V:    Yeah.
0403   DA:   What were the names of your friends you'd seen inside.
0404              (6.0)
0405   PA:   I think that's- (.) irrelevant yer honor.
0406   J:    O:: Over- Overruled
0407            [          ]
0408   DA:     (test-      )
```

```
0409              (7.5)
0410   V:    °mm(hh)
0411              (2.0)
0412         I don't remember (.) specifically who was there at that
0413         night because I'd seen (.) people I've (.) knowed
0414         there before,

                 .
                 .
                 .

0420   DA:   Can you name me one friend who was certainly there
0421         that night.
0422              (3.0)
0423   V:    The girl I was with?
0424              (1.3)
0425   DA:   Anybody else.
0426              (2.0)
0427   V:    No (.) it was very crowded n' I'd (.) seen people
0428         there before I don't remember.
0429   DA:   O.K. you went outside and you waited for at least ten
0430         minutes for one of these friends to emerge, is that correct?
0431              (1.2)
0432   V:    Mmhmm
0433   DA:   Who were you waiting for.
0434              (3.9)
0435   V:    I don't remember who it was.
0436   DA:   Aren'tchu just trying tuh come up with an excuse for why
0437         you had to wait outside there,
0438              (0.6)
0439   V:    No.
0440         [[
0441   DA:   Weren't you in fact waiting outside for somebody to go
0442         pardying with (.) anybody.
0433   PA:   Objection yer honor.
0444   J:    Overruled
0445              (1.5)
0446   V:    °No.
```

(5.49)   Trial 1: Recross following redirect

```
       DA:   >Didn't you testify in direct examination that you
             knew how many times you were struck in the face
             and say it was two!<
                  (4.5)
       V:    That was my head.
```

Put simply, is the utterance unit "no" an answer to a question unit act, or a rejection/denial to an accusation? In 5.49, it might well be the case that it is the syntactic properties of negative grammatical yes/no questions that specify accusation status, so that syntax takes assignment priority over sequencing. In this case, syntax is carrying the load of impeaching testimony or revealing inconsistency in it.

Furthermore, if syntax were irrelevant or secondary to sequential positioning, any size and type of response should be possible after an accusation – anything from a long narrative to a yes or no. If that were the case, sequential activities would indeed supersede the syntactic grounds for mapping function on to form. And if that were the case, different question types would not possess differential control capacity over answer size and type.

Yet, in fact, we have seen they do. There is quite clearly a delicate relationship between sequential activities and syntax which deserves more attention than conversation analysts have given it.

My position here is that sequential organization is tightly interlaced with not only syntax but also membership categorizations, formal legal procedures, and the implicatures of courtroom talk. Sequential, syntactic, and formal legal procedures are tightly interlocked and procedurally complementary. Sequential organization is the normative trajectory or trajectorial possibilities of talk-in-interaction; it propels the forward and backward looking movements of talk, shapes the internal organization of activity turns, and organizes the coherence between turns. More technically, sequential organization coordinates the transfer of turns, orders sequences of actions and their internal components, and provides opportunities for repairing problems in talk (Schegloff 1988a). Syntax is the constraint on response size and type, placing limitations on what and how much can be done in next turn. And formal legal procedure, of course, is the organizational framework for allocating participation rights and obligations, the system of enablement and constraint, based on structural location in the social organization of the court. Only attorneys can ask leading questions, for example, and these are permissible only during cross-examination.

In addition, during the rape trial, membership categorizations generate the production and derivation of moral inferences. These categorization practices lock in patriarchal domination through discourse practices to provide the penetrating thrust of blame-relevant inferences. Much of the testimony in the extracts we have seen and will see is organized around category-bound rights, obligations, actions and knowledge that a *bona fide* victim should normatively and morally possess. The systematically articulated power relations embedded in courtroom cross-examination draw on and reconstitute this mode of domination as a sense-making and legitimization apparatus.

A crucial point is in order here. Why is patriarchal domination being drawn on and reproduced through categorization work? Why invoke politically asymmetrical categorizations like patriarchy? What warrant is there for this particular designation? Could it not be that the relevant moral inferential work being transacted represents instead mundane, gender-neutral categorizations: doing credible or incredible testimony; doing honesty or dishonesty; doing consistency or inconsistency, etc.?

Such gender-neutral moral categorizations do indeed organize our descriptive practices and our constitution of facticity but only at a surface level! On a deeper level of social organization, the DA's descriptions of actions, ascriptions of blame and responsibility, involve judgmental and inferential practices from a patriarchal standpoint. Moral assessments of the V's performance conceal how male domination molds, shapes, and transforms our interpretations about particular incidents, about particular actions and inactions, so that we discover not rape but consensual sex (MacKinnon 1989: 172–83). As Giddens (1976: 113) puts it: "What passes for social reality stands in immediate relation to the distribution of power."

I suggested earlier two questions (though there are certainly more) which seem unavoidable if one is to take up the syntactical relationship between social actions. Having discussed the interaction between syntax and sequencing, I want to turn now to the second of these questions: to list and illustrate some of the social activities transacted through question and answer format. Once again, the following list is only illustrative, not exhaustive, and displays some of the discourse activities found in courtroom talk-in-interaction.

Meta-talk

The resources and opportunities for producing meta-talk are asymmetrically distributed between the DA and V. These discourse devices enable the DA to produce overt and covert blame-inferential comments about the V's talk: namely, that her testimony has been rehearsed or coached, that her recall has been selectively faulty, and that her testimony has been inconsistent and therefore lacks credibility.

(5.50)   Trial 2 (page 73, line 12)

> **DA:**   Did you ever say that three people got into your car?
> **V:**   Yes, I did.

DA: How often did you say that?
V: A few times.
DA: Before you talked to the prosecutor in this case?
V: Yes.
→ DA: Was that because you thought that made your story sound better?

(5.51) (page 108, line 6; Mrs Roberts is PA)

→ DA: Isn't it true that on direct examination by Mrs Roberts you never once answered a question with I don't know or I don't remember?

(5.52) Trial 2 (page 108, line 12; Mr Billings is DA)

→ DA: Isn't it true that on cross-examination by Mr Billings you on numerous occasions indicated you didn't know or didn't remember?

(5.53) Trial 2 (page 138, line 4)

→ DA: Didn't you in fact leave Stratman Park out of that statement because you thought it might be detrimental to you in the prosecution?

(5.54) Trial 1: Recross

→ DA: Have you been instructed to remain (.) ca::lm (.) and collected on this stand (1.0) by anybody (.) that that's the best way to get uh rape conviction=
PA: Objection your honor
  = [[
J: No- <u>SUSTAINED</u> AND THE (uh) JURY'S ORDERED TO DISREGARD THE LAST STATEMENT!
  (1.4)
  No::w Mr:: (.) Wasserman you know better n' that ...

Achieving topical relevance

Although the DA possesses the resources to organize the topic, frame testimony, and present evidence, and although the structural parameters of courtroom organization constrain footing transformations and restrict overt subversions by the V, topic shifts and transformations are only reduced, not eliminated. While the DA possesses most of the opportunity for orchestrating courtroom talk, the V still manages some control over testimony, despite the constraints preallocation imposes. Thus adherence to or departure from a given topical agenda involves the interactional coordination and power negotiations between DA and V. It constitutes an interactionally achieved and socially structured micro-mode of domination.

But the resources for achieving topical relevance are asymmetrically distributed: the DA's control of mechanisms to manipulate talk far exceeds the complementary capabilities of the V. The following device I refer to as *overt relevance binding*, because it exposes the DA's attempt to manage topical relevance more forcefully than simple questioning. In fact, the second face of power, setting the agenda, is organized covertly through the routine syntax of questioning. On the other hand, since the V can transform topical relevance the DA must mobilize overtly the first face of power, coercion, to retrieve the V's deletions (see Wrong 1979; Issac 1987; Clegg 1989; Lukes 1974). The following are two cases in point: lines 0226 in 5.55 and 0571 and 0578 in 5.56, both of which, interestingly, consist of relevance binding post DA's WH question and V's rather long and damaging (for the defense) answer.

(*5.55*) Trial 1

```
0217   DA:   When were you on yer ba::ck in the fie::ld?
0218   V:    When he first (1.9) pulled me outa the car? (1.0) and (0.8)
0219         uh (.) knocked me down (0.5) >when he wuz< (.) hit me a
0220         couple of times n he attempted to:: (.) force me to (   )
0221                                                         [
0222   DA:                                                  Were
0223         you bein dragged at that point?
0224   V:    No.
0225             (4.5)
0226 → DA:   Didn't you have (6.5) JUS TALKING ABOUT the fie::ld the
0227         second time (.) >that's it< (0.7) restricting these questions
0228         to that point n time (4.3) didn'ju tell (1.8) Brian you
0229         wanted to have intercourse with him out in that field?
0230             (0.9)
0231   V:    No sir I did not=
0232   DA:   =Didn't you do that b'cuz you couldn't ha::ve
0233         intercourse with him inside the car?
0234             (0.9)
0235   V:    No I did not
0236             (.)
0237   DA:   N wernchu angry out in the field b'cuz he- wuz
0238         (.) not particularly interested in it all?
0239             (0.9)
0240   V:    No sir.
```

(5.56)   Trial 1

0520	**DA:**	So one of the objectives, when you lef that pardy at
0521		the parking lot wuz to go out n pardy, is that correct?

.

.

.

0527	**DA:**	What's meant by <u>PARD</u>ying (2.2) yer- yer- what?
0528		nineteen? (0.6) <u>W</u>ere you nineteen at that time?
0529		(1.5)
0530	**V:**	°Yes
0531		(2.5)
0532	**DA:**	What's meant among- (1.2) youthful people (.)
0533		people yer age (.) Brian's age by <u>pardying</u>?
0534		(3.0)
0535	**V:**	Some take it jis to go en (1.3) with some frens,
0536		people en (.) have uh few drinks (1.3) en some do
0537		smoke (0.7) some do take th- pills.
0538		(2.6)
0539	**DA:**	Pardying
		[[
0540	**V:**	(Drugs)
0541		(1.2)
0542	**DA:**	Is it not true (.) pardying (.) among people yer <u>age</u>,
0543		(1.1) <u>does</u> <u>not</u> <u>mean</u> go to a <u>pardy</u>.
0544		(1.6)
0545	**V:**	That's true=
0546	**DA:**	=It implies (7.4) tuh many people that implies
0547		sexual activity dozen it?=
0548	**PA:**	=Objecshun yer honor
0549		(2.5)
0550	**J:**	((Clearing throat)) (2.3) Overru::led.
0551		(1.0)
0552	**DA:**	To many people yer age (.) that means sexual
0553		activity does it not?
0554		(2.6)
0555	**V:**	Tuh so::me yes (.) I guess.
0556		(1.3)
0557	**DA:**	En- at the very le::ast it means the use (.) of intoxikints.
0558		(1.1)
0559	**V:**	Yes.
0560		(2.1)
0561	**DA:**	So:: when- (.) they suggested- (0.3) who suggested
0562		that you go pardying?

```
0563                    (5.0)
0564   V:      I don't know who- first brought it up (.) they did (0.7) mention
0565                                              [        ]
0566   DA:                                        (then did)
0567                    (1.0)
0568   V:      Did mention that (.) uh (0.5) there would be frens
0569           who had the apartment (0.4) who'd be having uh pardy.
0570                    (1.9)
0571→ DA:      (So) the word pardying (.) les go pardy, something
0572           like that ( ) correct? not just go to uh pardy=
0573                          [              ]
0574   V:                     °mmhmm
0575   DA:      =correct?
0576   V:       °mmhmm
0577                    (.)
0578→ DA:      We're talkin about pardying (.) as it's defined by::
0579           (.) people yer age? correct?
0580                    (0.5)
0581   V:      Mmhmm (.) yeah
```

I wish to spend some time with example 5.56 above, because this case illustrates in some detail the inherent problems for not only achieving topical relevance but maintaining it as well. The DA begins the sequence with a transformation in the use of the term "pardy" on lines 0520–1, a transformation from an event-at-a-location descriptor to an activity descriptor. Occurring once again on lines 0527–8, the activity descriptor undergoes a process of derivational suffixation which transforms "pardy" to "pardying", and that process, in turn, sets the stage for a powerful defensive strategy in which both the DA and V collaboratively construct a definition of the term (beginning on line 0527). I call this strategy a *definition lure*.

Embedded within the definitionally lured question, generating its blame-implicative power, rests a finely crafted piece of categorization work. As defined previously, categorization work refers to the methods members of a culture employ to classify actors, actions, and events, and to manage informational particulars into morally constructed and hence interactionally motivated descriptions (see Sacks 1972; Jayyusi 1984; Erickson and Schultz 1982). As we also saw, categories may be conventionally tied to particular category-bound activities, the relevant activities members may warrantably ascribe to category incumbents. Bearing these points in mind, notice how the DA's definition lure ascribes the relevant category-bound activities – pardying – characteristic of specific category incumbents – "youthful people." Even though the V is a unique individual, a personal witness to the events that transpired during the rape incident, the categorization work embedded in the fine-grained procedures of talk functions to not only depersonalize her, but also, and even more crucially, overtly co-select her *and the defendant* as co-incumbents in the age-specific category youthful people: "DA: What's meant among- (1.2) youthful people (.) people yer age (.) Brian's age by pardying?"

That definition lures represent a collaborative accomplishment on the part of both the DA and V is evident from not only the DA's question but also the V's answer on lines 0537–9. Ironically, the V – not the DA – is the first to raise the relevance of alcohol and drugs as category-bound activities culturally bound to youthful people. Even so, she still hedges her answer against the damaging inferences being generated and thereby manages to avoid automatic category inclusion: pardying means drug and alcohol use only to "some" people her age. Once again, neither the question nor the answer directly address if pardying applies to the V personally, as opposed to the age-specific category of which she and the defendant are co-incumbents.

Starting on line 0542, the DA radically expands and transforms her definition, first in a negative/positive contrast format (lines 0542–7), and second, following the embedded objection sequence, in an "at the most/at the least" parallel contrast format (0552–7). Both contrast sequences upgrade the V's definition of pardying to include not just drug and alcohol use, but also, in a much more accusatory vein, sexual activity, and it is this latter category-bound activity that works to transform her victim category status into the co-incumbent-in-a-relationship category. Formulaically, the DA's realignment strategy unfolds as follows: (1) select the category "youthful people"; (2) co-select both the victim and the defendant as co-incumbents of this age-specific category; (3) ascribe the relevant category-bound activities youthful people engage in – drugs, alcohol, and sex; and (4) infer that, since both the victim and defendant are co-incumbents of the category youthful people, they logically engaged in the relevant category-bound activities culturally tied to that category. In so doing, the adversarial pair victim/rapist is transformed into a consensual sex relationship pair via the categorization work embedded in procedures of talk. In effect, rape is transformed into consensual sex, into a micro-enforcement of the social order, during the moment-to-moment performance of domination.

If we scrutinize the second contrast sequence, two further properties may be specified. After the objection overrule, the DA, as we have seen, upgrades the verb "implies" to "means" on lines 0552–3 to activate the first sequence of the second contrastive pair: "DA: To many people yer age (.) that means sexual activity does it not?" And that question creates the answer environment for the V's downgraded and twice hedged second assessment: "V: Tuh so::me yes (.) I guess." Yet because the resources with which to interpret and control testimony are asymmetrically distributed in court, the DA possesses the institutionally endowed power to selectively reinterpret and even override or retroactively delete the V's responses, so that her hedged answer on line 0555 is reformulated not as a minimal second assessment but as a maximal agreement. This is precisely what happens in the DA's next turn on line 0557. The DA's question "En- at the very le::ast it means the use (.) of intoxikints" creates an oblique reference that his/her own prior question was actually the first – yet elided and covert – part of the "at the most/at the least" contrastive sequence.

In the ensuing second part of the sequential contrast pair, another oblique reference becomes quite eminent, yet this time involving the V's "Yes" on line 0559. The contrastive "at the most/at the least sequential pair is linked by the discourse connective "and" (elided here as "en"), and when these connectives are mobilized they may function not only to coordinate compound sentences but to link compound sequences also. When the DA coordinates a question and answer pair through the discourse connective in the next question and answer pair to generate a sequential contrast pair (over the course of four turns from lines 0552–9), the answer in the second pair may hyper-project into prominence through the sequential override device, retroactively deleting the hedged assessment, and may therefore stand as an answer not just to the second question but to both the first and second question simultaneously: as an answer to sequential compound. Here, the V's "Yes" on line 0559 may be interpreted as an agreement to the compound contrastive sequence as a whole – as one question – and not as a sequal to just the second question. Because the V's strong agreement on line 0559 overrides – through the DA's contrastive pair – the weak and hedged assessment regarding sexual activity on line 0555, the former may be heard as an agreement to the DA's much more damaging question about sexual activity.

But while the DA may do considerable work to set up a definition, have the V accept it, and achieve, even momentarily, topical relevance, the mere creation and acceptance of a definition in no way secures its relevance on future occasions of use. Although the definition of the term pardying and the delicate negotiation over its meaning appear complete, the definition's privileged status becomes immediately jeoparized and imperiled when the DA continues to employ the term in subsequent questioning. In so doing, the DA opens up an opportunity space for the V to renegotiate the term's ascriptive implications, and, on lines 0564–9, she begins to exploit that opportunity, undermining the term's accusatory inferences and recovering, or perhaps better, renaturalizing its event-at-a-location semantic relevance. In the shifting sands of courtroom positioning and maneuvering, the V transforms the context of pardying from an impersonalized and categorized definition of sexual activity and drug use to a more "naturalized" and particularized event-at-a-location description. And that much appears evident as the DA, on line 0571, moves quickly to repair and rebind the previously secured meaning.

Attempting to repair the breach and recover the preferred meaning, however, exposes the depersonalized and artificial categorization work employed to impeach the V's credibility in the first place, primarily because the DA must hyper-bind or hyper-explain – persist at the same point (see Erickson and Schultz 1982: 121) – the original definition several times over the course of two sequences. Thus the DA on lines 0571–9: (1) (So) the word pardying; (2) les go pardy; (3) something like that ( ) correct?; (4) not just go to uh pardy; and (5) We're talkin about pardying (.) as it's defined by:: (.) people yer age? correct? An overly exposed form of impression management, hyper-binding, in essence, reveals the DA's attempt to manipulate testimony and denaturalize evidence.

I will return to comment on the relevance of definition lures for the DA's closing argument in the next section, but suffice it to note here that our categorization practices, how members classify reality, operate through the fine-grained and multiplex procedures of talk, and in the rape trial these procedures are instrumental in transforming the V's experience of sexual violence into consensual sex. Further, although the resources with which to direct the course and outcome of interaction are asymmetrically distributed between the DA and V, both must struggle to negotiate meaning, to make their accounts count, and to reproduce their systematic courtroom relationship as a micro-mode of domination.

Sequential poetics

The DA controls the resources to thread together widely disparate strands of testimony, which have been built out of the tissue of previous question and answer pairs, and to design *emergent and expansive yet tightly coherent sequential structures out of such pairs* (see Schenkein 1980; Jefferson and Schenkein 1978). Sequential puzzles, contrast sets, and three-part lists represent abstract combinatorial devices woven out of and emergent from base question and answer pairs. These sequential configurations and their creative improvisations constitute orderly transformations on and expansions of primitive adjacency pair structures, and when fully mobilized generate the most powerful blame-rhetorical devices in the DA's arsenal of strategic persuasive options: the conversational production of charisma (see Heritage and Greatbatch 1986; Atkinson 1984).

(5.57) Trial 1

0450	DA:	When you left the parking lot that night did'ju know(.)this-
0451		mister Winwoods first name at that point?
0452		(0.8)
0453	V:	Yes
0454		(2.8)
0455	DA:	Did'ju know his last <u>name</u>? when you left the parking lot
0456		that night?
0457		(0.5)
0458	V:	°No.
0459		(0.5)
0460	DA:	Did 'ju know Brian's last <u>name</u>? when you left the parking
0461		lot tha- that night?
0462		(0.5)
0463	V:	°No.
0464		(.)
0465	DA:	Did'ju know where Brian was <u>from</u>? when you left the
0466		parking lot- (.) that night?
0467		(1.0)
0468	V:	From Illinois.
0469		(1.1)
0470	DA:	Did'ju know where Winwood was <u>from</u>? when you left the
0471		parking lot that night?
0472		(0.7)
0473	V:	°No.
0474		(1.1)
0475	DA:	Did'ju know where Winwood was <u>work</u>? when you left the
0476		parking lot that night?
0477		(0.7)
0478	V:	°No.
0479		(.)
0480	DA:	Did'ju know where Brian <u>worked</u>? when you left the
0481		parking lot that night?
0482		(0.9)
0483	V:	°No.
0484		(4.2)
0485	DA:	Did he force you to get in- to his automobe::l in the parking
0486		lot?
0487		(0.8)

```
0488   V:     °No.
0489          (3.9)
0490 → DA:    How did'ju wind up in his automobe::l?
0491          (1.8)
0492   V:     I got in.
0493          (1.3)
0494 → DA:    WHY::::.
0495          (1.6)
0496   V:     Because he said we were goin to uh party at uh
0497          friend of of his house.
0498          (2.7)
0499 → DA:    But'chu didn't kno::w (.) his last name (.) where he
0500          worked(.) or where he was from correct?
0501          (1.0)
0502   V:     °Yes.
0503 → DA:    You didn't know uh thing about him did'ju?
0504          (1.0)
0505   V:     °No.
```

According to Mauet (1988: 220) in his classic trial textbook, cross-examination involves "the art of slowly making mountains out of molehills. Don't make your big points in one question. Lead up to each point with a series of short, precise questions" (also see Tanford 1983; Bailey 1985). And in 5.57, questions occurring in lines 0460, 0465, and 0480 are designed not so much for securing information but for building a series of progressive "facts," eliciting the V's agreement to those "facts," and assembling her answers to formulate an accusation. The cumulative and progressive establishment of these "facts" operates as a pre-sequence: as a preliminary to some forthcoming or projected action (Atkinson and Drew 1979). They set up the basis for accusation work. They are selected and designed as moves in a projected sequence. They function not so much for descriptive adequacy or for requesting information, as for pre-sequence inputs to sequential puzzles, contrast sets and three-part lists.

Questions about last name, residence, and place of employment constitute category-bound knowledge and obligations that a *bona fide* victim is held accountable for "owning." Because the V only knows the rapist's first name and not the last, for example, the inference is strongly suggestive of a casual relationship, which in turn may be symbolic of casual sex. Moreover, the absence of such knowledge is tied to and organized around the projected accusation as a preliminary. These these questions augur for a forthcoming accusation sequence is apparent not only from the DA's questioning, but also from the V's answers: her excuse in line 0496, and even more transparently, her answer "From

Illinois" in 0468. Just as the DA can engage in preliminary work to set up an accusation, so the V may similarly detect such maneuvering and attempt to deflect or derail the accusation. "From Illinois" appears designed for such work in mind, because not only is it treated as inadequate by the DA in line 0499, it is also treated as inadequate by the V in her subsequent response (and is treated as inadequate by both DA and V throughout the course of cross-examination and closing argument).

The questions about category-bound knowledge are followed by a two-part puzzle/solution sequence: *how*, a descriptive component (lines 0490–2), and *why*, an explanatory component (lines 0494–7). And these two puzzle pairs form the basis for a two-part contrast component, the first occurring as a *compressed contrast list* (line 0499), "But'chu didn't kno::w (.) his last name (.) where he worked (.) or where he was from correct?", and the second occurring through what I refer to as a *list summarizer*, "You didn't know uh thing about him did'ju?" (line 0503) – another expansive formulation built off of and on to the prior specific list members. The list summarizer, in turn, generates the feeding conditions which create the environment for and permit the application of further blame-relevant devices. One of these I refer to as a *post-posed contrast qualifier*, such as "except that he was good looking", a third type of contrastive and expansive device often appended to list summarizers, as in the example in 5.58 (line 07).

(5.58) Trial 1: DA closing argument

```
01        She:: was willing to go alon:::g with him (0.9)
02        in the beginning (0.8) without knowing
03        his last name
04        where he was from
05        where he was employed
                (1.4)
07        WHAT HE WAS ABOUT >except that he was good looking<
```

These three devices, occurring either singly or combinatorially and with their emergent improvisations, accentuate, articulate, and amplify the testimony they organize, and embody powerful impression management techniques generated through sequential manipulation of discourse style. Most importantly, the persuasive power of these rhetorical structures is independent of both message content and speaker identity (Heritage and Greatbatch 1986: 110; Atkinson 1984: 60; Tannen 1989). Puzzle/solution pairs create an aura of suspense. Contrast sets embody emphasis and irony through reverse polarity (positive versus negative) format; they amplify and underscore the V's inconsistency. And three-part lists project crescending completion points, emphasize list items, and convey cumulative blame inferences through rhythmically balanced and grammatically repetitive parallelistic structures – a pattern of equivalence and contrast relations (Atkinson 1984; Heritage and Greatbatch 1986; Tannen 1989). The rhythmic-like repetitive patterns embodied in these structures generate a "more of form equals more of content" conceptual metaphor, such that the V appears more and more inconsistent, more and more in violation of category-bound requirements (see Lakoff and Johnson 1980: 127). Parenthetically, the embedded three-part contrast list with a positive truth tag (0499 in 5.57) represents the most conducive device in the DA's arsenal of poetic repetitive strategies.

Such discourse mechanisms function in court as rhythmically interlaced and tightly integrated sense-making and coherence-producing packages. Occurring in discretely bound units, the sequential poetics of talk convey the normative sense and intelligibility of accusation work against the victim and aid in the production, comprehension, and coherence of blame ascription – the construction of meaning. The cumulative repetition and rhythmic patterns generated through such sequential poetics strengthen blame-implicative inferences against the V (Smith 1978; Jayyusi 1984) and reveal the processually unfolding and discourse mechanics of charismatic oratory: the persuasive power encompassing what Hall (1972) refers to as political impression management. Directly germane to his point, these expansive and emergent sequential structures are designed not only for producing charismatic legal rhetoric, but also with an eye to their persuasive influence on and treatment by a jury deciding the outcome of a rape trial. The devices anchor sequentially organized and systematically articulated power relations between the DA and V.

Contrasts, lists, and puzzles may occur in combinations of various sorts, as in examples 5.57 and 5.58 (see example 5.26 on pp. 128–9 as well), or they may occur in isolation, as in examples 5.59, 5.60, 5.61, and 5.62.

(5.59)   Trial 1

0226	**DA:**	Didn't you have (6.5) <u>JUS TALKING ABOUT</u> the fie::ld the
0227		second time (.) > that's it< (0.7) restricting these questions
0228		to that point n time (4.3) didn'ju tell (1.8) Brian you
0229		wanted to have intercourse with him out in that field?
0230		(0.9)
0231	**V:**	No sir I did not=
0232	**DA:**	=Didn't you do that b'cuz you couldn't ha::ve intercourse
0233		with him inside the <u>car</u>?
0234		(0.9)

0235	**V:**	No I did not.
0236		(.)
0237	**DA:**	N wernchu <u>angry</u> out in the field b'cuz he- wuz (.) not
0238		particularly <u>interested</u> in it all?
0239		(0.9)
0240	**V:**	No sir.

(5.60)	Trial 1	
0628	**DA:**	Did she <u>only</u> have <u>two</u> drinks?
0629		(4.1)
0630	**V:**	Yes- I think- if she did drink it was uh few.
0631		(1.5)
0632	**DA:**	Not many?
0633		(0.8)
0634	**V:**	No=
0635	**DA:**	=But she drove right across some strange peoples lawn
0636		didn't she?
0637		(2.6)
0638	**V:**	°Yes.
0639		(2.0)
0640	**DA:**	She was in a <u>pardying</u> mood wasn't she.
0641		(2.1)
0642	**V:**	Yes.
0643	**DA:**	So were you wern't you.
0644		(2.0)
0645	**V:**	Yes.
0646		(25.5)

(5.61)	Trial 1	
	DA:	Isn't it true that Brian to::ld you:: (3.0) that he had a
		girlfriend and a child (3.4) n'that he was very concerned wi-about
		them and that's why he could not perform that night.
		(1.1)
	V:	No
		(0.7)
	DA:	N'isn't true that Brian indicated to you:: (1.8) that he
		wasn't too sure he wanted to see you again (0.7) towards the end
		of that evening.
		(3.8)
	V:	No.
		(0.4)

DA: N'isn't true you became <u>EXTREMELY</u> angry about that
        (1.5)
V: No
        (1.6)
DA: I have no further questions your honor.
        (2.1)
J: Any re-direct.

(5.62) Trial 1

0134 DA: Those items that you've already sho::wn (to be) people's
0135   exhibit one two three ARE ACTUALLY in substantially
0136   the same condition they were that night aren't they?
0137   (3.2)
0138 DA: Was your sweater this wrinkled?
0139   (0.4)
0140 V: No.
0141   (.)
0142 DA: Were your pants that wrinkled?
0143 V: No
0144   (1.0)
0145 DA: Was this jacket that wrinkled?
0146 V: °No.
0147 DA: Then they're not in substantially the same <u>condition</u> are
0148   they?
0149   (2.5)
0150   <u>ARE</u> <u>THEY</u>?
0151 PA: Objection your honor=
0152 J: =No just uh minute (.)hhh let her answer (.) your fire'in
0153   about three questions (.) before she has uh.

In example 5.60, a contrast device appears on lines 0628–38, a device
marked with the contrastive marker *but* (see Schiffrin 1987: 176). Notice
especially that the device is expanded internally on lines 0632–4. Recall
that contrasts underscore and emphasize the irony in the V's account: the
incongruity between normative requirements and departures from those
requirements. And that incongruity can operate inferentially through our
culturally bound knowledge about social actions, that is, through
normative polarity alone. One procedure for dramatizing and amplifying
the contrast even further occurs through what I call an *embedded contrast
intensifier*, a device for preserving not only normative polarity but also
syntactic reverse polarity (positive/negative). In this case, the negated
contrast intensifier is embedded within the interstice between the contrast
components: "DA: Not many?" + "V: No." And, if that were not

enough, the contrast furnishes the structural environment for another expansive mechanism: a two-part contrast summarizer occurring on lines 0640–5.

I wish to make one final note on the devices presented above, this time occurring on the sequential list in example 5.61. As we saw, lists function as a type of incremental repetition, where each iteration substitutes an item – a word, phrase, or clause – in a particular structural environment. In the process, each repeating and each new component become increasingly and cumulatively more striking. In example 5.61, for instance, the repetition of the negative contracted auxiliary "isn't" pre-poses a truth clause in the negative interrogative frame "isn't it true that": an interactive frame for subsequent list members being joined with the elided discourse connective "and." In particular, look at just the DA's first turn in the sequence.

(*5.63*) Trial 1

    DA: Isn't it tru::e that Brian told you
            (3.1)
            that he had uh girlfriend and a child
            (3.2)
            and that he was very concerned (a)bout- them
            (.)
            and that's why he could not perform that night.
            (1.0)
    V: °No.

The creative and improvisational characteristics of natural language in use are clearly revealed in the DA's first turn above. Within the expanded sequential list is an embedded three-part intra-turn or compressed list – a list within a list – similar in structure to the intra-turn lists occurring in examples 5.57 and 5.58, though the list members above are governed through different syntactic and discourse connectives: in particular, "and" and "that."

Another pre-sequence property of courtroom cross-examination involves a much more macro dimension. On a macro or global discourse activity level, cross-examination occurs as a preliminary to the closing argument. The closing argument repeats, formulates, and summarizes the talk conducted in cross; selectively combines key strands of testimony into coherent blame-relevant arguments; transforms blame inferences and other allusions, innuendos, etc. into full-blown accusations and rationalizations; and derives transparent interpretations of blame and responsibility from blame-relevant inferences developed – but constrained to inferential form – during cross. The crucial nature of this part of the trial is stated most forcefully by Tanford (1983: 412): "the most important part of cross-examination may be the closing argument."

Consider, then, the relationship between example 5.57 on pages 171–2 with the following extract taken from the DA's closing argument, a contrast list with a list summarizer followed by a post-posed contrast qualifier.

(*5.64*) Trial 1: DA closing argument

```
01        She:: was willing to go alon:::g with him (0.9)
02        in the beginning (0.8) without knowing
03        his last name
04        where he was from
05        where he was employed
06              (1.4)
07        WHAT HE WAS ABOUT >except that he was good looking<
```

Compare, further, example 5.56 with example 5.65 below.

(*5.65*) Trial 1: DA closing argument

Linda Sims (1.7) without knowing him (1.4) Just concerned about his looks (1.2) gets into an automobile with him, takes OFF with him (.) Obviously has an objective, she knows they're going pardying (.) we've heard from her own mouth (.) on the witness stand (.) what pardying means?...

While the damaging definition of "pardying", despite being a joint production in cross-examination, was primarily orchestrated and assembled under the DA's direction, it "belongs" solely to the V in the DA's closing argument. The DA selectively reinterprets and transforms her hedged answers referring to a category as applying to her specifically: "from her own mouth." The V is, first, depersonalized and categorized in cross-examination and, second, personalized and particularized in the DA's closing argument. According to the DA, the V created and therefore "owns" the definition of pardying, owning it not by virtue of category incumbency but, crucially, by accepting it personally. That is how the DA interprets evidence and testimony. That is power.

Below are final examples to illustrate the macro pre-sequential character of question/answer sequences in cross-examination for their development and transformation in the closing argument.

(5.66) Trial 2 (page 103, lines 19–24, page 104, lines 1–10)

> DA: Do the words "Don't Touch" come right across your breasts
> when you have the shirt on?
>
> V: Above 'em.
>
> DA: Just above your breasts?
>
> V: Um-hmm.
>
> DA: Did you buy this to give a message to people not to touch
> your breasts?
>
> PA: I'll object to this. It is clearly irrelevant and immaterial.
>
> J: Objection sustained.
>
> DA: Didn't you buy this shirt with this writing above it to draw
> attention to your breasts?
>
> PA: Same objection, your Honor.
>
> J: Objection sustained.

(5.67) Trial 2: DA's closing argument (page 996, line 14; Mr Matthews is DA)

> DA: And again, as Mr Matthews points out, "Don't touch" is
> emblazoned across the breast, and that's where it would
> hang, and you saw the young women, doesn't mean don't
> touch. No decent young woman is going to walk around
> with that kind of thing emblazoned across their breast.

In a very transparent sense, this power to weave together previous
strands of testimony, to build repetitive and expansive structures out of
the fabric of question/answer pairs, and to create blame-relevant moral
inferences which undercut the V's accusation clarifies the intersecting
parameters of sequential, organizational, and patriarchal power: power
embodied through and driven by what I call socially structured talk.

Direct challenges to credibility

Much more generally, other social actions include accusations, displays of
doubt, skepticism, disbelief, or surprise, functioning to reveal inconsistency, requesting information much more overtly and directly; and V's
answers, as we have seen, often constitute denials, excuses, justifications,
rebuttals, and so on.

(5.68) Trial 2 (page 139, line 4)

> → DA: Miss Belcher, isn't it a fact that the reason you're in court
> testifying today is this all got blown out of proportion when

you were stopped on the way back to St Louis by a police
officer for a speeding ticket?
V: No.

(5.69)   (page 139, line 17)

→ DA: Ma'am, isn't it a fact that this is all a cover-up for a wild
evening of pleasure for you on Chouteau Island?
V: No.

(5.70)   Trial 2 (page 810, line 9)

DA: What do you mean by concerned?
V: I don't think I was really scared then. I was just kind of
worried.
DA: Just kind of worried?

Pursuing a response

The conversational resources for initiating a topic, pursuing or abandoning a
response, and deleting/overriding a response, with the particular and
general perquisites such devices inherit, are asymmetrically distributed
between DA and V.

(5.71)   Trial 1

0618	DA:	You were <u>attracted</u> to Brian weren't you.
0619		(5.9)
0620	V:	I thought he was a nice (2.3) clean looking (.) man.
0621	DA:	He was <u>attractive</u> looking <u>correct</u>.
0622		(1.5)
0623	V:	°Yeah.
0624	DA:	And <u>basically</u> when you left that parking lot all you knew
0625		about <u>him</u> was that he was a good lookin <u>man</u> (.8) isn't
0626		that true
0627		(2.9)
0628	V:	°Yeah.
0629		(12.5)
0630	DA:	When you got over...

(5.72)   Trial 1

DA: Can you drink over at Saint Louis?
(0.9)

V:	No.
	(1.0)
→ DA:	So you come over here so you c'n git some <u>alcohol</u> is that correct?
	(1.0)
→ V:	That's not the sole purpose (.) no.
→ DA:	That's <u>one</u> of the purposes is it not?
	(1.4)
V:	Yeah.

Extracts 5.71 and 5.72 introduce these power resources rather dramatically. In 5.72, the DA's "So you come over here so you c'n git some alcohol is that correct?" consists of a *general exclusive* characterization: a superordinate categorization that maximizes getting or using alcohol. That is the primary reason for crossing a state line. In contrast, the V's elaborated response "That's not the sole purpose (.) <u>no</u>." consists of a *negative inclusion contrast*: a device that minimizes or downgrades the DA's superordinate categorization, treats it as a contrast subordinate categorization among a covert list of items, and thereby includes and contrasts it with perhaps dancing, socializing, and drinking. In this sense, getting some alcohol may be treated as a subordinate category, as an incumbent with other subordinate categories, under a superordinate category like "a night out." The V rejects the hierarchical status of the DA's categorization, and places it in direct contrast with a list of co-incumbent items.

The DA's pursuit power is organized around a *positive inclusion* categorization "<u>That's</u> one of the purposes is it not?" which selectively accentuates and partially retrieves the prior formulation. This selective accentuation sustains the relevance of and asserts the supremacy of the prior question about alcohol, elevating that reason through a positive upgrade following the V's negative downgrade: juggling the description from (1) "purpose", to (2) "not sole purpose," and (3) transforming "not sole purpose" into "one of the purposes."

A similar type of negotiation and juggling over descriptions occurs in 5.71, which also demonstrates not just the power of the DA to pursue a topic, but also the power of the V to shift topics and to elaborate the answer frame provided by the DA's question. The V shifts the DA's question "You were <u>attracted</u> to Brian weren't you," a question about the V's possible sexual interest toward her assailant, into an answer organized around the less accusatory and impersonal perception about his looks: "I thought he was a nice (2.3) clean looking (.) man." In this example, the DA's question revolves around a category-bound activity related to the category "relationship" or, at the very least, the genesis of a relationship between the V and the defendant. Since the V was "attracted" to Brian, she had a personal, intimate, and, according to patriarchal logic, sexual interest in him. The V's description of the defendant as a "nice, clean looking man," however, represents not just a category shift but also her detached, impersonal, and de-sexualized assessment of his looks, a symbolic characterization about the nature of their relationship.

Although the DA relinquishes pursuit of the prior topical category (line 0621), the V's topic shift is tracked and pursued with a considerably upgraded and blame-inferential formulation: "He was <u>attractive</u> looking <u>correct</u>." Since the DA fails to secure an overt and direct admission that the V was attracted to the defendant and to therefore gain an admission that an intimate relationship existed, he/she must employ a backward operating inferential logic. This logic in action operates as follows. First, the DA attempts to establish a relationship between the V and the defendant via "You were <u>attracted</u> to Brian weren't you." Second, once the V has rejected that assessment by transforming the membership category from "relationship" to the impersonal "looks" assessment, thereby undermining the utterance's moral significance, the DA upgrades and reformulates her assessment, an assessment – as it turns out – the V agrees with (that is, that the accused was "attractive looking"). And, third, the category "relationship" or even "sexual relationship" is inferentially and retroactively produced through this upgraded looks assessment. Because the defendant was "<u>attractive</u> looking," the V must have been "attracted" to him, and because she was attracted to him, then, according to patriarchal ideological standards of sexual access, there was quite possibly not just a relationship but a *sexual* relationship between them. Failing to obtain a direct admission from the V, the DA manages to secure one covertly and inferentially. The V's sexual interest in and relationship with the defendant must be retroactively inferred from a mundane yet motivated description about his looks.

Moreover, in both these extracts the DA pursues a response with upgraded formulations, but just as importantly, that pursuit power appears just as much designed to pursue a *copied*, not elaborated, answer through more conducive tag components as to pursue a topically coherent response. Looked at in this light, courtroom cross-examination constitutes a self-explicating transaction (Pollner 1979) in which the V is socialized to courtroom identity position practices, to the moment-to-moment contextualized unfolding of courtroom order, and sanctioned through the DA's pursuit of answers (in copied form) to produce and reproduce the hierarchical arrangements of courtroom social organization.

Because the conversational resources for pursuing a response are asymmetrically distributed across courtroom position practices, the resources for abandoning and overriding talk allow the DA considerable leverage for literally interpreting what counts as reality and for deciding what constitutes knowledge! In extract 5.57 above, notice how the V's answer about the defendant's residence "From Illinois" is transformed and deleted in both the DA's specific and general formulations. When an intra three-part list is mobilized, the list as a whole is true or false, not any specific list items, because of the gestalt-like unity it possesses (Jayyusi 1984). In extract 5.56 above, notice how the applicability of "pardying" applies to the V: "tuh some yes I guess" is overridden by the DA and literally treated as meaning: partying equals sexual activity and intoxicants and that applies to the V. Notice further in extract 5.65 that the blame-relevant definition of "pardying" becomes the V's definition in closing argument: as the DA puts it, "we've heard from her own mouth."

Since the V's turn environment is limited to answering questions, the ability to make comments about the DA's questions or interpretations of testimony and evidence is severely but not totally constrained. Her gradational movements to elaborate testimony and to gloss answers are structurally and strategically vulnerable to similar constraints; the DA is under no constraint to honor the politeness rituals of natural conversation. And since questions may be designed to maximize conducivity and possess blame inferential loadings of various scope, the power to question, as I have mentioned, may be much more important than the answer. Even if the V answers unfavorably to the DA, her utterances, as we have seen, may be overridden, deleted, and transformed.

The epistemological power of courtroom disciplinary regimes

The courtroom micro-mode of domination imposes its strict disciplinary power on witnesses on the stand not only through questioning strategies but also through epistemological and ontological strictures. Specifically, attorneys impose standards governing, first, what passes for reality, the ontological facticity of what happened, and second, but even more important, what is the basis of that knowledge, the epistemological status of reality claims (how do we know what we know?). Since reality claims always presuppose epistemological practices, the possibility of reality disjunctures (Pollner 1987) or interpretative asymmetries (Coulter 1975, 1979) – of varying degrees of magnitude – emerges as an endemic condition of courtroom logic. But the point I have stressed throughout this study is most relevant here. Since the DA imposes the standard for determining the legitimacy of accounts, an option largely though not completely foreclosed to the V, he/she can seriously undermine the facticity of the V's account, making the V appear indecisive, inconsistent, and incompetent (see Molotch and Boden 1985). In fact, the DA possesses the power to not only set those standards but to continually and locally upgrade them, insisting on more and more rigorous evidence, requesting finer and finer discriminations and thus setting impossible criteria for warranting the facticity of her claim. Extract 5.73 illustrates the mutual elaboration and dialectical interweaving between patriarchal and legal modes of domination (see example 5.48 on pages 160–1).

(5.73) Trial 1

```
0420   DA:   Can you name me one friend who was certainly there that
0421         night?
0422              (3.0)
0423   V:    The girl I was with?
0424              (1.3)
0425   DA:   Anybody else?
```

Epistemology filters strain the V's account through legal strictures of evidence, a micro-exercise of disciplinary power (Foucault 1979), and may work (beyond the purely legal) to undercut her account by trading on the patriarchal myth that women are too emotional or hysterical to be credible witnesses. Here notice how the DA can hold the V to a strict account of her friends' names, not allowing her to gloss such knowledge, as might be the case in natural conversation. The DA cuts out and limits the gradational particulars which might justify discrepancies or absence of knowledge. Even if the V attempts an answer, which she does through "The girl I was with?" in line 0423, the DA can continuously request more specific knowledge: "Anybody else?" These "upgrade requests" for more specific knowledge permit the DA to define the criteria for determining the legitimacy of accounts, what Molotch and Boden (1985: 273) refer to as the third face of power. Epistemology filters establish the epistemological criteria for warranting the facticity of reality claims.

The final illustration of the DA's use of epistemology filters as an exercise of disciplinary power involves the following.

(5.74) Trial 1

```
0348   DA:   You say- that (.) Brian's car led the way over to::: (.) this
0349         Glen Carbon area.
0350              (.)
0351   V:    Mmhmm=
0352   DA:   =>How do you know that was Glen Carbon<?
```

```
0353              (.)
0354    V:        There's uh:: (1.5) water tank? Maybe? Uh big silver bubble=
0355                                                         [      ]
0356    DA:                                                  (what)
0357    V:        =thing (1.0) that says- Glen Carb- Glen Carbon
0358              (3.6)
0359    DA:       (OK) but you don't actually know whether or not you
0360              were in Glen Carbon (1.6) or had you been told you were
0361              in Glen Carbon at that point in time?
0362              (1.3)
0363    V:        I was told that was (2.0) uh part of Glen Carbon.
0364              (0.5)
0365    DA:       By the police officers?
0366    V:        °Mmhmm
0367              (1.2)
0368    DA:       (OK) so you don't actually know it was Glen Carbon (2.8)
0369              of your own personal knowledge
0370              (0.7)
0371    V:        No I assumed it when I'd seen (that    big      )
0372                                             [
0373    DA:                                      And when the police
0374              officers told you.
```

In this extract consider first that power operates most efficiently when it flows smoothly and covertly through the mobilization of presuppositions, syntactic options, and topical relevance: when the V mirrors the presuppositions, copies the answer frame, and attends to the topic embedded in and provided by the DA's prior question. Second, when these strategic power mechanisms break down (as we have seen), when the V contests their taken-for-granted operation, the DA and V enter into complex negotiations with back-up power systems. And third, such power confrontations involve, on the one hand, provocative maneuvering on an overt level, where the DA wields power through overt coercion and the V through disobedience, and, on the other hand, subtle manipulations on a covert level, where both the DA and the V maintain the taken-for-granted trajectory of actions.

Bearing these points in mind, extract 5.74 illustrates that covert power manipulations may be exercised as a first confrontational strategy. When these fail, the DA may then mobilize and wield more overt, coercive procedures in an attempt to overcome the initial resistance. On line 0352 the DA raises a question about locational knowledge: "How do you know that was Glen Carbon?" The V's response is organized around generally – in most contexts – sound evidence for warranting such knowledge claims on lines 0354–7: "There's uh:: (1.5) water tank? . . . that says- Glen Carb- Glen Carbon." But the DA (lines 0359–73) cuts out and fails to honor the indexical particulars that the V offers as evidence, insisting that her account meet even more stringent standards of warrantability. Even if the V possesses direct perceptual evidence that she was in the town in question, but the police have told her she was there also, then her knowledge claim is "contaminated" and thereby invalidated as an epistemological basis for making the statement. Cook-Gumperz defines this sort of (covert) persuasive power in the following.

> Persuasion is not letting up when the intent of a single speech act is misunderstood or does not have its intended effect, and continuing verbally to attempt to influence the actions of another without resort to direct action or verbal imperatives . . . I describe persuasion as a verbal suggestion which is repeated more than once in an attempt to bring an alternation in the activity or belief of another person. One interesting feature of persuasion is the need to use *more than a single verbal strategy or utterance* in order to persuade, *verbal arguments* must be constructed and utterances must be multiple and most probably varied. (1981: 40; emphasis in the original)

The final (overt) confrontation in this battle occurs on lines 0371–4. In this case, the V starts to repeat the evidential basis for knowledge about place location, but her turn is interrupted and, as it turns out, usurped by the DA. Notice that the interruptive completer is precision timed and strategically placed to coordinate subordination: an interruptive conjunction, "and," pre-posing a subordinate clause, "when the police officers told you." Interlacing syntactic, sequential, and socially structured forms of power, *coordinating subordinators* highlight not just the mutual collaboration and coordination in the construction of a turn sequence, but also the asymmetrical resources and micro-synchronized processes of overt coercive power involved in courtroom cross-examination: the interactive construction of an answer and the negotiated production of domination.

Hence, while the DA and V negotiate domination in consort, the DA possesses the overt coercive power to neutralize the V's answers through interruptions, and to usurp her turn through coordinating subordinators and other preemptive completers (Lerner 1987) – to warrantably collaborate in the production of the V's answers.

These social activities and conversational devices represent the types of interactional work going on during the reproduction of courtroom disciplinary regimes and patriarchal modes of domination. As I have

hown, the resources with which to pursue, abandon, override, and delete
opics and responses, the ability to interpret reality and to determine the
egitimacy of accounts, and the stylistic options with which to assemble
multiplex sequential structures represent the processes of power which
produce and reproduce the asymmetrical relationship between DA and V,
in particular, and patriarchal modes of domination in general.

More generally, and building on my comments in the previous
chapters, while feminists have dealt exclusively with patriarchal structures
and legal statutes in an effort to understand, explain, and alleviate rape,
applying this knowledge to promote social change, they have systematically ignored the courtroom talk through which rape is discovered-in-
action and reproduced as a social structure of domination. Research on
rape has systematically ignored how members' talk draws on and
reproduces the interpenetrating moments of micro-institutional modes of
domination, on the one hand, and patriarchal modes of domination on
the other. Having discussed courtroom talk in some detail, demonstrating
its relevance for discovering rape, I turn next to a more thorough
discussion of social structure. In chapter 6, the final chapter of this study,
I will theoretically elaborate the twin themes of social structure and
power, and situate the procedures of talk within the structurational
theory of Anthony Giddens.

NOTES

1   In this study, I am claiming that the courtroom institutional mode of
    domination is procedurally consequential for sequential operations: that this
    speech exchange system transforms, in systematic fashion, the organization of
    turn-taking, sequencing, and repair. By contrast, patriarchal modes of
    domination, while not procedurally consequential for sequential operations,
    do generate the sense and meaning of male hegemony *in conjunction and
    interaction with sequential operations*. Sequential structures package and
    produce the blame implicative coherence of patriarchal social structures. For
    patriarchal structures to influence sequential operations I would have to prove
    inter alia that the rape trial is somehow different from the sequential structures
    in murder, manslaughter, fraud, burglary, robbery, and assault trials, to
    mention but a few. I would have to prove, further, that the differences are due
    to patriarchy and not to some other mode of domination such as race or class.
    Finally, I would have to prove that significant differences exist between trial
    talk and natural conversation and that those differences are patriarchally or
    gender driven. I strongly doubt, however, that patriarchal structures exert any
    influence over sequential structures in the rape trial.

2 Atkinson and Drew (1979: 209–15) are the only ones to even address the relevance of objection sequences. They actually raise the possibility of an objection opportunity space but then fail to develop the idea – I suspect because they may have lacked the necessary data.

6

From Social Structure to the Duality of Structure

In this final chapter I shall integrate the empirical analyses presented in previous chapters into a more comprehensive and formal theoretical framework. I shall do so to address Marx's augural paradox: "Men make their own history, but they do not make it just as they please; they do not make it under circumstances chosen by themselves, but under circumstances directly found, given and transmitted from the past" (1972: 437).

But just how do men and women draw on and reproduce historically inherited structural arrangements when making history? How does the obdurate facticity of these structural circumstances emerge from recursively organized structuring practices to become external and constraining on members? Much more narrowly, how are the social facts of both rape and legal institutions regenerated and regrooved in and through the structurational processes embedded in courtroom talk? Just how are these social facts transmitted from the past? And, just as important, when do we make and remake these dominational histories under structural conditions inherited from the past?

THE IDEA OF SOCIAL STRUCTURE

When addressing Marx's paradox, most sociologists consider the primal if not exclusive reference point to be in the second half of Marx's often quoted statement – the idea of social structure (Merton 1957, 1975; Blau 1975: introduction; Blau 1977; Wallace 1983; Stinchcombe 1975; Porpora 1987, 1989; Smelser 1986, 1988; Bhaskar 1979, 1989; Mayhew 1980, 1981; Issac 1987; Layder 1985, 1987, 1990; Cohen 1989; Giddens 1976, 1984; Rubinstein 1986; Coulter 1982; J. Wilson 1983; Maynard and Wilson

1980; Sztompka 1986). Despite the term's ambiguous and differentiated usage (R. Williams 1983; Porpora 1989), the idea of social structure possesses a generic overarching system of referential properties which encompasses several prominent conceptual dimensions.

The generic attributes of social structure are found in Durkheim's concept of social facts (Ritzer 1988: 470; Rubinstein 1986: 80; Bhaskar 1989: 76):

> The system of signs that I employ to express my thoughts, the monetary system I use to pay my debts, the credit instruments I utilize in my commercial relationships, the practices I follow in my profession, etc., all function independently of the use I make of them. . . . Thus there are ways of acting, thinking, feeling which possess the remarkable property of existing outside the consciousness of the individual. Not only are these types of behavior and thinking external to the individual, but they are endued with a compelling and coercive power by virtue of which, whether he wishes it or not, they impose themselves upon him. (Durkheim 1982: 51)

Social structure, according to Durkheim, refers to the objective, pre-existent, and external constraints on social action. This statement can be broken down along the following lines. First, social structure is objective because it consists not of random or idiosyncratic events, but of repetitive, patterned, and relatively enduring activities that operate independently of the sociologist's conceptual apparatus; it is something that is objectively real. Second, social structure is pre-existent because it is bequeathed to us already fashioned through the social practices of prior generations; it is a product we did not create. Third, social structure is an external fact *sui generis* because it functions as an autonomous collective reality with a distinctively emergent nature and logic, a transcendent, superindividual reality that persists and achieves continuity even through successive cohorts of fresh individuals; it is not a psychological or individual attribute nor is it reducible to such psychic levels (Mandelbaum 1959; Gane 1988; Lukes 1985). And, last, social structure is constraining because it exerts, both morally and physically, an accountable pressure on the individual, inducing conformity to social conventions and imposing bounds on the universe of possible social activities and human choices.

As I have demonstrated throughout this study, language performance in many respects possesses these institutionalized characteristics; it is an external and collective property that compels conformity through successive generations of cohorts (see Durkheim 1982: 248; Gane 1988: 34–6). Individuals do not invent or make these institutionalized linguistic properties when talking, but instead confront them as external, pre-existent determinants of their action. Needless to say, most sociological concepts and theories, to varying degrees of sweepingness, are used either overtly or covertly with these properties in mind: classes (Wright 1978), role sets (Merton 1957; Coser 1975), modes of production (Marx 1977), patriarchy (Weedon 1987; Walby 1989), rape (MacKinnon 1987, 1989), conversation (Schegloff 1972), language (Labov 1972; Bernstein 1971), deviant behavior (Merton 1957), labor markets (Bibb and Form 1977), suicide (Durkheim 1951), power (Clegg 1989), personality (Kanter 1977; Kohn 1977), race and disadvantage (W. J. Wilson 1987), the distribution of social positions (Blau 1977).

Beyond these overarching social fact properties there are several prominent substantive conceptions of social structure employed within sociology. While the following represents the more prominent conceptualizations, these are neither exhaustive nor mutually exclusive. More categories could be listed, and despite claims to the contrary most conceptions overlap to some degree.

First, social structure limits the scope of action within and between a structurally delimited and differentially distributed range of options. Robert Merton's theory of structurally induced deviant behavior is the clear prototype for this conception (Sztompka 1986: 182; Stinchombe 1975: 12; Merton 1957, 1975: 34–5). Structural constraints, the articulation between opportunity and normative structures, affect the choice and hence action among a range of possible alternatives – the modalities of behavioral adaptation. For Merton, the choice between conforming or deviant behavior as structurally available solutions is an adaptation to the individual's location within an opportunity structure that differentially distributes the means to achieve normatively prescribed goals. In contrast to its impact on the upper classes, social structure exerts strong pressures on members of the lower classes toward deviation when pursuing wealth, power, and prestige (Merton 1975: 35; Messner 1988).

The idea of social structure as setting bounds on the range of human choice and action operates not only at a macro level, but in a crudely deterministic fashion, on a micro-structural dimension as well (see Clegg 1989: 101). Illustratively, attorneys and witnesses on the stand possess differential participation rights to mobilize question and answer strategies in court. These participation rights are generated through and based on structural location in the courtroom, and are anchored in a configuration of courtroom relationships. Attorneys are constrained to choose – in a narrow syntactic sense – between WH questions on the one hand and yes/no question types on the other. Similarly, given either a WH or yes/no question, witnesses are constrained to mirror that question form in the answer frame. Although attorneys and witnesses have the freedom to choose actions from a restricted range of alternatives, the choice options themselves are both prestructured and differentially (or, more accurately asymmetrically) distributed not only through courtroom social organiza tion but also through the syntactic-sequential design of question strategies. Put briefly: the idea of social structure operating as structural constraint, restricting and foreclosing interactional options among differentially positioned actors, incorporates both macro and micro level of social reality. Agency is, in effect, constrained by if not dissolved into social structure.

Second, social structure refers to statistical correlations among social facts (group properties): patterns of lawlike regularities operating autonomously from agential processes and even culture; social fact explained mechanically in terms of other social facts (Blau 1977; Mayhew 1980, 1981; Rubinstein 1986; Porpora 1987). This hyper-structuralist and positivistic sociology draws its inspiration from Durkheim's work or concomitant variation (1982: 151), the prototypic example being "the suicide rate varies inversely with the degree of social integration" (Durkheim 1951).

More recently but just as structurally, William J. Wilson (1987) has put forth an analysis of poverty, households headed by women, and out-of-wedlock births found in the black underclass. Wilson demonstrates that the rise in households headed by women among the black underclass poverty, and out-of-wedlock birth is strongly correlated with the Male Marriageability Pool Index (MMPI): the ratio of employed males per 100 females of the same age and race. Since marriage is strongly related to an encouraging economic situation for young people, and since females do not marry unemployed males, there is an inverse relationship between the MMPI and the existence of female householders: the higher the MMPI the lower the number of female householders and out-of-wedlock births conversely, the lower the MMPI the higher the number of female householders and of out-of-wedlock births (W. J. Wilson 1987: 95)

Such lawlike relationships between demographic/aggregate variables – females facing a shrinking pool of marriage partners and similar types of population distributions among social positions – form the image of social structure for hard structuralism. Once again, this particular image envisions a social structure of interrelated aggregate variables which operates over the heads of actors, beyond their subjective orientations, and without their culturally embedded and context-sensitive interpretations.

Third, social structure is conceptualized as a systematic organization and complex articulation of human relationships among social positions (Porpora 1987, 1989). Here actors are portrayed as structurally located, tightly anchored within networks of social relations and relationships.

The key terms in this formulation are relations and relationships: the elements of a structure are less important than the configurations among them.

> This image of a configuration among elements that has distinctive significance can be exemplified by the arrangement of dots in a cross or in a square, since the cross or the square we see is not an inherent property of the dots but results from the relationships among them in the way they are arranged, which is probably the most specific meaning of the statement that the whole is greater than the sum of its parts. (Blau 1975: 10)

In this definition we only know the positions of husband and wife, for example, when we have previously conceptualized the relation of marriage, and, just as important, the relationships of domination, exploitation, and reciprocity in which such positions are structurally embedded (see Smelser 1988: 103–4; Walby 1990: 61–89; Hochschild 1989; Weedon 1987: 3; Bhaskar 1989: 4).

As the above remarks intimate, this conceptualization cuts in two major directions. The first, a Mertonian micro dimension, emphasizes the multirelational configuration and synchronization of role sets, status sets, status sequences, and (more fashionably) position-practice relationships. The second, a Marxist-realist macro dimension, emphasizes the real underlying mechanisms – human relationships of power and domination among social positions or categories – which generate manifest forms of activity. Both, however, conceptualize the idea of social structure, not as statistical or lawlike correlations among aggregate variables, or as mere aggregations of repetitive micro-interactions across space/time (see Collins 1981a, 1981b, 1988a, 1988b), but as systems of human relationships among social positions (Merton 1957: 370; Merton 1976: 216; Coser 1975; Handel 1979; Crothers 1987: 93; Issac 1987; Manicas 1987; Layder 1990). I will discuss some implications of the first dimension later in this chapter, but for now I want to define more fully the second strand of this conceptualization.

The interest in "how", the real underlying mechanisms which generate observable social and physical reality, captures the core imagery of realist philosophy of science, from Chomsky's transformational generative grammar to more recent developments in Marxian social science (see Keat and Urry 1982). As we noted in chapter 3, realists are less interested in laws than in the "real operative mechanisms or devices which may or may not yield specific, observable outcomes" (Outhwaite 1987b: 175; also see Outhwaite 1987a; Keat and Urry 1982; Issac 1987). These real underlying structures generate the surface regularities and repetition we observe in everyday events. The association between underlying structure and the particular events produced is not, however, deterministic: structures are associated only with the contingency of particular outcomes.

In the physical world, to illustrate, Noam Chomsky (1986) has demonstrated that humans are born with a genetic language program which forms the initial state (genetically encoded linguistic principles prior to any linguistic experience) of the language organ: a language acquisition device. Since a child's linguistic experience involves an impoverished – not a degenerate – stimulus for language acquisition, the child cannot acquire knowledge of language through the various learning processes, that is to say, trial and error, conditioning, abstraction, association. Instead, the initial state of language acquisition is genetically determined, something that operates and unfolds like any other biophysical organ, such as the liver, heart, kidney. The realist imagery is clear. Chomsky answers the question, "How is knowledge of language acquired?" by describing real structures at an underlying, not directly observable, level of reality.

At the social level, Marxist theorists depict underlying systems as relations of production: human relationships of domination, exploitation, and competition among and within classes. The positioning of classes relative to one another and to the forces of production structures the interests, motives, and practices of individual capitalists and workers, and generates various causal effects in the political economic system (McQuarie and Spaulding 1989; Porpora 1987, 1989). As Heilbroner (1985), Bowles and Gintis (1986), Appelbaum (1988), and Bluestone and Harrison (1982, 1989) have noted, the nature and logic of capitalism – the drive to amass capital – constrains capitalists (in competition with other capitalists and labor) to move operations overseas and cannibalize smaller firms, to bust unions, reduce pay, and increase working hours, to pollute the environment, externalize costs, and to accumulate, reinvest, and innovate. Moreover, this underlying structure unleashes contradictory tendencies which create cyclical crises and other forms of economic and political instability. Appelbaum gives an excellent illustration of this process. It is in the interest of each profit-maximizing and competition-sensitive capitalist to cut labor costs, but when implemented collectively this rational economic behavior reveals a structurally embedded contradiction:

> This leads individual capitalists to adopt labor-saving technological innovations that – across the entire economy – result in increasing automation, the systematic impoverishment of labor, and ultimately a loss of market demand for the goods that are produced. This, in turn, leads to crises of overproduction and underconsumption. Furthermore, the impov-

erishment of labor undermines legitimacy and leads to social unrest, further destabilizing the system. (Appelbaum 1988: 139)

The image of social structure captured here moves toward the dialectic interweaving of structure and action. Action is structure driven, but because of contradictory system requirements it can also collectively transform social structure, the transformation from competitive to monopoly capitalism being a particular case in point. Moreover, these underlying structures only create the conditions for surface actions, ontological potentials which may or may not be realized during the course of history.

But while the class relations of production model is seductive as a prototype model for structural analysis and thinking, it clearly embodies an economistic narrowness which reduces nonclass and noneconomic forms of domination to direct or indirect expressions of class structure (Giddens 1981a: 242; Giddens 1989: 264–5; Wright 1989: 88–90). While patriarchy (along with ethnicity), for example, is interconnected with class relations, it constitutes a relatively autonomous mode of domination with a distinct underlying logic. As Walby notes: "patriarchy both pre-dates and post-dates capitalism, hence it cannot be considered to be derivative from it" (1989: 214; also see Walby 1990; MacKinnon 1987, 1989; Connell 1987: 46; Bowles and Gintis 1986: 92–120). More accurately, patriarchy, ethnicity, class, the state, and other structures of domination must be reconceptualized to yield the operation of autonomous yet intersecting modes of domination.

Seen in this light, patriarchy functions within a nexus of social structures as a conjuncture of structures of domination (Porpora 1987: 119) – a heterogeneous mosaic of domination (Bowles and Gintis 1986). As an autonomous social structure, however, its distinct underlying generative mechanisms must be explicated. Bearing this point in mind, patriarchy is not a system in which domination, exploitation, and oppression are organized around class relations of production. Rather, it is a system in which these human relationships are organized around the social positions or categories of men and women. It is an underlying system of social relations in which men dominate and exploit women.

Moreover, according to Walby there are relatively autonomous yet intersecting substructures within the social structure of patriarchy itself: "the patriarchal mode of production, patriarchal relations in paid work, patriarchal relations in sexuality, male violence, patriarchal relations in the state, and patriarchal relations in cultural institutions" (Walby 1990: 20), each, in turn, embodying and generating a specific set of practices (also see Connell 1987).

Male violence – interacting minimally with state, cultural, and sexual substructures – as a patriarchal social structure constitutes an underlying mechanism which generates surface relational patterns between (among other combinations of people) men and women. I have delineated these repetitive social facts in some detail. Although females are routinely and systematically raped by men, the interpretation that counts – the standard for the act's criminality – does not emerge from the victim's emotional and physical pain but from male standards of legitimate sexual practice. That is power. Male and female relationships are constrained by and influenced in and through these pre-existing asymmetrical structures of power.

The major issue here is that the idea of social structure embodies a distinction between modularity and uniformity. Social structure is modular, a system of interacting subsystems possessing distinct properties. Social structure is not a single, homogeneous system emanating from a single source, a single mode of domination. Rather, it designates a totality of interacting systems – patriarchy, ethnicity, class – each functioning with a specific set of underlying relational properties and practices, each in turn operating with a specific set of interacting submodules endowed with a diversity of heterogeneous submodule-specific properties and practices – violence, the legal system, sexuality.

The courtroom, for example, is embedded within the legal submodule because it contributes to the discovery of rape as a crime, and, as a patriarchal submodule, it interacts with other submodules such as violence and sexuality, since both components are irremediably interlaced when interpreting rape as a criminal act. But while interacting with other submodules, such as patriarchal ideologies, the courtroom system is still autonomous. It has, as we have seen, a distinct set of discourse organizational properties independent of patriarchy. It is, as we have seen, a micro-mode of domination which imposes strict disciplinary power on courtroom participants. And as we have seen, it thrusts a powerful epistemology – particular techniques of knowing – into prominence, and invests the findings with ontological status, with what passes for knowledge, what constitutes reality (Smart 1989: 4, 26). I will discuss the intersection between patriarchy and courtroom modes of domination more thoroughly later.

Intrasocietal class reductionsm, therefore, asserts the causal primacy of class as the dominant mode of exploitation in modern society. But this is little more than dogma, for the causal primacy of one or the other mode of domination, as well as the manner and degree of their articulation, is a historically variable and therefore empirical issue. The structuring dimensions of gender and ethnicity may indeed be much more deeply engraved in forms of social organization on the one hand, and in social action on the other, than other modes of domination, such as class or the state (Giddens 1989).

Before turning to the last idea of social structure, I want to make several more or less general and critical points about the images considered thus far. Social structural analysis marks the pre-existing collective circumstances that constrain members' actions. Social structure refers to the relational properties that exist from an actor's structural location in a social system, and emerges from collectively patterned relationships and interactions across time and space. Agential processes are largely predetermined through structural location in relational systems and, if considered at all, operate derivately as secondary variables which are typically filtered through class, gender, or, more generally, location-based interests, motives, and opportunities (see Porpora 1987, 1989). Within this structural reductionstic framework, social structure chronologically precedes and independently influences social action, so that action is treated as epiphenomenal, as a residual concept which, to varying degrees, is dissolved into structure.

But social structures do not do anything. If social structure exists and persists it is only because members make social facts happen, and if social structure pre-exists and constrains it is only because members interpret, reify, and reproduce such properties as stubborn facticities for one another in ultra-detailed live interactional performances. The reification of social structure is produced and reproduced through the performance of knowledge as a mode of practical consciousness, not through reified and abstract analytic concepts, and since these structures are produced by members for one another, it constitutes a process that must be explicated, not taken as given.

What I turn to next, then, is not another idea of social structure, at least not in the orthodox images just considered, but rather a depth explication of the mutual and simultaneous elaboration of structure and action. In it, Marx's augural paradox is revitalized to reveal not just the second nor just the first, but both sides of the structure/action issue: how the social facts of rape and legal institutions are constituted – are produced and reproduced – through the structuring performances of members to become external constraints on action, to become reifying facticities across time and across space, in sum, to become historically inherited collective circumstances which recursively shape and facilitate social interaction.

THE THEORY OF STRUCTURATION

The drive to reconcile and articulate the robust linkage between structure and action implicates the most pressing conceptual and empirical dilemma confronting contemporary sociology (Alexander et al. 1987; Collins 1986; Giddens 1976; Ritzer 1990). But developing a model to pry open this "new window to the sociological imagination" (Alexander and Giesen 1987: 37) has proved elusive indeed, for a battery of well-entrenched dualisms – social structure versus action, macro versus micro, society versus individual, determinism versus freedom – has fixed and restricted the linguistic parameters under which the debate is held.

Anthony Giddens's structuration theory is the only model to resolve the conflicts posed by these dualisms. Giddens ascribes analytical primary neither to social structure nor to action, but instead locates both within a duality of structure: structure is recursively drawn on and reproduced by members in interactional performance. As he puts it:

> Structure is both the medium and the outcome of the human activities which it recursively organizes. Institutions, or other large-scale societies, have structural properties in virtue of the continuity of the actions of their component members. But those members of society are only able to carry out their day-to-day activities in virtue of their capability of instantiating those structural properties. (Giddens 1987: 161)

It is the remaining task of this chapter to trace and capture the sprawling maze of conceptual forks encompassing this deceptively simple formulation, and to illustrate its relevance for rape trial talk. Of course, any task of this sort is necessarily selective, and in the context of Giddens's work this is especially so, for structuration theory is not, in the orthodox sense, a formal theory *per se*, but a complex system of intersecting sensitizing concepts, a system directing attention to the constitution of society through the mutual and simultaneous elaboration of structure and action (Turner 1986: 460).

Structure versus action

As we have seen, social structural analysis emphasizes the external constraints on social interaction, and it is these structural features that form the chief terrain for sociological thinking. Fully eclipsing agential processes, social structure operates, first, mechanically outside of action, over the heads of actors, and, second, statically like an anatomical pattern, like the "skeleton of a body" or the "girders of a building" (Giddens 1977, 1981b).

On the other hand, theories of action proclaim the relative autonomy and epistemological/empirical primacy of the interaction order, and assert that social structure is merely a reification or hypostatisization of a dynamic reality; that social structure is just a gloss for the motives, reason, accounts, or, more generically, the knowledgeability of actors; that once pared of metaphysical props social structure simply reflects the aggregate outcome of meanings and interpretations woven from and threaded through contextualized moments of negotiated interaction; and last, that it is not social structure at all, but instead the self-propelled character of social action which represents the primary object of analysis for sociology (see Knorr-Cetina and Cicourel 1981; Collins 1981a, 1981b).

What emerges, then, from both formulations crystalizes into the antagonistic poles of a dualism: on the one hand, structural analysis neglects the knowledgeability of actors and the negotiated processes of interaction; on the other hand, action theory neglects the systemic patterns and structural features of society which shape and facilitate the performance of interaction.

In place of these stark either/or dualisms, Giddens advocates a radical reconstruction of both structure and action organized not around a dualism, but around a duality of structure. Rather than ascribing primacy to either structure or action, Giddens reconstructs both so that structures are simultaneously embedded in and recursively reproduced through interactional performances. Recursivity is the central theme in Giddens's work: "Recursivity refers to the fact that human social activities are not brought into being by social actors but are continually recreated by them via the very means whereby they express themselves as actors. In and through their activities agents reproduce the conditions that make these activities possible" (1984: 2).

The starting point for structuration theory, then, is not how structure constrains social action, nor how an aggregate of repetitive actions or interactions produce structure, but rather how structure is embodied in interaction and how the structural properties of that interaction are, by virtue of the real-time and local production of performances, thereby reproduced. Society is constituted in and through the mutually elaborative and gestalt-like texture of structure shaping action as action reproduces structure in recursively organized systems.

In structuration theory, social structure is not external to agents, something operating over their heads, behind their backs. Instead, structures are employed by actors to reproduce the systemic patterns and structures found in social reality. As Giddens notes: "Structure is not 'external' to individuals; As memory traces, and as instantiated in social practices, it is in a certain sense more 'internal' than exterior to their activities in a Durkheimian sense" (1984: 25). This dynamic structuring of structure, the forming of form, elevates the performance of structural properties to center stage: to how social structure is recursively drawn on and reconstituted in interactional performance. Cohen captures this point well when he notes: "In structuration theory it is the performance of conduct per se which stands out as the center of concern" (1989: 23).

The linguistic analogy

But what are these processes of structuration? What is drawn on? Any attempt to even broach this question must consider this first: the conceptual imagery Giddens invokes draws heavily from Chomsky's structural linguistics, in particular, and other forms of structuralism, such as those developed by Claude Lévi-Strauss and Roman Jakobson, more generally, as the following quote illustrates:

> When I speak a sentence, the sentence is generated by, and understood by the listener in terms of, an "absent totality": that "absent totality" is the rest of language, which has to be known for the sentence to be either spoken or understood. The relation between the speech act and the rest of the language is a moment/totality relation between "presence" (the spoken words) and "absences" (the unspoken, taken for granted knowledge of the rules and resources that constitutes "knowing a language"). . . . One should notice that in this sense structure does not exist anywhere in time-space – as speech acts do – except in the form of memory-traces in the human brain, and except in so far as it is instantiated in speech acts, writing, etc. (Giddens 1981b: 170)

Let me use an example – in radically simplified form – to illuminate how this linguistic model underpins Giddens's conception of structure. First, consider knowledge of language or, less ambiguously perhaps, knowledge of grammatical competence and the formation of polar interrogatives and tag questions. Tag questions, as we have seen, may consist of the empty auxiliary verb "do" (with contracted negative) plus pronoun at the end of a statement, as in "Tom drinks, doesn't he?" On the other hand, yes/no questions consist of subject/verb inversion, as in "Does Tom drink?", where the empty auxiliary is inserted to the left of the subject noun phrase. And finally we may have the simple statement "Tom drinks" or, alternatively, "Tom does drink." The point I wish to make here is this: part of what is referred to as knowledge of language consists of our unconscious knowledge about systematic rules of grammar, including the formation of tags, yes/no questions, and statements, and in the cases just considered, such knowledge consists of an underlying form that acts as the structural input to transformational rules that generates *do* – an underlying structure which generates surface structures and which may or may not be realized at the surface level (Akmajian and Heny 1975: 1–22).

Consider another sentence: "The dog barked, then ran." Although there is no subject noun phrase for "ran" in the second conjoined sentence, as competent speakers of English we know the tacit subject of "ran" is "the dog." Similarly, if the above sentence is revised to read "The dog barked, then he ran," we also know that "he" is a pronominalization of "the dog." An underlying structure of "The dog barked, then the dog ran" – which may or may not be realized at the level of surface structure – accommodates such tacit knowledge of sentence structure, an underlying structure drawn on via optional deletion or pronominalization transformations in the second conjoined sentence to create synonomous surface structures.

Additionally, and from a related point of view, knowledge of language involves not just linguistic competence but pragmatic competence as well, a component of knowledge of language dealing with how we produce and understand language. The sentences "Tom drinks" and "Tom drinks, doesn't he" could, under the appropriate felicity conditions, perform an accusatory speech act: that Tom is a drunkard, and is missing work because of problem drinking. At the moment of production, speakers and hearers draw on a welter of taken-for-granted assumptions about the nature of language, the nature of performance systems, and the nature of their knowledge about the world. And simultaneously, each instance in which such language conventions are produced, each instance when rules are drawn into a new temporal moment, contributes to the reproduction of the structural conditions for generating further speech acts.

> When I utter a sentence I draw upon various syntactical rules (sedimented in my practical consciousness of the language) in order to do so. These structural features of language are the medium whereby I generate the utterance. But in producing a syntactically correct utterance I simultaneously contribute to the reproduction of the language as a whole. (Giddens 1982: 37)

Thus, for Giddens, social structure is conceived in quite different terms than in the orthodox ideas considered previously. In fact, he rarely uses the term social structure (see Giddens 1989: 256) because of the connotations of constraint and exteriority associated with orthodox usage. "I have introduced the above usage of structure to help break with the fixed or mechanical character which the term tends to have in orthodox sociological usage" (Giddens 1984: 18).

In contrast, structure refers not to the patterning, organization, and articulation of social interctions and relationships through time and across space – how most sociologists employ the term social structure and what Giddens conveys through the concept of system – but as an absent set of rules and resources which exist, first, only when instantiated in action and, second, when otherwise stored as memory traces. Following the linguistic analogy, structures never exist as a patterning of presences, never all at once, but as a continuous interplay of presence and absence during structurational performances (Giddens 1984: 16): they are subject de-centered and exist out of time and space, except when instantiated. Following the linguistic analogy further, just as underlying "do" and the implicit subject noun phrase "the dog" are drawn in the reproduction of sentences, so the concept of structure is designed by Giddens to depict structurational performances: how actors wield, implement, and manipulate structures in the reproduction of social practices and social systems.

There is one last point about the linguistic analogy. That structure is reproduced by the very practices it recursively organizes bears a bit of elaboration, for the idea that structure is merely reproduced would quite rightly spawn a welter of objections, not least of which is the fact that social change becomes problematic. But if we look again at the analogy to language and compared Giddens's account, notice that reproduction and recursivity are not being used in the strict linguistic sense. Recursion in linguistics refers to repetitive or iterative application of sentence generating rules, the main formal mechanism which accounts for the creativity of language. This device refers to a machinery which permits a finite set of rules to generate a potentially infinite number of sentences, given the application of the appropriate insertion rules in the relevant section of the grammar. For instance, in the following example

NP → Det + N (+ Prep Phrase)

Prep Phrase → Prep + NP

there is a potentially infinite output of prepositional phrases which may occur after a noun in a noun phrase: "the dog in the coat in the car on the street . . . belongs to my father." And I think Giddens wants to retain this aspect of creativity; structures are not just constraining but enabling as well.

But notice that, in the example above, sentence structure does not change. Recursivity for Giddens is quite different, and it is here that he departs significantly from the linguistic model. The interactional competence of actors during the performance of social action is always bounded by the unintended consequences of their actions, on the one hand, and the unacknowledged conditions for producing future action on the other (see Chodorow 1978). Since unintended consequences condition social reproduction, the possibility for change is inherent in each new social action, possibly transforming or sustaining structural properties: "All reproduction is necessarily production. The seed of change is there in every act which contributes towards the reproduction of any 'ordered' form of life" (Giddens 1976: 102). Put even more accurately: "every process of action is a production of something new, a fresh act; but at the same time all action exists in continuity with the past, which supplies the means of its initiation" (Giddens 1979: 70).

So although actors are constrained by the unintended consequences of prior actions, which may limit the subsequent options they can pursue, reproduction of structure is also enabling and may facilitate creative social action in various ways, in various contexts, and in various historical periods. I will return to these twin notions of enablement and constraint later on, but for now I wish to address a more fundamental issue.

Structuration and the duality of structure

What is structuration? How and through what mechanism is it transacted? Structuration refers to how actors draw on structural properties via the duality of structure during the reproduction of interactional systems. The duality of structure is the mechanism which articulates the structural properties of collectivities, and the dynamic, situated, and interactional performance of those properties – the process of structuration – during the course of social reproduction, reproducing (more accurately, contributing to the reproduction of) the very conditions that makes such performances possible: "structure is both the medium and the outcome of the structurational performances it recursively organizes" (Giddens 1984). As Cohen notes: "Structuration refers to the simultaneous reproduction of structure and systemic relations which occur as patterns of interaction are reproduced in the duality of structure" (Cohen 1989: 88). And elsewhere he states that structuration refers to the "reconciliation of structure and action provided by the duality of structure. To neglect reproduction of regularities in practice makes it impossible to determine how enduring structural properties are generated and sustained. To neglect structural properties makes it impossible to determine the conditions agents require to reproduce such regularities" (p. 31).

The duality of structure represents the intersecting linking moment between the production of interaction, on the one hand, and the reproduction of structural properties of collectivities on the other. It binds the interplay of presence, manifestations of structure implicated in interactional performance, and absence, underlying structural properties of collectivities, during the course of social reproduction. The duality of structure captures the reciprocal interaction between structure and action – between moment and totality – as it connects the most ephemeral social action to historically inherited collective circumstances. These structural properties, like conceptions of structure in structuralism, exist out of time and space save for their instantiations, and are subject de-centered, thus exhibiting institutionalized properties of collectivities.

Through the closely related concepts of duality of structure and structuration, Giddens captures the idea of structure not as an external, autonomous, and mechanical social fact, but as an active and dynamic structuring process: as structurational performance. For Giddens, the *sui generis* facticity of social structure is bracketed, and since there are no internal dynamics of structure, only actors, drawing on institutionalized properties in interactional performance, make social facts happen. Structure is not mysteriously outside of action; structure is embodied in action. In this analytic maneuver, Giddens preserves a concern for both the structural properties inherited from the past on the one hand, and the richly detailed interactional production of those properties on the other. In contrast to the other ideas of social structure, social reproduction is much more complex than any notion of class, race, or gender based interests and motivations can ever even remotely hope to grasp. Like other glosses severed from real live interactional performance, interactionless reproduction packs little (if any) explanatory punch;

> social reproduction is not an explanatory term: it always has itself to be explained in terms of structurally bounded and contingently applied knowledgeability of social actors. It is worth emphasizing this, not merely in respect of criticizing orthodox functionalism, but also in regard of the not infrequent tendency of Marxist authors to suppose that "social reproduction" has magical explanatory properties – as if merely to invoke the term is to say something. (Giddens 1981b: 172–3)

Rules and resources

Still more precisely and formally, what does it mean to say that structures are drawn on and implicated in the constitution of interaction? How is structuration transacted via the duality of structure? More comprehensively and formally, structuration refers to the reproduction of systemic and relatively enduring patterns of interaction across time and space via the duality of structure – how rules and resources are implemented in practice. The key element in this formulation is that structure refers to rules and resources recursively drawn on in interactional performance to produce and reproduce social systems (Giddens 1984: 16–30). Rules represent tacit and transsituational procedures or conventions: the mutual knowledge members possess regarding the meaningful constitution and appropriate performance of social action. And, most critically, the rules of mutual knowledge constitute structural properties of collectivities which enter into the reproduction of institutionalized activities.

Two rule components are subsumed under mutual knowledge: first, constitutive or signification rules, and second legitimatization or regulative rules. The first component refers to the meaning, interpretation, and contexts of social activities; the second refers to the normative and moral coordination of such activities, to the legitimate methods of performing them, and to the types of sanctions necessary to secure such appropriate performances. It should be kept in mind that these two aspects of mutual knowledge, while analytically distinguishable, are not substantively discrete but intricately interwoven and therefore non-isolable structures. They enter into the constitution of social life simultaneously interlaced.

What do structural rules look like? What direction should be taken when considering them in the context of rape trial talk? Since this is such a pivotal concept in structuration theory, it deserves to be clarified and illustrated with some precision. According to Cohen (1989: 237), "Rules are formulae or generalizable procedures which may be applied in an indefinite number of specific situations." And, much more specifically, Giddens states the following:

> By rules that are intensive in nature, I mean formulae that are constantly invoked in the course of day-to-day activities, that enter into the structuring of much of the texture of everyday life. Rules of language are of this character. But so also, for example, are the procedures utilized by actors in organizing turn-taking in conversation or in interaction. (1984: 22)

(Also see Giddens 1984: 23, 77; Turner 1986: 471–2; Cohen 1989: 39–40, 99.)

As I have demonstrated throughout this study, the collectively governed procedures of talk constitute a generic organizing structure for the synchronization and coordination of social interaction, a kind of structural template which can be systematically adapted and transformed to manage the restricted speaker options found in trials. As such, these procedures represent a major mechanism of the duality of structure whereby the flow of social activity is produced and sustained. Within the courtroom, the sequential, syntactic, and discourse procedures of talk-in-interaction interact with patriarchal ideologies and methods of practical reasoning to fashion the powerful thrust of blame-implicative attributions against the victim. The moral-interpretative order is constituted, in large part, through such intensive rules of talk and sense-making procedures.

But while mutual knowledge of rules specifies the conditions for the constitution of meaning and the moral order, how rules are interpreted and made to count depends on the effective mobilization of resources, that is to say, power:

> The use of power in interaction can be understood in terms of resources or facilities which participants bring to and mobilize as elements of its production, thus directing its course. These thus include the skills whereby the interaction is constituted as "meaningful", but also . . . any other resources which a participant is capable of bringing to bear so as to influence or control the conduct of others who are parties to that interaction, including the possession of authority and the threat or use of force . . . The reflexive elaboration of frames of meaning is characteristically imbalanced in relation to the possession of power, whether this be a result of the superior linguistic or dialectical skills of one person in conversation with another; the possession of relevant types of "technical knowledge"; the mobilization of authority or "force," etc. "What passes for social reality" stands in immediate relation to the distribution of power; not only on the most mundane levels of everyday interaction, but also on the level of global cultures and ideologies, whose influence indeed may be felt in every corner of everyday social life itself. (Giddens 1976: 112–13)

Such dominational resources incorporate the capabilities for making things happen: the power-activating mechanism for rules, the methods by which meaning and norms are activated in interactional performance. Like rules, resources come in two components, the first being allocative resources – the capacity to control material goods and property – and the second being authoritative resources – the asymmetrically institutionalized capacities actors possess and wield to control the shape of interactional performances. Moreover, just as the semantic and normative aspects of rules are not substantively discrete practices, but are simultaneously enmeshed in the production of interaction, the mobilization of resources is similarly interlaced with the rule component during the production of institutionalized activities. Morality, meaning, and power are decomposed analytically not empirically. As Giddens has noted and as I have demonstrated empirically in some detail, since resources possess no autonomous influence during the constitution of society and since power is not a mere reflex of structure, the possession and implementation of resources always interacts with aspects of mutual knowledge to activate strategies of control during interactional performances (Cohen 1989). Together, both rule and resource structures are drawn on and thereby reconstituted in strategic interactional performances.

This conceptual equality and dynamic interplay between mutual knowledge and resources of domination has been well documented in the discussion of courtroom interaction. The DA possesses the authority to ask questions and compel the V to answer them by virtue of structural location in the social organization of the courtroom. But this positioned authority requires mutual knowledge about what types of questions to ask, when to ask them, and how to weave expansive and emergent sequential structures out of the fabric of base question/answer pairs. As I have shown, the DA cannot ask particular types of questions or comment on the victim's answer, at least overtly. Similarly, the V cannot ask questions, or answer in any way she pleases. And as we have witnessed in detail, both the DA and V run the risk of judicial sanctions for violating the moral order of the court.

Both the DA and V must manipulate the sequential, discourse, and syntactic structures of talk, and must exploit or finesse the evidentiary, procedural, and statutorial constraints to their advantage. The DA, for example, must strategically negotiate and thereby reproduce his/her strategic advantage against the complementary resources of not just the V, but also (and just as important) those of the PA and J. In addition to this sequential/linguistic capital, the DA employs methods of practical reasoning and patriarchal ideologies as interpretative moral rules which impose male definitions of reality on the rape incident, thereby reproducing the patriarchal moral order through which rape is legitimated and de-criminalized. These interpretative rules are not gender neutral, even though appearing so at the surface. At deeper levels of social organization they are patriarchally driven through authoritative resources. Indeed, this interactional process highlights the power of ideology in cementing relations of domination by concealing underlying patriarchal interests and male/female differences.

Thus processes of structuration involve this dynamic interplay and mutual elaboration among semantic, regulative, and dominational structures, structures drawn on and reproduced during the constitution of social interaction. Neither rules nor resources operate independently of one another, but, instead, the chronic interpenetration of rules and resources permits the DA to regenerate his/her structural advantage over the V through strategies of control. Analytically, these structurational processes via the duality of structure require unprecedented scrutiny not only to the description of structures, but also to the negotiated features of interaction, since, at the level of strategic interaction, rules constitute contested claims which must be upheld through the effective mobilization of sanctions, relational power outcomes which necessarily depend on the reciprocal and contingent activities of interactional participants; "normative elements of social systems are contingent claims which have to be sustained and 'made to count' through the effective mobilization of sanctions in the contexts of actual encounters" (Giddens 1984: 30).

And most importantly, none of this denies the systematically asymmetrical power relations exhibited in social systems, for at the level of strategic interaction: "Power is expressed in the capabilities of actors to make certain 'accounts count' and to enact or resist sanctioning processes; but these capabilities draw upon modes of domination structured into social systems" (Giddens 1979: 83).

The novelty of Giddens's approach rests in the idea that the structuration of social systems involves analyzing how actors draw on and mobilize structural rules and resources in interactional performance. That structures of dominational resources are drawn on and reproduced means that actors strategically manipulate those resources to direct the course and outcome of interactions with others – to enact and resist sanctioning procedures and to employ strategies of control during the interactional performance of action. Since subordinate actors have access to power resources also, since they can potentially subvert and invert asymmetrical power relationships via the dialectic of control – the capacity of the weak to wrest control from the strong, even in a fleeting instance – superordinates must apply knowledge to sustain and reproduce their strategic autonomy over the complementary counterstrategies of subordinates (Giddens 1985: 7–12). More technically, the dialectic of control captures the fact that power is always bi-directional, even in the most systematically asymmetrical relationships, since subordinates possess varying degrees of power in relation to superordinates. In the courtroom, despite the imbalanced degree of autonomy and dependence characterizing the power relationship between the DA and the V, the latter possesses the capability to exercise counterstrategic options against the former, however limited her options may be at various times and in various contexts (see also Hall 1985). The reproduction of domination is never automatic. It is always something that must be worked for.

Before leaving this discussion of rules and resources, a conceptual point bears mentioning. When Giddens discusses the structuration of social systems as a social performance, he is referring to the implication of structure in concrete instantiations, manifestations of institutionalized properties in interactional performance, and not to the structural properties of collectivities. Structural properties – the conditions actors need to reproduce institutionalized activities – are recursively drawn on or implicated in interactional performance, and exist simultaneously as the reproduced outcome of that performance. In this way Giddens maintains not only a distinction but also the connection between the moment of the production of interaction, on the one hand, and the reproduction of structural totality on the other.

Such a terminological and conceptual distinction connects structures of signification, domination, and legitimation with the communication of meaning, the use of power, and the implementation of sanctions respectively during the course of social reproduction. For example, resources are structural properties of collectivities; strategies and counter-strategies of control are processes of power or aspects of structure that are employed during interactional performance via the duality of structure. During the performance of institutional activity, strategies of control refer to specific techniques or processes of power embedded within particular contexts of domination (Giddens 1985: 11). Power, in this formulation, is the capacity to achieve outcomes in and through the reproduction of structures of domination and in the context of strategic interactional performances. But as mentioned earlier, because both superordinates and subordinates possess reciprocal opportunities for action, however asymmetrical those opportunities may be, superordinates must possess and wield not just resources but also knowledge concerning how to employ those resources effectively in order to maintain their strategic advantage over the complementary counterstrategies of subordinates. As we saw from the example on "pardying" (on pages 166–7), just possessing the resources to control the flow of talk is of little value unless one knows how to effectively wield it, for instance, knowing when to stop questioning on a topic. The empirical collaboration between rules and resources must therefore operate simultaneously to generate the moral/interpretative meaning of the rape incident during the trial.

The conceptual distinction between the production of action and the reproduction of structure is an important yet confusing point to make, and I repeat it here only for terminological consistency and continuity with Giddens. With this point in hand, the reciprocal interaction between structure and action addressed in this study focuses primarily, though not exclusively, on the concrete procedures of structuration embedded in courtroom talk, how structure is implicated in action, not on the structural properties of collectivities.

To summarize this discussion of rules and resources. Once structures are reconceptualized as rules and resources they are transformed into structurational mechanisms and devices. Once this occurs, a structure is not just constraining but enabling as well – something actors employ to reproduce the systematic facts of social reality, something agents exercise in action, something "structurational." None of this denies the asymmetrical arrangements built into social systems. Although I have consistently noted the asymmetrical distribution of options characterizing the relationship between DA and V, this study has explored the reproduction of that imbalanced relationship: the constitution and performance of inequality. Regardless of how deeply and intensively our social arrangements bite into space and time and become external facticities for members, such constraints (and enablements) must be reproduced in interactional performance.[1]

And for purposes of this study, the equal coalition and dynamic interweaving of rules and resources contribute to the structuring of both legal and patriarchal systems of interaction, lending them systemic form and promoting their institutional fixity across time and space. Specifically, rape as a systematic legal discovery, as a social fact, is constituted and reconstituted through sequentially driven, institutionally anchored, and socially structured forms of talk – a "structurational" totality.

Social systems

A final point remains to be broached: what is the object that is being structurated in Giddens's theoretical framework? Rules and resources are drawn on to reproduce stable patterns of social interaction and social relationships across space and time: they reproduce systematicity. In contrast to structures which exist out of time and space, save in their instantiations, Giddens uses the concept of social system to refer to the descriptive and syntagmatic features of social life, to the continuity of form. The term social system, what most sociologists refer to as social structure, deisgnates the patterning, articulation, and organization of social interaction and social relationships across space and time. Systems exist as the surface aspects of social life. Structures exist as the underlying mechanisms – rules and resources – which generate and reproduce that systematicity via the duality of structure. In so doing, the duality of structure connects the production of interaction to the reproduction of social systems across time and space.

This facet of structuration theory captures Giddens's conception of the problem of social order. In contrast to Talcott Parsons, the problem of order is not an issue of motivational compliance or of internalization of norms, but a problem concerning how order is ordered, how structure is structured, in sum, how the relatively enduring patterns of social life are constituted in moment-to-moment performances. Even though social systems exhibit structural properties, systems are distinct from structures, for, once again, structure conveys something actors employ to structurate social systems – to produce regularity. I will show later that the pattern and shape of both legal and patriarchal systems of interactions are structured by practices independent of both systems. These structuring features of social interaction shape the systemic form of reproduced practices (not just that form exists but how it is constituted), yet are not reducible to them, even when deeply implicated in their production.

A major corollary to system reproduction involves the role of routinization, an integral, though vastly overrated, component in the structuration process. Routinization crystalizes and consolidates the taken-for-granted character of everyday social interaction. It nestles deep into the tacit regions of practical consciousness, thereby contributing to the fixity and to the stretching away of interactional practices across time and space. These habitual or nonmotivated aspects of practical consciousness are rigorously implicated in the relatively enduring, repetitive, and systemic patterns of social interaction and social relationships. Routinization hardens those patterns and hence contributes to the reproduction of structures and institutions via the maintenance of agential ontological security systems: actors trust the predictable and familiar and find a calming sense of security in them. According to Giddens's logic, the routine helps actors maintain a sense of ontological security, which in turn helps generate the powerful thread of continuity in everyday social life. It makes for the underlying trust in the social fabric as an incorrigible facticity, and reproduces the predictability and continuity of actions across time and through space. The recursivity of social reproduction continually regrooves the taken-for-granted character of social practices and institutions, and regenerates the familiar reassuringness of everyday attitudes. The rigid and penetrating facticity of the routine is therefore instrumental in system reproduction. In fact, the continuity of system coordination and the gravitational pull of social structure depend, in large measure, on routinized social practices (see also Berger and Luckmann 1967: 230; Turner 1988: 63–5).

But even though the routinization of interactional patterns and practices constitutes the social cement of social reproduction, maintaining the actor's stable psychological existence, such stable and reassuring cognitive outlooks not only wax but wane, since de-routinization exists as an endemic condition of all social processes – whatever the prima facie rigidity of such systems. The dislocation of routines – in a radical sense when the taken-for-granted practices of mundane reality are breached or, less drastically, the transformation of routines, when established practices are (perhaps more slowly) progressively altered – implicates a transformation in social reproduction: radical disjunctures that threaten or destroy the predictability and continuity of institutionalized routines. Thus while routines may indeed lend continuity to social reproduction, especially when power freezes them in place, they may also be dislocated and fractured.

I think a major caveat is in order when discussing routinization. While everyone is jumping on the routinization bandwagon, becoming infatuated with it, the point must be re-emphasized that the routine is always a skilled and systematic accomplishment. It is always brought off by members' ceaseless and chronic interactional work. When looked at in fine-grained interactional performance, there is little routine about it. Appeal to routinization, therefore, packs an extremely weak explanatory punch (see Schegloff 1986).

To summarize the distinction between system and structure. Giddens employs the concept of social system to refer to the patterning, articulation and organization of social interactions across space and time. Social systems are not structures, but possess structural properties. Systems are best conceived as forms. On the other hand, when considering structures, we are looking at how that form is formed – how it is structured, what gives it systematic shape. When considering structures, we are looking at the often subtle and taken-for-granted mechanisms agents employ to reproduce the systematicity of social forms and practices across space and time – not individual actions or actors, or collective properties, but relatively enduring, structured, and institutionalized procedures of interaction. Structures involved in the reproduction of patriarchal violence and legal systems lend themselves to the institutional fixity of these modes of domination, but are nevertheless distinct from those systems, since they can be implicated in an array of different systems as well. The structures of talk, while reducible neither to patriarchy nor to legal institutions, nevertheless contribute to the systemness of both. One of the most famous criminal trial attorneys, F. Lee Bailey, captures this observation in the following, so eloquently put it is worth quoting at length:

> Cross-examination is not peculiar to the trial of cases. It is used everywhere in daily life, albeit in primitive forms. . . . Cross-examination is used in the board rooms of corporations, by executives who are trying to advance themselves through illuminating the shortcomings of others. It is used by wives on their husbands, when lipstick is found where it ought not to be, and on their children when a deficiency is discovered in the cookie jar. It is

used by husbands on their wives, when a new wrinkle has mysteriously appeared on the left front fender of the new family car. It is used by military leaders, when a hapless field commander is trying to explain why he had to retreat from a position he was ordered to hold. It is used by representatives of the news media when they are questioning politicians and other public figures. It is used in virtually every walk of life where there is human communication. (Bailey 1985: 135–6)

SYSTEMIC FACTS OF RAPE AND LEGAL INSTITUTIONS

Given this distinction between structures and systems it will be helpful to repeat some of the systemic patterns of rape and legal institutions presented in chapter 1.

According to Russell (1984: 283–4), 44 percent of the women in her sample suffered either rape or an attempted rape during their lifetime. Of these cases, only 9.5 percent of nonmarital rapes and attempted rapes were reported to the police, and of this percentage only 2 percent resulted in an arrest, while only 1 percent resulted in a conviction. Breaking these cases into category of relationship between rapist and victim, and then considering reporting of rapes of each category, Russell discovered the following (pp. 61, 97):

- 28 percent of rapes were by dates, boyfriends, or lover/ex-lover, and of these cases, reporting of rapes were 1 percent for date rape, 10 percent for boyfriends, 3 percent for lover/ex-lover;
- 23 percent of rapes were by acquaintances, and of these 7 percent were reported;
- 16 percent of rapes were by strangers, and of these 30 percent were reported; and
- 7 percent of rapes were by friends of the victim, and in these cases 2 percent were reported.

In the Koss study (Warshaw (1988: 11), 25 percent of women in the sample suffered either a rape or an attempted rape, and in 84 percent of the cases the woman knew her assailant. The latter percentage should hardly be surprising since 57 percent of the rapes or attempted rapes occurred on dates. Similar to Russell's findings, Koss found that only 5 percent of the rapes and attempted rapes were ever reported to the police. This low percentage should not be surprising either, for only 27 percent of the women raped identified themselves as rape victims.

Similar to the findings in these two studies, Koss (1988) found that 54 percent of all women report some form of sexual victimization, with 15 percent experiencing rape. In these cases, 84 percent of all rapes involve either a close acquaintance or a date, and most strikingly, none of those in that 84 percent reported the rape to the police.

Finally, Adler's study of English rape trials deserves re-mention here, if only for the fact that she demonstrates how blaming the victim operates as a systemic courtroom fact (1987: 43): de-criminalizing rape by discouraging reporting, and victimizing the victim on the stand if she does report, the latter making it likely that defendants will be acquitted of rape charges during the trial. In this study, 29 percent of the defendants entered guilty pleas, while 71 percent of the defendants went to trial. Of this 71 percent, 44 percent were convicted of rape, 46 percent were acquitted, 8 percent were convicted of other sexual offenses, and 2 percent were retried. The chances for acquittal if the case goes to trial are excellent for those accused of rape, and compared with other offenses rapists and their attorneys are much more likely to take advantage of this state of affairs than in other criminal cases. According to Adler (p. 7), 60 percent of those tried for rape offenses pleaded not guilty in 1976, compared with 34 percent pleading not guilty for homicide, 28 percent for all sexual offenses, and 12 percent for burglary.

In addition to the systematic aspects of rape, their are regular patterns and systematic relationships in courtroom examination. The legal institution in general, and courtroom cross-examination of the V in particular, constitute a relatively enduring system of interaction and relationship in which defense attorneys dominate victims on the stand. This mode of domination has been referred to as blaming the victim, a system which functions within a position practice structure in which the DA asks questions and the V answers them.

Since rape trials *contribute* to the reproduction of such social facts (MacKinnon 1987, 1989; Adler 1987), the next step in a depth explication of rape involves the structural devices and processes that reproduce these legal-institutional and patriarchal systems in courtroom talk. What is the social organization of rape's legal facticity? I turn next to examine how these systematic social facts are generated and sustained.

THE COURTROOM CONSTITUTION OF RAPE AS A CRIMINAL SOCIAL FACT

This narrow definition of rape as a locally produced linguistic process is necessary because different audiences may have varying interpretations of the act. But while rape may be differentially defined by different audiences – the victim (Russell 1984; Warshaw 1988), the community (Bourque 1989), legal practitioners (LaFree 1989; Adler 1987), the assailant (Scully and Marolla 1984; Scully 1990) – the objectivity and criminality (not the violation) of rape as a pre-existing criminal social fact is embedded within our social institutions, our cultural practices, and above all our language, and it is precisely this pre-eminently social linguistic construction of rape that is the center of focus here (see Weedon 1987).

A second definitional caveat is in point also. As mentioned in chapter 3, the rapes under consideration in this study fall broadly into the category of acquaintance and/or date rape. These are rapes that Estrich (1987: 1–7) refers to as simple rapes: rapes in which there is some type of relationship between the assailant and victim; rapes in which the victim and assailant know one another; rapes in which little physical (extrinsic) violence is present; rapes in which an extralegal victim precipitation logic is employed; and rapes in which the "contributory behavior" of the victim forms the primary defense strategy (see Fenstermaker 1989: 257–71). By contrast, aggravated or real rape refers to an act of sexual assault in which none of these minimizing conditions are present: the victim and assailant(s) are strangers, some type of extrinsic violence is present such as guns, knives, and beatings, and the primary defensive strategy will be much less likely to employ a victim precipitation logic. Bearing these points in mind, let's turn to the duality of structure in rape trial talk.

(1) Rape trial talk represents the reproduction of two autonomous yet tightly interlaced modes of domination: legal institutions, the rules and resources governing the procedures of talk and the introduction of evidence in court; and second, patriarchy, the rules and resources of male hegemony in society. Operating through courtroom talk, this two-tiered system of legal and patriarchal domination contributes to the de-criminalization and hence legalization of rape first by discouraging victims from reporting rapes, and second by acquitting rapists during the trial (MacKinnon 1989). When this happens, not only are the social facts of rape and patriarchy reproduced but so also is the legal system of domination as it operates in and through the trial micro-mode of domination, a strict and powerful disciplinary apparatus in its own right. More accurately, through the real live performance of institutionalized sexism during the discovery of rape, both patriarchal and legal modes of domination are drawn on and thereby reproduced.

While patriarchy interacts with courtroom talk to discover rape and reproduce the legal system as a source of structural constraint and enablement, this is not to say that courtroom actors draw on patriarchy exclusively or even primarily to reproduce legal-institutional modes of domination. Although patriarchy contributes to the reproduction of legal systems on a number of fronts – evidentiarily and ideologically – during the rape trial, courtroom talk more generally draws on and thereby reproduces legal modes of domination, a system bearing some degree of autonomy from patriarchy even in the rape trial. Why make the distinction? The legal system possesses a distinct set of organizational properties – mechanisms of talk, admission of evidence, and procedural restrictions – which are reproduced independently of patriarchy. These properties are exhibited in other types of trials, such as murder, theft, assault and the like, trials in which rape and patriarchy are simply irrelevant (McBarnet 1984: 328–35). In the previous chapter I demonstrated that the social organization of courtroom talk operates within a distinct speech exchange logic: that access to sequential and syntactic structure is asymmetrically distributed across social positions, in particular that attorneys and witnesses on the stand possess imbalanced degrees of access to the sequential and syntactic mechanisms of talk; that turn allocation, turn order, turn type and distribution of turn type are relatively fixed; that talk unfolds sequentially according to global activity structures including selection of jury, opening statements, direct and cross-examination of witnesses, closing statements; and that local activity types such as objection sequences transform not only the participation network of the court but also the organization and trajectory of sequential activities.

Moreover, although courtroom speech exchange systems possess a distinct set of organizational properties, the previous chapter also illustrated that trial talk still preserves many of the local management features of natural conversation. These generic conversational social facts enter significantly into the structuration of trial talk and therefore into legal modes of domination. As we witnessed previously, syntactic options become available and must be exercised from moment to moment, as must be the size, content, and transfer of conversational turns. Additionally, adjacency pairs and the emergent/expansive structures built out of the tissue of these pairs must be locally produced and interactionally managed. While interacting within a logic of the courtroom speech exchange system, these devices function more generally as part of our collectively inherited and culturally shared everyday linguistic practices.

How do these practices relate to the duality of structure? First, institutional and conversational syntactic-sequential devices contribute to the performance of meaning in talk – the semantic or signification component of mutual knowledge. Second, the rules driving the performance of meaning combine with norms of legitimation to sanction or regulate the appropriate performance of social actions, and in so doing, they provide the normative sense of courtroom order. And finally, the meaningful and normative constitution of courtroom talk requires the mobilization of power to enact sanctions and to control and direct the pattern of interaction, power drawing on modes of domination structured into the legal system. Chapter 5 (examples 5.2 to 5.5 on pages 106–7) illustrated in rather dramatic fashion the interaction between the rules of mutual knowledge and the mobilization of authoritative resources during the constitution of meaning in courtroom cross-examination. In example 5.2, the J quashes the V's attempt to ask a question: "V: Can I ask a question? Can I? J: No . . ." In example 5.4, the DA suppresses the V's attempt to alter topical relevance and expand the answer beyond a mirrored yes/no answer: "DA: Ma'am would you answer that yes or no, did you give him a statement?" While power may indeed function most impressively when running silently through routinized practices, the V's overt breach of those routines followed by the DA's or J's overt sanctioning of her violations in next turn normatively rebind and thereby reproduce the moral and sequential order of courtroom ritual. This dual binding first, through routine courtroom practice and, second, through overt sanctioning of breaches in the routine accentuates, explicates, and dramatizes the courtroom order for all witnessing participants (à la Durkheim) – freezing those practices into place. Much more covertly and much less dramatically, the DA exercises yes/no questions, self-explicating transactions, tags, conducivity, definition lures, relevance binding, and other devices to constrain the V's answer to just yes or no, thereby attempting to deny her any chance to elaborate in the answer frame and attempting to force her to collaborate in her own interactional undoing (see Molotch and Boden 1985: 285; Foucault 1979: 170).

I used the term "attempt" above to underscore the dialectic of control found in courtroom cross-examination of the victim. While her sequential and linguistic options are limited relative to the DA, the V still possesses powerful opportunities for action. The V, as we saw in chapter 5, often transforms topical relevance, asks questions that expand into statements during her repair initiations, and forces the DA to rebind definitional lures. When the DA exercises the WH-type question option, an opportunity space is opened for numerous types of creative action on the V's part, not all of which, of course, deliver positive outcomes. Even if a yes/no question option is employed, the V is not completely constrained to mirror that question type in the answer frame. Indeed, on numerous occasions the V breaks frame, produces expanded answers, and thus elaborates the context for her actions and inactions during the incident. And although the asymmetrical distribution of speaking rights based on inequality structured into the legal mode of domination and on the syntactic design of questioning function to constrain her answers, those very same constraints operate, paradoxically, as enablements too. While the DA, by virtue of his/her structurally superordinate position, may overtly or covertly suppress the V's answers or coerce a compressed yes/ no in the answer frame, the unbridled exercise of such strategies of control is constrained or tempered because of a co-present but nonparticipating audience: the jury. As we have seen in striking detail, the DA wants to give favorable impressions to the jury, while simultaneously avoiding or minimizing unfavorable ones. For the jury, overt strategies of control may not only function to suppress and constrain the V's answer, but may also be interpreted as concealing testimony, as an attempt by the DA to hide something. As Giddens puts it: "there are major asymmetries in the constraint/enablement relation. One person's constraint is another's enabling" (1984: 176).

The sequential and linguistic capital with which to organize and direct the flow of courtroom talk is systematically asymmetrical. There is no arguing about that. But power always runs in bidirectional currents, even in the most hierarchically arranged relationships, and in the rape trial the V possesses and wields counterstrategies of control at various times, in various contexts, and with various outcomes in negotiated interactions against the DA. There is no arguing about that either. A polar interrogative will not always yield a question-mirrored answer in next turn. Contrary to Molotch and Boden (1985: 276, 285) and Clegg (1989: 101), yes/no answers to polar interrogatives and other yes/no questions are not just structurally determined by the syntactic design of questions or by the authoritative power of the DA or even both. As I have shown and emphasized throughout this study, if the DA wants to reproduce his/ her strategic autonomy over the complementary activities of the V on the stand, getting yes or no answers to polar interrogatives and other yes/no questions, then he/she must work for it. The reproduction of the legal system of domination is not automatic. The social organization of the courtroom's facticity is never just prestructured. The disciplinary power (Foucault 1979: 215) embodied in it always represents a locally produced and structurally conditioned social fact. Reproduction is always something participants must accomplish and negotiate during the performance of knowledge.[2]

(2) Patriarchal ideologies reproduce rape as a systematic social fact by furnishing the topical content of courtroom talk. In addition to courtroom rules and resources, the categorization work that assesses the V's actions and inations during the incident – the ascription of blame and

the allocation of responsibility – operates as a distinct patriarchal system of mutual knowledge and domination, a system deeply interwoven with legal institutional talk during the rape trial. Patriarchal domination – a system organized around the subordination and sexual control of women – propels a second set of signification and legitimization structures: the patriarchal meanings that define how females should act and behave as legitimate victims during the rape incident. These normative meanings are shaped by and interpreted through patriarchal ideological standards, not gender-neutral ones, even though such neutral categorizations appear at the surface level of interaction. At the surface, membership categorizations are organized around the V's complicity in the rape: that she had consented to sex with her assailant, that she was a willing participant in the very state of affairs she is complaining about and for which she is blaming others, or, at the very least, that she had "asked for it" through her actions and inactions, her "acts of commission and omission" (Scully 1990: 42).

This victim-precipitation logic (Amir 1971, 1975; Fenstermaker 1989) embodies patriarchal rules and resources for assessing both the victim's and the rapist's action: for ascribing blame, and for allocating responsibility for the incident – for making sense of what happened. In courtroom talk, the performance of the victim and the rapist during the incident is understood and interpreted through this interrelated web of constitutive and regulative rules of mutual knowledge. In this structural formulation, the sexual practices and attitudes organizing male and female relationships constitute socially structured and thus objective forms of discourse, that is, power-driven male standards for sexual access, and not the subjective intentions or meanings of individual men and women.

Since this conception of ideology is central both to the content of rape trial talk and to Giddens's structuration theory it needs to be elaborated in some detail. According to Giddens (1984: 33), ideology refers to the "asymmetries of domination which connect signification to the legitimation of sectional interests." And, in a similar vein, Thompson (1984: 131) claims that "to study ideology is to study the ways in which meaning (signification) serves to sustain relations of domination." In both definitions, ideology permits hegemonic groups to reproduce their domination over subordinates by "making their own sectional interests appear to others as universal" (Giddens 1979: 6). More operationally, Cohen (1989: 194–5) claims that ideology is deeply enmeshed in routine modes of practical consciousness, where it "reifies the facticity of prevailing systems and the power relations embedded in them."

Recent advances in the study of ideology brought about by Giddens (1979, 1984), Thompson (1984), Van Dijk (1989: 23–7), Wuthnow 1987:

145–85), Lamont and Wuthnow (1990: 294–301), and others situate it firmly in the midst of our cultural language practices: "Ideas circulate in the social world as utterances . . . hence to study ideology is . . . to study language in the social world" (Thompson 1984: 2). And it is precisely this conception of ideology that in the context of the rape trial captures patriarchal power embodied in the self-concealing properties of talk: talk as the medium of ideology (ibid: 1–15). "Talking ideology" shapes, intensifies, and reproduces our emotions about social reality and the moral order (see Wuthnow 1987: 145), and, as such, represents a constitutive form of social action.

> once we recognize that ideology operates through language and that language is a medium of social action, we must also acknowledge that ideology is partially constitutive of what, in our societies, "is real." Ideology is not a pale image of the social world but is part of that world, a creative and constitutive element in our social lives. (Thompson 1984: 5–6)

And, more formally and thoroughly:

> The analysis of ideology is fundamentally concerned with *language*, for language is the principal medium of meaning (signification) which serves to sustain relations of domination. Speaking a language is a way of acting, emphasized Austin and others; what they forgot to add is that ways of acting are infused with forms of power. The utterance of the simplest expression is an intervention in the world, more or less effective, more or less endowed with institutional authority. "Language is not only an instrument of communication or even of knowledge," writes Bourdieu, "but also an instrument of power. One seeks not only to be understood but also to be believed, obeyed, respected, distinguished." (ibid.: 131)

More specifically, ideology contributes to the reproduction and reification of patriarchy as a mode of domination, and, even more specifically, to the phenomenon of rape as a micro-enforcement of the social order.

In this conception of ideology, the constraining and reifying facticity of patriarchal systems of domination penetrate deep into consciousness during rape trial talk, disqualifying the victim's experience (Smart 1989: 26) and transforming the act of rape into consensual sex (MacKinnon 1989).[3] If rape occurs so systematically and routinely in violent patriarchal societies like the US, why is this form of sexual terrorism *not* discovered as a crime. Why is patriarchal ideology so powerful? And, more important, how is that power generated and reproduced in courtroom talk?

(3) As the mobilization of meaning to legitimate modes of domination, ideology reveals how talk, meaning, and moral categorizations are drawn on by actors with asymmetrical resources and with differential access to the power-driving mechanisms of discourse to graft the patriarchal content of talk on to sequential/discourse structures, creating a multiplex interacting sytem of patriarchal and legal domination.[4] And in the restricted opportunity structure of the court, certain positions are institutionally endowed with the resources to make their accounts count – "to make their meaning stick" (Thompson 1984: 132). Since courtroom questioning between the DA and V is limited to syntactic question and answer pairs, accusations and other blame work must be transacted inferentially through irony, innuendo and other rhetorical practices. These blame-inferential practices craft the fine-grained meaning and sense of patriarchal ideologies through design in sequential structure: that is, through puzzle/solution pairs, contrast sets, three-part lists, and through expansive combinatorial variations of these devices. While the generic structural rules of language use are governed under the legal mode of domination, they nevertheless, in courtroom context, provide the penetrating and cumulative thrust of patriarchal blame-inferential practice. They provide the powerfully persuasive coherence, cogency, and rhythm of the defense attorney's interrogation of the victim.

While the procedural constraints of the court prohibit the use of anything but syntactic questions during courtroom examination of the witness, and while rape reform statutes have eliminated introduction of the victim's sexual history, an ironic effect of these constraints is that they have simultaneously enabled the DA to construct delicately interlaced and expansive blame sequences out of the tissue of base question/answer pairs; structures are not just constraining but enabling as well. When manipulated effectively, these microtechniques of power generate blame inferentially. In fact, when fully functioning, these syntactic-sequential mechanisms produce the charismatic oratory found in the DA's talk, powerful rhetorical skills through which covert attacks against the V are conducted. Such charisma is located not in individual personalities, or in structural location, but in the interactional manipulation of words, utterances, and sequences. The DA reproduces his/her strategic advantage over the V not only through restricted access to speaker options but also through the effective exercise of charismatic microtechniques of power, rhetorical options almost entirely foreclosed to the V. When considering even the most systematically asymmetrical relations of power (that is to say, domination), structuration theory focuses not on structural position or on cultural practice but instead on the mutual elaboration of both in position practices (see Cohen 1989: 207–10).

The substance or ideological content to which these devices are applied appear, at the surface, as gender-neutral sanctimony categorizations: that the victim had precipitated her own sexual assault on the one hand or that she had engaged in consensual sex on the other. Victim-precipitation logic exercises such a gravitational pull on our interpretations of the incident because rules of sanctimony are indeed gender-neutral categorizations for negotiating blame and attributing responsibility across a range of different contexts. They constitute rules of mutual knowledge which enter into the structuring of both legal and patriarchal systems via the rape trial, yet are not part of either system. More formally, the rule of sanctimony works as a powerful blame-interpretative mechanism, a tight interweaving of signification and legitimation rule structures, and as a transsituational procedure it applies generically across a diverse range of contexts and encompasses a heterogeneous array of activities in which blame and responsibility assessment are relevant (see my previous discussion on page 43).

The point I wish to stress however is this: At an underlying level of social organization these normative and signification rules embody and embrace patriarchal ideologies for interpreting the sexual assault, concealing while simultaneously generating the male standard which makes the act look more like consensual sex rather than a criminal act of rape. The rules of sanctimony, on closer scrutiny, disclose ideological penetrations which mask patriarchal sectarian standards. In rape trial cross-examination of the V, generic rules of sanctimony lock on to patriarchal standards as an interpretative base from which to judge the victim's normative departure; the V is judged according to the male all-or-nothing, impersonal, and aggressive standard of sexual practice and access (Russell 1984: 162; Russell 1975: 257–75; MacKinnon 1987, 1989; Scully and Marolla 1985b; Schur 1984, 1988; Baca-Zinn and Eitzen 1990: 249–53). Within a system of hegemonic masculinity (Connell 1987: 183), males first interpret and then act on a female's actions through their own normative sexual preferences (Cancian 1987: 77; Johnson 1988: 117–22; Hansell 1988). At the same time, this underlying male standard for interpreting sexual practice is concealed at surface levels of action as gender neutral and therefore appears as a structureless member's categorization, and it is this standard which embodies the legal definition of rape: "The law sees and treats women the way men see and treat women" (MacKinnon 1989: 162). As MacKinnon (1982, 1983), Smart (1989), Connell (1987: 245) and others have noted, the legal system disqualifies the female perspective on sexual practice:

The crime of rape is defined and adjudicated from the male standpoint, presuming that forced sex is sex and that consent to a man is freely given by a woman. Under male supremacist standards, of course, they are. . . . Interpreted this way, the legal problem has been to determine whose view of that meaning constitutes what really happened, as if what happened objectively exists to be determined . . . the rape law . . . presumes a single underlying reality, rather than a reality split by the divergent meanings inequality produces. (MacKinnon 1989: 180)

Reproducing rape is a dynamic process in which the act of rape is transformed into and "naturalized" as routine consensual sex in the legal system (see Connell 1987: 245). This operation can be broken down as follows: The force and violence of rape are discovered through courtroom talk. But since courtroom talk embodies and conceals patriarchal standards – the standard – for interpreting the rape incident, that very same sectarian ideology imposes its definition on and thereby legitimates the incident. Patriarchal ideology shapes, constrains, and organizes our interpretations of particular incidents of rape (MacKinnon 1989: 182). Patriarchal ideology functions as a dominational resource for interpreting the sexual reality of the incident: a resource powering and concealing the sense of what happened. If a woman dates a man, if she goes off with him to an apartment, if she kisses him, and so on (endlessly), then, according to the legal system, she has consented to sexual intercourse. Thus the force and violence the female experiences as rape is transformed into sex during courtroom cross-examination, and as this transformational process unfolds, patriarchy is legitimated and reproduced in live performance (ibid.: 237; Connell 1987: 107, 184).

Let me illustrate the interaction between legal and patriarchal systems in considerably more detail by drawing on a piece of data analyzed in chapter 5 (example 5.26 on pages 128–9, abridged here for convenience sake).

Puzzle/answer →	**DA:**	The first time you became concerned was when.
sequence	**V:**	When he parked the car.
Contrast with →	**DA:**	But you weren't concerned for your safety
embedded three-		when you left the parking lot?
part list	**V:**	No
	DA:	N' you weren't concerned for your safety when when your girlfriend drives across somebody else's lawn?

V: No

DA: N' you weren't concerned when Brian
          follows the wild lady wh- just driven across
          somebody else's lawn

This segment of talk is structurally organized around a puzzle/solution pair followed by an expanded contrast list in the next three sequences – a rather elegant illustration of the emergent and improvisational design aspects of natural language use. But in the courtroom system, these design features are differentially distributed across a network of position practices. Within that network, the DA possesses the legal-institutionally endowed capacity to lock on to and exercise these restricted speaker options to manage the topical relevancies found in cross-examination talk and to limit, organize, and direct the V's participation in that talk.

In this data segment, the DA wields this sequential capital to construct and establish a spatiotemporal matrix through which blaming the victim or sanctimony is generated. More formally, I referred to this device as a (reversible) spatiotemporal interval marker, a sequentially propelled ideological penetration which establishes the cumulative strength of blame-implicative assessments against the V. Notice how spatiotemporal markers function through contrast lists, and in particular, notice how the inverted reference to and organization of time/space function to discover rape. After the puzzle sequence, in which the V specifies the time and place she first became concerned for her safety, each new question progressively updates the V's state of unconcern during precise spatiotemporal intervals, and simultaneously inverts the normatively relevant and spatiotemporal moment for "being concerned": the V was "concerned for her safety when he parked the car," but not at three previous times in three previous places. During this operation, each unfolding question/answer sequence assembles an articulation node connecting a new spatiotemporal moment with its predecessors, a cumulation of historic moments in which the V not only omits basic precautions to prevent a rape, but also fails to exhibit the normatively required and category-bound mental state of a bona fide victim. The multiplex meshing of rules and resources inverts the relevant spatiotemporal matrix, and simultaneously propels the dominational relationships concealed as a gender-free normative order, an order unfolding as a historically naturalized succession of moments mapped on to sequential structures.

Through differential and restricted access to speaker options, the DA designs a spatiotemporal reality within the framework of courtroom talk, and manages the relevance of space and time for the gender order: an arbitrary yet socially structured inversion of normatively relevant space and time. While the physical world of time and space may indeed consist of logical discontinuities in nature, the social world of time and space encompasses a cultural process organized around discretely layered intervals of structurally bound and interactionally achieved relevance.

In a less abstract vein, the socially structured relevance of time/space is generated by grafting or mapping spatiotemporal markers on to combinatorial variations in puzzle and contrast list sequences. These structural rules and resources combine to generate the ideological sense of the incident, to discover rape, and to blame the victim, and as generic transsituational procedures they represent structuring features contributing to the reproduction of both patriarchal and legal systems. But while these rules and resources contribute to that structuration, they are not part of either system. Although the mechanisms of talk are mobilized and systematically adapted to manage the details of courtroom interaction, they function more generically as both charismatic discourse mechanisms and powerful sense-making practices: generating the local productional sense of patriarchal ideology. In this regard, patriarchal interpretations of the rape incident are mobilized as dominational resources through socially structured, organizationally anchored, and sequentially driven forms of talk.[5] When both courtroom and patriarchal reproduction systems collide and fuse in that talk, social structure is instantiated in action and thereby reproduced. This is the articulating moment of the duality of structure: not just when but how we make history under conditions inherited from the past.

From this structural formulation, *reproducing rape does not directly address whether the V consented to sex, but ascertains instead whether she consented to male sexual standards and only then, indirectly and derivatively, to sex.* This is not a mental or psychological experience but a socially structured, culturally mediated, and interactionally negotiated process of normative alignment and realignment: the reproduction of gender identity within the patriarchal order.

How are gender identities negotiated and performed? How does gender categorization operate? Consider a further example, almost identical to the example analyzed above.

Trial 1: Defense attorney's closing argument

> She calmly entered the car. There can't be any <u>question</u> I don't
> think in <u>anybody's</u> mi:::nd (1.4) that at the very <u>least-</u> (0.6)
> she was <u>willing</u> to engage in <u>some sort</u> of sexual <u>activity</u> (2.1)
> There couldn't be any <u>question</u> in the DEFENDANT'S mind
> at that point in time that she'd be <u>willing</u> to.

If a woman "calmly enters a man's car" then she cannot have been raped, for she must have consented. This is how rape functions not as a violation but as an enforcement of the social order. The rape trial is, for the defense, an attempt to align and realign the V's actions to fit patriarchal standards of sexuality and sexual access – that is, through a mode of domination. Conversely, the rape trial is, for the prosecution, an attempt to resist that realignment and create a lack of fit. The procedure functions in the following manner: (1) women are normatively accountable for exhibiting expressive and vulnerable types of behavior; (2) they are, nevertheless, supposed to be cautious, suspicious, and scared; yet (3) if a woman is too independent, she consents to male sexual standards. Formulaically, (1) turns into (3) and suspends (2). For example, when a woman is friendly and expressive – trying to meet a man – she gets raped, then blamed because she was not rational, suspicious, and cautious. And of course, since the V was not rational, cautious, and suspicious, she could not have been really innocent and friendly in the first place but must have been independent enough to "ask for it." And, of course, when the female is independent, her actions are realigned to fit the patriarchal standard. West and Zimmerman summarize this theoretically in the following way: "Gender . . . is the activity of managing situated conduct in light of normative conceptions of attitudes and activities appropriate for one's sex category" (1987: 127). And later in the same article they state that: "a person engaged in virtually any activity may be held accountable for performance of that activity as a *woman* or a *man*, and their incumbency in one or the other sex category can be used to legitimate or discredit their other activities" (p. 137).

Indeed, the V's performance during the incident is realigned in courtroom talk to discredit her version of what happened and to hold her normatively accountable for a performance aligned to the male and not the female sex category.

Consider a final and closely related example. Like society in general, the rape trial ensnares a woman within a web of shifting gender-structured contradictions: rational and irrational; dependent and independent; trusting and suspicious. She should be expressive, emotional, and vulnerable yet simultaneously instrumental, cautious, and calculating (Schur 1984; Lipman-Blumen 1984). During cross-examination and closing arguments, the defense attorney mobilizes the ambivalence embedded in the gender-structured order to create a virtual minefield of double-bind situations against the victim. But the minefields are not just patriarchally organized. They are also generated through the syntactic-sequential design of courtroom questioning and the epistemological practices of the legal regime – through organizationally endowed power.

Consistent with the position advocated throughout this study, patriarchal and legal modes of domination interact to discredit the V's account of what happened during the rape incident.

Below, the defense attorney depicts the victim as too dependent, confused, and emotional to produce credible testimony, yet simultaneously and within the very same line of questioning, portrays her as cold, calculating, and rational, as someone maliciously motivated to obtain a conviction against the defendant.

(6.1)	Trial 1

```
031   DA:   In preparation for yer testimony he::re, what documents
032         have you read?
033               (3.1)
034   V:    My-(1.9) my medicul? (1.4) uh- (0.5) uh paper sayin
035         that I had released my medicul records.
036               (2.1)
037   DA:   Are you tellin me you didun read this statement=
038                                    [   ]
039   V:                                 no
040   DA:   =that you- gave to-
041               [   ]
042   V:          my statement yes.
043               (1.2)
044   DA:   Which statement?
045               (0.7)
046   V:    That I gave to:: (.) (hh) Mister Kuba.
047               (2.2)
048   DA:   WHEN did'ju las read that °statement?
049               (2.0)
050   V:    Friday.
051               (2.6)
052   DA:   WERE there ITEMS in that statement thit- (.)
053         you didn't remember indipendently but- you
054         remembered after you read >reread the statement<?
055   V:    Yes.
056               (2.0)
057   DA:   So thit essenchely what yer testifying to here in court (.) is
058         the statement that you gave to detective Kuba is that correct?
059   PA:   Objecshun °yer honor.
060               (1.3)
061   DA:   °It's cross examinashun °yer honor.
062               (3.7)
063   J:    Overru::led.
```

```
064          ((Cough))    (1.0)
065   DA:    Essenchuly yer testifying to what waz in the
066          statement >izint that correct<?
067               (0.8)
068   V:     I- (.) testified °as to what happened.
069               (0.7)
070   DA:    Well WHAT were the items that you hadn't remembe::red
071          when you- remember as of Friday?
072               (6.2)
073   DA:    Or donchew remember that?
074               (1.0)
075   V:     I don't know.
076               (2.7)
077   DA:    So you don't know what you do and don't remember?
078          izat accurate?
079   PA:    Objecshun yer honor he's BAjuring the witness=
080   J:     =Yeah- uh- uh- (hhh) no- ah- susta::ined? Uh:: refraze yer
081          yer question.
082               (3.5)
083   DA:    (hhh) (1.0) Are you telling me that you don't know what you
084          remember without the statement en you en you don't know
085          what you(::r) Are you tellin me you don't know (.) what
086          items you remember without reading the statement=
087   PA:    =Objecshun yer honor she has testified that (.)
088          she stated (0.5) what she remembered? (0.7) She testified
089          as to what she remembered as to WHAT HAPPENED!
090   J:     I think what she has testified to thet sayz- (.)
091          her testimony toda::y (.) wuz refreshed (.) some what (.)
092          on certain items (by) the statement she read Friday.
093               (.)
094   DA:    OK- I- MAM what items wuz (it) were (1.0) WHAT WERE
095          THE ITEMS?        (1.9)              that you didn't=
096                       [                            ]
097                       ((Slight audience laughter))
098   DA:    =remember until las Friday?
099               (6.0)
100   DA:    When you said you didn't know already when you- when I
101          asked you that question- are you still saying you don't know?
102   V:     (No-) I don't know specificly.
```

On line 052, the defense attorney starts the cross-examination by making a pivotal distinction between (1) the victim's statement to detectives shortly after the rape incident and (2) the present status of her

memory or recollection about that incident. As a provisional characterization, that the victim's statement objectively reports what happened
during the incident, that her statement is not isolable from her present
recollection, and that it would be considered more or less unremarkable
for the statement to "contaminate" the status of her present knowledge
since the latter is presumably built out of the former, illuminate taken-
for-granted and glossed aspects of mundane knowledge claims which are
routinely transgressed during courtroom cross-examination. Breaching
this mundane order, the DA exposes an embedded and covert presuppositional grid for assessing the factual status of accounts, and proposes
an epistemological disjuncture between two competing methods for
warranting the facticity of knowledge claims: first, through an indirect
and dependent statement about reality and, second, through a direct and
independent recollection about reality.

But this interchange is not just about statement and recollections. It is
about reality and representations of reality. It is about making an
invidious comparison between an independent, direct, and preferred
recollection of reality on the one hand, and an inferior written
representation of reality on the other. It is about a direct observation of
reality preserved in memory versus an indirect written document –
produced in collusion with police detectives – representing an observation.
Beyond the arbitrary bifurcation between reality and statements about
reality looms an additional – yet just as powerful – implication of
courtroom epistemological practice grafted on to or smuggled into the
two methods of warranting the facticity of knowledge claims. That is, the
V should recount such a devastating life event – an act possessing serious
emotional and physical consequences for both her and the defendant –
not only in specific detail, but also spontaneously and without rehearsal
(most prominently displayed on line 031: "In preparation for yer
testimony . . ."). And reading the statement imperils that seriousness and
downgrades the impact of the incident on the V – a subtle impeachment
of her credibility. The V's rehearsed performance lacks the necessary
credibility for passing the stringent knowledge requirements imposed by
the DA, and fosters the impression that she has "polished" her testimony.
As I have shown, the DA routinely unveils the V's exercise of such
impression management tactics as a major strategy for discrediting her
testimony, for undercutting the status and facticity of her knowledge
claims, and for displaying to the jury that she is not an ingenuous victim
as claimed, but rather a crafty, cold, and calculating woman "bent" on
revenge against the defendant. Thus a symbolic nexus of contradictions
works to characterize the V as malicious and calculating because she has
rehearsed for courtroom testimony, yet, ironically and simultaneously,

confused and dependent because that very same testimony has been contaminated by the statement she gave to the police.

After establishing that the V read the statement, the DA begins a lins of questioning through polar interrogatives to establish what particular "items" were remembered independently – that is, through memory without help from the statement. When the V states remembering (on line 055) some unspecified number of items from reading the statement, the DA (on line 057) in next turn formulates "items in the statement" as referring not to a mere portion of the statement but to the statement as a whole: as a sole equivalent reference to just "the statement." Even though the V ostensibly possessed some unknown degree of knowledge about the incident independently from the statement, the mere fact of reading the statement "contaminates" the purity of her total knowledge base.

So as a first strategy the DA attempts to assess the existence of knowledge contamination from the statement, and if the V recalls items through the statement, then the statement and not an independent recollection furnishes the basis of her testimony. As mentioned above, the presupposition of this strategy involves first setting up an invidious distinction and a hierarchical contrast between an independent recollection of reality on the one hand and a dependent reference to reality via the statement on the other. I call this first strategy *determining the existence of knowledge contamination.*

If the V contests the knowledge contamination formulation and attempts to suppress the disjuncture, which in this case she does, a second presupposition becomes automatically operative. The second presupposition poses a much more difficult, much more powerful epistemological hurdle for substantiating knowledge claims. It presupposes the existence of a sharply differentiated boundary separating statement from recollection items and that the V is capable of locating these different item types. The DA's puzzle presupposes that, given the existence of this sharply bounded pair of item categories (not permitting gradations in category membership of course), the V can specify in next turn which items were remembered through the statement and which were remembered independently without it. Since the V contests the DA's formulation (DA: "essenchely what yer testifying to here in <u>court</u> (.) is the statement". . . . V: "I- (.) testified as to what happened") on line 068, and since, in so doing, she claimed a direct, unmediated reference to reality and not merely an indirect reference through the statement, the DA engages the second, even more powerful strategy, which is set up and presupposed through the first, through determining the mere existence of knowledge contamination. Once the V claims that the testimony refers to reality, the DA moves to secure a separate and distinct identification for each specific item from the V – to separate what items were remembered through reading the statement from those remembered independently without it. This sets up several points of impeachment strategy.

First, the V failed to remember items about the incident without depending on the statement: 052–4 DA: "WERE there ITEMS in the statement thit- (.) you didn't remember indipendently but- you remembered after you read >reread the statement<?" and 065–6 DA: "Essenchuly yer testifying to what waz in the statement >izint that correct<?" Second, she failed to separate and specify the remembered from the forgotten particular items; she failed to differentiate which items were read and then remembered through the statement from those recollected solely from memory about the rape incident (which took place six months prior to the trial): 070 DA: "Well WHAT were the items that you hadn't remembered?" and 073 DA: "Or donchew remember that?" V: "I don't know." Third, given the first two specific memory failures, the stage is set for the DA's general formulation or summary involving not just the current spate of testimony, but also a discrediting character assessment, namely that, on line 077, the V "does not know what she does and does not remember." And last and cumulatively via the first three strategies, the DA ushers into prominence a symbolic inference that, as an incumbent in the gender category "female," the V's credibility, in general, and her perception about the events that transpired during the incident, in particular, are too confused, emotional, and dependent to constitute credible testimony.

The DA's strategy creates a no-win, double-bind situation for the V. Given that the statement is separate from both her memory about the incident and the incident itself, and given that it represents a nonpreferred method for warranting knowledge claims, if the V agrees with the DA's formulation in lines 057 and 065 "yer testifying to . . . the statement", then she is talking about the statement and not reality. On the other hand, once the statement has been read and the epistemological contamination of knowledge claims activated, the V must specify and separate what items were remembered through the statement from those recounted independently in order to talk about the incident, to talk about reality, and to thereby substantiate the facticity of knowledge claims. Given the existence of knowledge contamination, the V must determine and display the extent of contamination and specify the inclusion/exclusion of items. Only then, presumably, could such knowledge become authorized as a factual depiction of reality, as a serious contender for, or competing version of, what happened. I call this second strategy *determining the extent of knowledge contamination*.

But, of course, the V could never accomplish such a task, could never meet such stringent criteria for warranting the facticity of knowledge claims and suppressing the disjuncture. Nor, of course, could anyone. That much appears evident from the ensuing objection sequence on lines 087 to 092. Just as the V displays a dependence on and confusion about the statement, so she ultimately exhibits a further dependence on the PA and J to formulate the gist of her answers and to "repair" her confused testimony: a process limited to more than just the judge's statement, "J: her testimony toda::y (.) wuz <u>refreshed</u> (.) somewhat . . ." The damaging implications of the testimony thus far culminate in her final answer on line 102 which builds off of, depends on, and is cued from, the responses of both the J and the PA: "V: (No-) I don't know <u>specifically</u>." In the process, the V looks even more confused and dependent. Her character and testimony appear even more discredited. At the outset, the local linguistic production of moral character keeps the jury's attention riveted on V's difficulty in answering questions. Indeed, courtroom disciplinary regimes denigrate and jeopardize the unproblematic facticity of mundane knowledge claims, and, as Dorothy Smith (1990: 80) continually reminds us, this ability to authorize the facticity of one version of reality while suppressing the facticity of competing versions is a form of power. In this regard, courtroom interaction reflects a preoccupation with not just category-bound knowledge, but the epistemologically filtered and purified basis of that knowledge, what Molotch and Boden (1985) call the third face of power.

But there is more. The interaction exhibited within this extract is designed to make the V appear confused on the stand, just as she was during the incident, just as she was during the police investigation, just as women are in society more generally, and when a jury acquits a rapist, or when a woman declines to report a rape, or when attorneys, judges, and juries treat such gender categorizations as relevant and tactical resources for assembling and assessing the meaning of the incident, that is how structural constraints and enablements function in practice to reproduce the systemic outcomes of both rape and the legal order. Just as women are dependent on men in society, so the V in court is dependent on the police, the statement, and the judge or attorneys to answer for her, to pronounce in their words what she is saying, and to explain and reformulate her testimony. In just this way, patriarchy is drawn on and reproduced as a resource of symbolic domination in courtroom talk. In just this way, gender identities are negotiated and performed through talk-in-interaction. And in just this way, courtroom talk captures the pariarchally organized, institutionally structured, and interactionally achieved reproduction of gender identity. More generally, this is how patriarchy and the legal system represent the historically inherited structural conditions which shape and facilitate social interaction, conditions which are embodied in and reproduced through such interaction.

Before closing, I'd like to mention an applied matter that rape reformists mention in passing, but never pursue, which illustrates the relevance, for both sociologists and policy advocates, of structuration theory for rape law reform. According to structuration theory, inequality, asymmetrical relationships, and the asymmetrical distribution of options are embedded in social systems of interaction. Systems are not structures. When looking at structures, Giddens is referring to rules and resources which operate via the duality of structure: the devices actors wield to reproduce systematic relationships and patterns of interaction. Bearing this point in mind, the rape reform movement has focused on, first, the systematic relationship between the DA and V via rape shield and other statutorial changes, and, second, the patterned legal outcomes involving the rape trial. But writers on rape reform have completely ignored the underlying interpretative and linguistic devices which structurate the DA/V relationship and which reproduce those regularities. Rape reform statutes attempt to redress the imbalance of power in the DA and V system, but without even considering the sequential, discourse, and syntactic structures that are employed – in powerfully creative and emergent ways – to reproduce that system. As I have demonstrated in quite some detail, power is not nor could it ever be a mere reflex of structure. It must always be worked for. A good case can be made that the limits of law reform are a direct result of concentrating exclusively on static social system properties and outcomes, while ignoring the rules and resources which agents wield to structure that system. As I have also demonstrated in quite some detail, the presence of the past must be enacted and reproduced – negotiated, sustained, and transformed – in the dynamic micro-second moments of the present, which is of itself but another historical moment in a recursively cumulative progression. This is not to say that statutorial reform is unimportant and unnecessary. But if blame is operating inferentially through powerful sequential/syntactic devices, then a bottom-up approach to rape reform, focusing on the procedures of talk-in-interaction, would serve as the interactional complement and necessary corrective to the limitations of statutorial reform. I offer this research with that hope in mind.

NOTES

1   Prestructured constraints must be reproduced, even when considering the most hardened patterns, and when looked at within the framework of

structuration theory, constraints are ultimately rooted in the context of action where actors confront and negotiate them. Their "given" properties must be interpreted and reproduced within the situated performance of interaction (see Giddens 1984: 176; Cohen 1989: 219–29).

2   This should not suggest that the asymmetrical distribution of options is unimportant or that their constraining power is weak. But to discover the constitution and reconstitution of these options, I employ a methodological suspension toward systemic properties, and concentrate instead on the structuration of asymmetrical relationships and interactions. As Cohen (1989: 229) remarks: "The distribution of structural courses of action do not represent the constitution of inequality but only the institutionalized conditions agents encounter in the reproduction of inequality."

3   Constraint here refers to the gravitational pull the local production of ideology imposes on our interpretations of the rape incident (see Giddens 1984: 172–80).

4   Ideology may not be directly grafted on to sequential structure. More technically and very tentatively, it may first be sealed and concealed in gender-neutral membership categorization devices, and then mapped on to sequential structure.

5   For lack of a more elegant phrase, I coined the notion of socially structured talk to capture the multiplex interpenetrations among sequential, organizational, and patriarchal structures – the structurational totality. Blame work is conducted inferentially through powerful and sophisticated rules of mutual knowledge, and through differential access to the procedures of talk. When coupled with patriarchal ideology, these procedures produce the accusatory sense of what happened during the incident. The criss-crossing and articulating moments among norms, meaning, and male sexual hegemony are embedded in sequential lists, contrast sets, and puzzles.

References

Adler, C. 1985: An exploration of self-reported sexually aggressive behavior. *Crime and Delinquency*, 31.2, 306–31.

Adler, Z. 1987: *Rape on Trial*. London: Routledge and Kegan Paul.

Akmajian, A. and Heny, F. 1975: *An Introduction to the Principles of Transformational Syntax*. Cambridge: MIT Press.

Alexander, J. 1982: *Theoretical Logic in Sociology*, vol. 1. Berkeley: University of California Press.

—— 1984: Social-structural analysis: some notes on its history and prospects. *Sociological Quarterly*, 25.1, 5–26.

Alexander, J and Giesen, B. 1987: From reduction to linkage: the long view of the micro–macro link. In J. Alexander et al. (eds), *The Macro–Micro Link*, Berkeley: University of California Press, 1–41.

Alexander, J., Giesen, B., Munch, R. and Smelser, N. (eds) 1987: *The Micro–Macro Link*. Berkeley: University of California Press.

Amir, M. 1971: *Patterns in Forcible Rape*. Chicago: University of Chicago Press.

—— 1975: Forcible rape. In L. Schultz (ed.), *Rape Victimology*, Springfield, Ill.: Charles Thomas, 43–58.

Appelbaum, R. 1988: *Karl Marx*. Beverly Hills: Sage.

Atkinson, J. 1984: *Our Master's Voices*. London: Methuen.

—— 1985: Refusing invited applause: preliminary observations from a case study of charismatic oratory. In T. van Dijk (ed.), *Handbook of Discourse Analysis*, vol. 3, New York: Academic Press, 161–8.

Atkinson, J. and Drew, P. 1979: *Order in Court*. Atlantic Highlands: Humanities.

Atkinson, J. and Heritage, J. (eds) 1984: *Structures of Social Action*. New York: Cambridge University Press.

Atkinson, P. 1988: Ethnomethodology: a critical review. In W. Scott and J. Blake (eds), *Annual Review of Sociology*, vol. 14, Palo Alto: Annual Reviews Incorporated, 441–65.

Austin, J. L. 1975: *How to Do Things with Words*. Cambridge: Harvard University Press.

Baca-Zinn, M. and Eitzen, S. 1990: *Diversity in American Families*. New York: Harper and Row.

Bailey, F. Lee 1985: *To Be a Trial Lawyer*. New York: John Wiley.

Baron, L. and Straus, M. 1989: *Four Theories of Rape in American Society*. New Haven: Yale University Press

Bart, P. and O'Brien, P. 1985: *Stopping Rape*. New York: Pergamon.

Benson, J. 1981: Organizations: a dialectical view. In M. Zey-Ferrel and M. Aiken (eds), *Complex Organizations: Critical Perspectives*, Glenview: Scott, Foresman, 263–82.

Berger, P. and Luckmann, T. 1967: *The Social Construction of Reality*. New York: Doubleday.

Bernstein, B. 1971: *Class, Codes and Control*, vol. 1. Boston: Routledge and Kegan Paul.

Bhaskar, R. 1979: *The Possibility of Naturalism*. Atlantic Highlands: Humanities.
—— 1989: *Reclaiming Reality*. New York: Verso.

Bibb, R. and Form, W. 1977: The effects of industrial, occupational and sex stratification on wages in blue-collar markets. *Social Forces*, 55, 974–96.

Bilmes, J. 1988: The concept of preference in conversation analysis. *Language in Society*, 17, 161–81.

Blau, P. 1977: *Inequality and Heterogeneity*. New York: Free Press.
—— (ed.) 1975: *Approaches to the Study of Social Structure*. New York: Free Press.

Bluestone, B. and Harrison, B. 1982: *The Deindustrialization of America*. New York: Basic.
—— 1989: *The Great U-Turn*. New York: Basic.

Blumberg, R. 1984: A general theory of gender stratification. *Sociological Theory*, 2, 23–101.

Boden, D. and Zimmerman, D. H. (eds) 1991: *Talk and Social Structure*. Cambridge: Polity.

Borgida, E. and Brekke, N. 1985: Psycholegal research on rape trials. In A. Burgess (ed.), *Rape and Sexual Assault*, New York: Garland, 313–42.

Borgida, E., Fraser, P. and Swim, J. 1987: Prosecuting sexual assault: the use of expert testimony on rape trauma syndrome. In R. Hazelwood and A. Burgess (eds), *Practical Aspects of Rape Investigation*, New York: Elsevier, 347–60.

Bourque, L. 1989: *Defining Rape*. Durham: Duke University Press.

Bowles, S. and Gintis, H. 1986: *Democracy and Capitalism*. New York: Basic.

Brannigan, A. and Lynch, M. 1987: On bearing false witness. *Journal of Contemporary Ethnography*, 16.2, 115–46.

Briere, J. and Malamuth, N. 1983: Self-reported likelihood of sexually aggressive behavior: attitudinal versus sexual explanations. *Journal of Research in Personality*, 17, 315–23.

Brown, G. and Yule, G. 1983: *Discourse Analysis*. New York: Cambridge University Press.

Brown, P. 1987: *The Art of Questioning*. New York: Macmillan.

Brownmiller, S. 1975: *Against our Will*. New York: Simon and Schuster.

Burawoy, M. 1985: *The Politics of Production*. London: Verso.

Burgess, A. 1987: Public beliefs and attitudes concerning rape. In R. Hazelwood and A. Burgess (eds) *Practical Aspects of Rape Investigation*, New York: Elsevier, 3–18.

—— (ed.) 1985: *Rape and Sexual Assault*, vol. 1. New York: Garland.

—— (ed.) 1988: *Rape and Sexual Assault*, vol. 2. New York: Garland.

Burgess, A. and Hazelwood, R. 1987: 'The Victim's Perspective', in R. Hazelwood and A. Burgess (eds) 1987.

Burgess, A. and Holmstrom, L. 1985: Rape trauma syndrome and post traumatic stress response. In A. Burgess (ed.), *Rape and Sexual Assault*, vol. 1, New York: Garland, 46–60.

Burt, M. 1980: Cultural myths and supports for rape. *Journal of Personality and Social Psychology*, 38.2, 217–30.

Burt, M. and Albin, R. 1981: Rape myths, rape definitions, and probability of conviction. *Journal of Applied Social Psychology*, 11.3, 212–30.

Button, G. and Lee, J. (eds) 1987: *Talk and Social Organization*. Philadelphia: Multilingual Matters.

Cancian, F. 1987: *Love in America*. New York: Cambridge University Press.

Caringella-Macdonald, S. 1988: Marxist and feminist interpretations on the aftermath of rape reforms. *Contemporary Crisis*, 12, 125–44.

Chambliss, W. (ed.) 1984: *Criminal Law in Action*. New York: Macmillan.

Chodorow, N. 1978: *The Reproduction of Mothering*. Berkeley: University of California Press.

—— 1989: *Feminism and Psychoanalytic Theory*. New Haven: Yale University Press.

Chomsky, N. 1986: *Knowledge of Language*. New York: Praeger.

Clayman, S. 1988: Displaying neutrality in television news interviews. *Social Problems*, 35.4, 474–92.

—— 1989: The production of punctuality: social interaction, temporal organization, and social structure. *American Journal of Sociology*, 95.3, 659–91.

Clegg, S. 1989: *Frameworks of Power*. Newbury Park: Sage.

Cohen, I. 1987: Structuration theory and social praxis. In A. Giddens and J. Turner (eds), *Social Theory Today*, Stanford: Stanford University Press, 273–308.

—— 1989: *Structuration Theory*. New York: St Martin's.

Cohen, P. 1969: *Modern Social Theory*. New York: Basic.

Collins, R. 1975: *Conflict Sociology*. New York: Academic.

—— 1981a: Micro-translation as a theory-building strategy. In K. Knorr-Cetina and A. Cicourel (eds), *Advances in Social Theory and Methodology*, London: Routledge and Kegan Paul, 81–108.

—— 1986: Is 1980s sociology in the doldrums? *American Journal of Sociology*, 91.6, 1136–55.

—— 1987: Interaction ritual chains, power and property: the micro–macro connection as an empirically based theoretical problem. In J. Alexander et al.

(eds), *The Micro–Macro Link*, Berkeley: University of California Press, 193–206.

—— 1988a: *Theoretical Sociology*. Chicago: Harcourt, Brace and Jovanovich.

—— 1988b: The micro-contribution to macro sociology. *Sociological Theory*, 6.2, 242–53.

Connell, R. 1987: *Gender and Power*. Stanford: Stanford University Press.

Cook-Gumperz, J. 1981: Persuasive talk: the social organization of children's talk. In J. Green and C. Wallat (eds), *Ethnography and Language in Educational Settings*, Norwood: Ablex, 25–50.

Coser, R. 1975: The complexity of roles as a seedbed of individual autonomy. In L. Coser (ed.), *The Idea of Social Structure*. New York: Harcourt, 237–64.

Coulter J. 1975: Perceptual accounts and interpretative asymetries. *Sociology*, 9, 395–96.

—— 1979: *The Social Construction of Mind*. Totowa: Rowman and Littlefield.

—— 1982: Remarks on the conceptualization of social structure. *Philosophy of the Social Sciences*, 12.1, 33–46.

Crothers, C. 1987: *Robert K. Merton*. London: Tavistock.

Cuff, E. and Payne, G. 1984: *Perspectives in Sociology*, 2nd edn. Boston: Allen and Unwin.

Danet, B. 1980: Baby or fetus? Language and the construction of reality in a manslaughter trial. *Semiotica*, 32.3–4, 187–219.

Danet, B. and Bogoch, B. 1980: Fixed fight or free-for-all? An empirical study of combativeness in the adversary system of justice. *British Journal of Law and Society*, 7, 36–60.

Danet, B., Hoffman, K., Kermish, N., Rafn, H. and Stayman, D. 1980: An ethnography of questioning in the courtroom. In R. Shuy and A. Shnukal (eds), *Language Use and the Uses of Language*, Washington, D.C.: Georgetown University Press, 222–34.

Davidson, J. 1975: Ending structures in conversation. Unpublished Ph.D. dissertation, University of California, Irvine.

—— 1984: Subsequent versions of invitations, offers, requests, and proposals dealing with potential or actual rejection. In J. Atkinson and J. Heritage (eds), *Structures of Social Action*, New York: Cambridge University Press, 102–28.

Davis, K. 1988: *Power under the Microscope*. Providence: Foris.

Della Fave, L. 1986. Toward an explication of the legitimation process. *Social Forces*, 65.2, 476–500.

Drew, P. 1985: Analysing the use of language in courtroom interaction. In T. van Dijk (ed.), *Handbook of Discourse Analysis*, vol. 3, New York: Academic, 133–48.

—— 1990: Strategies in the contest between lawyers and witnesses in court examinations. In J. N. Levi and A. G. Walker (eds), *Language in the Judicial Process*, New York: Plenum, 39–64.

—— 1992: Contested evidence in courtroom cross-examination: the case of a trial for rape. In P. Drew and J. Heritage (eds), *Talk at Work*, Cambridge: Cambridge University Press, 470–520.

Durkheim, E. 1951: *Suicide*. New York: Free Press.

—— 1982: *The Rules of Sociological Method*. New York: Free Press.

Emerson, R. 1969: *Judging Delinquents*. New York: Aldine.

Erickson, F. and Shultz, J. 1982: *The Counselor as Gatekeeper*. New York: Academic.

Ervin-Tripp, S. 1969: Sociolinguistics. In L. Berkowitz (ed.), *Advances in Experimental Social Psychology*. New York: Academic.

—— 1987: About, to and by women. In D.l Brouwer and D. de Haan (eds), *Women's Language, Socialization and Self-Image*, Providence: Foris, 17–26.

Estrich, S. 1987: *Real Rape*. Cambridge: Harvard University Press.

Fenstermaker, S. 1989: Acquaintance rape on campus: responsibility and attributions of crime. In M. Pirog-Good and J. Stets (eds), *Violence in Dating Relationships*, New York: Praeger, 257–71.

Fielding, N. (ed.) 1988: *Actions and Structure*. Beverly Hills: Sage.

Fine, G. 1990: Symbolic interactionsm in the post-Blumerian age. In G. Ritzer (ed.), *Frontiers of Social Theory*, New York: Columbia University Press, 117–57.

Finkelhor, D. 1984: *Child Sexual Abuse*. New York: Free Press.

Fisher, S. 1988: *In the Patient's Best Interest*. New Brunswick: Rutgers University Press.

Fisher, S. and Todd, A. (eds) 1983: *The Social Organization of Doctor–Patient Interaction*. Washington D.C.: Center for Applied Linguistics.

Fishman, P. 1978: Interaction: the work women do. *Social Problems*, 25, 397–406.

Foucault, M. 1979: *Discipline and Punish*. New York: Vintage.

—— 1980: *Knowledge/Power*. New York: Pantheon.

Francis, D. 1986: Some structures of negotiation talk. *Language and Society*, 15, 53–79.

Frankel, R. 1983: The laying on of hands: aspects of the organization of gaze, touch and talk in the medical encounter. In S. Fisher and A. Todd (eds), *The Social Organization of Doctor–Patient Communication*, Washington D.C.: Center For Applied Linguistics, 19–54.

—— 1984: From sentence to sequence: understanding the medical encounter through microinteractional analysis. *Discourse Processes*, 7.2, 135–70.

—— 1990: Talking in interviews: a dispreference for patient initiated questions in physician–patient encounters. In G. Psathas (ed.), *Interaction Competence*, Lanham: University Press of America, 231–62.

Freeman, J. (ed.) 1989: *Women: A Feminist Perspective*. Mountain View: Mayfield.

Frohmann, Lisa, 1991: Discrediting victim's allegations of sexual assault: *Social Problems*, 38.2, 213–26.

Galbraith, J. 1983: *The Anatomy of Power*. Boston: Houghton Mifflin.

Gane, M. 1988: *On Durkheim's Rules of Sociological Method*. London: Routledge.

Garfinkel, A. 1981: *Forms of Explanation*. New Haven: Yale University Press.

Garfinkel, H. 1967: *Studies in Ethnomethodology*. Englewood Cliffs N.J.: Prentice-Hall.

—— 1988: Evidence for locally produced, naturally accountable phenomena of order, logic, reason, meaning, method, etc., in and as of the essential quiddity of immortal ordinary society. *Sociological Theory*, 6.1, 103–9.

Garfinkel, H. and Sacks, H. 1970: On formal structures of practical actions. In J. McKinney and E. Tiryakian (eds), *Theoretical Sociology*, New York: Appleton-Century Crofts, 102–28.

Giddens, A. 1976: *New Rules of Sociological Method*. New York: Basic.

—— 1977: *Studies in Social and Political Theory*. New York: Basic.

—— 1979: *Central Problems in Social Theory*. Berkeley: University of California Press.

—— 1981a: *A Contemporary Critique of Historical Materialism*. Berkeley: University of California Press.

—— 1981b: Agency, institution, and time-space analysis. In K. Knorr-Cetina and A. Cicourel (eds), *Advances in Social Theory and Methodology*, London: Routledge and Kegan Paul, 161–74.

—— 1982: *Profiles and Critiques in Social Theory*. Berkeley: University of California Press.

—— 1984: *The Constitution of Society*. Berkeley: University of California Press.

—— 1985: *The Nation-State and Violence*. Berkeley: University of California Press.

—— 1987: *Social Theory and Modern Sociology*. Stanford: Stanford University Press.

—— 1989: A reply to my critics. In D. Held and J. Thompson (eds), *Social Theory of Modern Societies*, New York: Cambridge University Press, 249–301.

Giddens, A. and Turner, J. (eds) 1987: *Social Theory Today*. Stanford: Stanford University Press.

Goffman, E. 1967: *Interaction Ritual*. Garden City: Anchor.

—— 1972: The neglected situation. In P. Giglioli (ed.), *Language and Social Context*. Baltimore: Penguin, 61–6.

—— 1981: *Forms of Talk*. Philadelphia: University of Pennsylvania Press.

—— 1983: The interaction order. *American Sociological Review*, 48.1, 1–17.

—— 1987: The arrangement between the sexes. In M. Deegan and M. Hill (eds), *Women and Symbolic Interaction*, Boston: Allen and Unwin, 51–78.

Goodchilds, J., Zellman, G., Johnson, P., and Giarrusso, R. 1988: Adolescents and their perceptions of sexual interactions. In A. Burgess (ed.), *Rape and Sexual Assault*, vol. 2, New York: Garland, 245–70.

Goode, E. 1990: *Deviant Behavior*. Englewood Cliffs: Prentice-Hall.

Goode, W. 1986: Individual choice and the social order. In James Short (ed.), *The Social Fabric*, Beverly Hills: Sage, 39–62.

Goodwin, C. 1981: *Conversational Organization*. New York: Academic.

—— 1989: Turn-construction and conversational organization. In B. Dervin, L. Grossberg, B. O'Keefe and E. Wartelly (eds), *Rethinking Communication*, Newbury Park: Sage, 88–102.

Gordon, M. and Riger, S. 1989: *The Female Fear*. New York: Free Press.

Greatbatch, D. 1986: Aspects of topical organization in news interviews. *Media, Culture and Society*, 8, 441–55.

—— 1988: A turn taking system for British news interviews. *Language in Society*, 17, 401–30.

Grimshaw, A. 1981: *Language as a Social Resource*. Stanford: Stanford University Press.

Groth, N. 1979: *Men Who Rape*. New York: Plenum.

Hall, P. 1972: A symbolic interactionst analysis of politics. *Sociological Inquiry*, 42, 35–75.

—— 1979: The presidency and impression management. In *Studies in Symbolic Interaction*, vol. 2, Greenwich, Conn.: JAI Press, 283–305.

—— 1980: Structuring symbolic interaction: communication and power. In *Communication Yearbook*, vol. 4, New Brunswick: Transaction, 49–59.

—— 1985: Asymmetric relationships and processes of power. In H. Farberman and R. Perinbanayagam (eds), *Foundations of Interpretative Sociology: Original Essays in Symbolic Interaction*, Greenwich: JAI Press, 309–44.

—— 1987: Interactionism and the study of social organization. Draft copy prepared for *Sociological Quarterly*, 28, 1–22.

Hall, R. 1987: *Organizations*, 4th edn. Englewood Cliffs: Prentice-Hall.

Handel, W. 1979: Normative expectations and the emergence of meaning as solutions to problems: convergence of structural and interactionist views. *American Journal of Sociology*, 84, 855–81.

—— 1982: *Ethnomethodology: How People Make Sense*. Englewood Cliffs: Prentice-Hall.

Hansel, M. 1988: Rape: a sociological analysis. Paper presented at the Midwest Sociological Society meetings, Minneapolis.

Harris, S. 1984: Questions as a mode of control in magistrates' court. *International Journal of Sociology of Language*, 49, 5–27.

Hart, H. L. A. 1961: *The Concept of Law*. London: Oxford University Press.

—— 1965: The ascription of responsibility and rights. In A. Flew (ed.), *Logic and Language*, Garden City, N.Y.: Doubleday-Anchor.

Hazelwood, R. and Burgess, A. (eds) 1987: *Practical Aspects of Rape Investigation*. New York: Elsevier.

Heath, C. 1986: *Body Movement and Speech in Medical Interaction*. New York: Cambridge University Press.

Heilbronner, R. 1985: *The Nature and Logic of Capitalism*. New York: Norton.

Heiman, W. 1987: Prosecuting rape cases: trial preparation and trial tactic issues. In R. Hazelwood and A. Burgess (eds), *Practical Aspects of Rape Investigation*, New York: Elsevier, 329–46.

Held, D. and Thompson, J. (eds) 1989: *Social Theory of Modern Societies*. New York: Cambridge University Press.

Henley, N. 1977: *Body Politics*. Englewood Cliffs: Prentice-Hall.

Heritage, J. 1984: *Garfinkel and Ethnomethodology*. Cambridge: Polity.

—— 1985: Analyzing news interviews: aspects of the production of talk for an overhearing audience. In T. van Dijk (ed.), *Handbook of Discourse Analysis*, vol. 3, New York: Academic, 95–119.

—— 1989: Current developments in conversation analysis. In D. Roger and P. Bull (eds), *Conversation*, Philadelphia: Multilingual Matters, 21–47.

Heritage, J. and Greatbatch, D. 1986: Generating applause: a study of rhetoric and response at party political conferences. *American Journal of Sociology*, 92, 110–57.

Heritage, J. Clayman, S. and Zimmerman, D. 1988: Discourse and message analysis. In R. Hawkins et al. (eds), *Advancing Communication Science*, Newbury Park: Sage, 77–109.

Herman, J. 1989: The rape culture. In J. Freeman (ed.), *Women: A Feminist Perspective*, Mountain View: Mayfield, 20–44.

Hochschild, A. 1989: *The Second Shift*. New York: Random House.

Holmstrom, L. 1985: The criminal justice system's response to the rape victim. In A. Burgess (ed.), *Rape and Sexual Assault*, vol. 1, New York: Garland, 189–98.

Holmstrom, L. and Burgess, A. 1983: *The Victim of Rape*. New Brunswick: Transaction.

Horney, J. and Spohn, C. 1991: Rape law reform and instrumental change in six urban jurisdictions. *Law and Society*, 25.1, 117–53.

Houtkoop, H. 1987: *Establishing Agreement*. Providence: Foris.

Hudson, R. 1975: The meaning of questions. *Language*, 51.1, 1–31.

Issac, J. 1987: *Power and Marxist Theory*. Ithaca: Cornell University Press.

Jayyusi, L. 1984: *Categorization and the Moral Order*. Boston: Routledge and Kegan Paul.

Jefferson, G. 1973: A case of precision timing in ordinary conversation: overlapped tag-positioned address terms in closing sequences. *Semiotica*, 9, 47–96.

—— 1979: A technique for inviting laughter and its subsequent acceptance/declination. In G. Psathas (ed.), *Everyday Language*, New York: Irvington, 79–86.

Jefferson, G. and Schegloff, E. 1975: Sketch: some orderly aspects of overlap in natural conversation. Paper presented at the meeting of the American Anthropological Association, December 1975.

Jefferson, G. and Schenkein, J. 1978: Some sequential negotiations in conversation. In J. Schenkein (ed.), *Studies in the Organization of Conversational Interaction*, New York: Academic, 155–72.

Johnson, A. 1980: On the prevalence of rape in the United States. *Signs*, 6.1, 136–46.

Johnson, M. 1988: *Strong Mothers, Weak Wives*. Berkeley: University of California Press.

Kanin, E. J. 1975: Selected dyadic aspects of male sex aggression (1969). In Leroy Schultz (ed.), *Rape Victimology*, Springfield: Charles C. Thomas, 59–76.

—— 1984: Date rape: unofficial criminals and victims. *Victimology: An International Journal*, 9, 95–108.

—— 1985: Date rapists: differential sexual socialization and relative deprivation. *Archives of Sexual Behavior*, 14, 219–31.

Kanter, R. 1977: *Men and Women of the Corporation*. New York: Basic.

Keat, R. and Urry, J. 1982: *Social Theory as Science*, 2nd edn. Boston: Routledge and Kegan Paul.

Kedar, L. (ed.) 1987: *Power through Language*. Norwood: Ablex.

Kelly, L. 1988: *Surviving Sexual Violence*. Minneapolis: University of Minnesota Press.

Kerbo, H. 1982: *Social Stratification*. New York: McGraw-Hill.

Knorr-Cetina, K. and Cicourel, A. (eds) 1981: *Advances in Social Theory and Methodology*. London: Routledge and Kegan Paul.

Kohn, M. 1977: *Class and Conformity*, 2nd edn. Chicago: University of Chicago.

Kollock, P., Blumstein, P. and Schwartz, P. 1985: Sex and power in interaction: conversational privileges and duties. *American Sociological Review*, 50, 24–46.

Koss, M. 1988: Hidden rape: sexual aggression and victimization in a national sample in higher education. In A. Burgess (ed.), *Rape and Sexual Assault*, vol. 2, New York: Garland, 3–26.

Koss, M. and Harvey, M. 1987: *The Rape Victim*. Lexington, Mass.: Stephen Greene.

Koss, M., Gidycz, C. and Wisniewski, N. 1987: The scope of rape: incidence and prevalence of sexual aggression and victimization in a national sample of higher education students. *Journal of Consulting and Clinical Psychology*, 55.2, 162–70.

Kuhn, T. 1970: *The Structure of Scientific Revolutions*, 2nd edn. Chicago: University of Chicago Press.

Labov, W. 1982: *Sociolinguistic Patterns*. Philadelphia: University of Pennsylvania Press.

LaFree, G. 1989: *Rape and Criminal Justice*. Belmont: Wadsworth.

Lakoff, G. and Johnson, M.l 1980: *Metaphors We Live By*. Chicago: University of Chicago Press.

Lamont, M. and Wuthnow, R. 1990: Betwixt and between: recent cultural sociology in Europe and the United States. In G. Ritzer (ed.), *Frontiers of Social Theory*, New York: Columbia University Press, 287–315.

Largen, M. 1985: The anti-rape movement: past and present. In A. Burgess (ed.), *Rape and Sexual Assault*, vol. 1, New York: Garland, 1–13.

—— 1988: Rape-law reform: an analysis. In A. Burgess (ed.), *Rape and Sexual Assault*, vol. 2, New York: Garland, 271–92.

Layder, D. 1985: Power, structure and agency. *Journal for the Theory of Social Behavior*, 15.2, 131–49.

—— 1987: Key issues in structuration theory: some critical remarks. In J. Wilson (ed.), *Current Perspectives in Social Theory*, vol. 8, Greenwich: JAI Press, 25–46.

—— 1990: *The Realist Alternative*. New York: St Martin's.

Lee, J. 1987: Prologue: talking organization. In G. Button and J. Lee (eds), *Talk and Social Organizations*, Philadelphia: Multilingual Matters, 19–53.

Lenski, G. 1984: *Power and Privilege*. Chapel Hill: University of North Carolina Press.

Lerner, G. 1987: Collaborative turn sequences: sentence construction and social action. Unpublished doctorial dissertation, University of California at Los Angeles.

Levinson, S. 1979: Activity types and language. *Linguistics*, 17.5, 356–99.

—— 1980: Speech act theory: the state of the art. *Language and Linguistics Teaching Abstracts*, 13.1, 5–24.

—— 1981: Some pre-observations on the modelling of dialogue. *Discourse Processes*, 4.2, 93–110.

—— 1983: *Pragmatics*. New York: Cambridge University Press.

Lieberson, S. 1985: *Making it Count*. Berkeley: University of California Press.

Lipman-Blumen, J. 1984: *Gender Roles and Power*. Englewood Cliffs: Prentice-Hall.

Loftus, E. 1975: Leading questions and the eyewitness report. *Cognitive Psychology*, 7, 560–72.

Loftus, E. and Zanni, G. 1975: Eyewitness testimony. *Bulletin of the Psychonomic Society*, 5, 86–8.

Loh, W. 1981: Q: What has reform of rape legislation wrought? A: Truth in criminal labelling. *Journal of Social Issues*, 37.4, 28–52.

Lottes, I. 1988: Sexual socialization and attitudes toward rape. In A. Burgess (ed.), *Rape and Sexual Assault*, vol. 2, New York: Garland, 192–220.

Luckenbill, D. 1980: Power: a conceptual framework. *Symbolic Interaction*, 2, 97–114.

Lukes, S. 1974: *Power: A Radical View*. London: Macmillan.

—— 1985: *Émile Durkheim*. Stanford: Stanford University Press.

McBarnet, D. 1984: Victim in the witness box: confronting victimology's stereotype. In W. Chambliss (ed.), *Criminal Law in Action*, New York: Macmillan, 328–35.

McHoul, A. 1978: The organization of turns at formal talk in the classroom. *Language in Society*, 7, 183–213.

MacKinnon, C. 1979: *Sexual Harrassment of Working Women*. New Haven Conn.: Yale University Press.

—— 1982: Feminism, Marxism, method and the state: an agenda for theory. *Signs*, 7.3, 515–44.

—— 1983: Feminism, Marxism, method, and the state: toward feminist jurisprudence. *Signs*, 8.4, 635–58.

—— 1987: *Feminism Unmodified*. Cambridge: Harvard University Press.

—— 1989: *Toward a Feminist Theory of the State*. Cambridge: Harvard University Press.

McQuarie, D. and Spaulding, M. 1989: The concept of power in Marxist theory. *Critical Sociology*, 16.1, 3–26.

Mandelbaum, M. 1959: Societal facts. In P. Gardiner (ed.), *Theories of History*, New York: Free Press, 476–87.

Manicas, P. 1980: The concept of social structure. *Journal for the Theory of Social Behavior*, 10.2, 65–82.

—— 1987: *A History and Philosophy of the Social Sciences*. New York: Blackwell.

Mannheim, K. 1964: On the interpretation of Weltanschauung. In *Essays on the Sociology of Knowledge*, ed. P. Kecskemeti, London: Routledge and Kegan Paul, 33–83.

Marsh, J., Geist, A. and Caplan, N. 1982: *Rape and the Limits of Law Reform*. Boston: Auburn House.

Marx, K. 1972: The eighteenth brumaire of Louis Bonaparte. In *The Marx-Engels Reader*, ed. R. Tucker, New York: Norton, 416–525.

—— 1977: *Selected Writings*, ed. D. McClellan. New York: Oxford University Press.

Mauet, T. 1988: *Fundamentals of Trial Techniques*. Boston: Little Brown.

Mayhew, B. 1980: Structuralism versus individualism. Part 1: Shadowboxing in the dark. *Social Forces*, 59, 335–75.

—— 1981: Structuralism versus individualism. Part 2: Ideological and other obfuscations. *Social Forces*, 59.3, 627–48.

Maynard, D. 1980: Placement of topic changes in conversation. *Semiotica*, 30, 263–90.

—— 1984: *Inside Plea Bargaining*. New York: Plenum.

—— 1988: Language, interaction, and social problems. *Social Problems*, 35.4, 311–34.

Maynard, D. and Wilson, T. 1980: On the reification of social structure. In Scott McNall (ed.), *Current Perspectives in Social Theory*, Greenwich: JAI Press, 287–322.

Mehan, H. 1979: *Learning Lessons*. Cambridge: Harvard University Press.

—— 1987: Language and power in organizational process. *Discourse Processes*, 10.4, 291–301.

Merritt, M. 1976: On questions following questions (in service encounters). *Language in Society*, 5, 315–57.

Merton, R. 1957: *Social Theory and Social Structure*. New York: Free Press.

—— 1975: Structural analysis in sociology. In P. Blau (ed.), *Approaches to the Study of Social Structure*, New York: Free Press, 21–52.

—— 1976: *Sociological Ambivalence and Other Essays*. New York: Free Press.

Messerschmidt, J. 1986: *Capitalism, Patriarchy, and Crime*. Totowa N.J.: Rowman and Littlefield.

Messner, S. 1988: Merton's social structure and anomie. *Deviant Behavior*, 9, 33–53.

Mills, C. W. 1959: *The Sociological Imagination*. New York: Oxford University Press.

Moerman, M. 1988: *Talking Culture*. Philadelphia: University of Pennsylvania Press.

Moerman, M. and Sacks, H. 1988: On "Understanding" in the analysis of natural conversation. In M. Moerman, *Talking Culture*, Philadelphia: University of Pennsylvania Press, 180–6.

Molotch, H. and Boden, D. 1985: Talking social structure. *American Sociological Review*, 50.3, 273–87.

Muehlenhard, C. 1989: Misinterpreted dating behaviors and the risk of date rape. In M. Pirog-Good and J. Stets (eds), *Violence in Dating Relationships*, New York: Praeger, 241–56.

O'Barr, W. 1982: *Linguistic Evidence*. New York: Academic.

Outhwaite, W. 1987a: *New Philosophies of Science*. New York: St Martin's.

—— 1987b: Laws and explanations in sociology. In R. J. Anderson, J. A. Hughes and W. W. Sharrock (eds), *Classic Disputes in Sociology*, Boston: Allen and Unwin, 157–83.

Parsons, T. 1937: *The Structure of Social Action*. New York: Free Press.

Peyrot, M. 1982: Understanding ethnomethodology: a remedy for some common misconceptions. *Human studies*, 5.4, 261–84.

Pfeffer, J. 1981: *Power in Organizations*. Marshfield, Mass.: Pitman.

—— 1982: *Organizations and Organization Theory*. Cambridge: Ballinger.

Philips, S. 1984: The social organization of question and answers in court-room discourse: a study of changes of plea in an Arizona court. *Text*, 4, 225–48.

—— 1987: On the use of WH questions in American courtroom discourse: a study on the relation between language form and language function. In L. Kedar (ed.), *Power through Language*, Norwood: Ablex, 83–112.

Pirog-Good, M. and Stets, J. (eds) 1989: *Violence in Dating Relationships*. New York: Praeger.

Polk, K. 1985: Rape reform and criminal justice processing. *Crime and Delinquency*, 31.2, 191–205.

Pollner, M. 1979: Self-explicating transactions. In G. Psathas (ed.), *Everyday Language*, New York: Irvington, 227–53.

—— 1987: *Mundane Reason*. New York: Cambridge University Press.

Pomerantz, A. 1975: Second assessments: a study of some features of agreements/disagreements. Unpublished Ph.D. dissertation, University of California, Irvine.

—— 1978: Compliment responses: notes on the cooperation of multiple constraints. In J. Schenkein (ed.), *Studies in the Organization of Conversational Interaction*, New York: Academic, 79–112.

—— 1984: Agreeing and disagreeing with assessments: some features of preferred/dispreferred turn shapes. In J. Atkinson and J. Heritage (eds), *Structures of Social Action*, New York: Cambridge University Press.

Porpora, D. 1987: *The Concept of Social Structure*. New York: Greenwood.

—— 1989: Four concepts of social structure. *Journal for the Theory of Social Behavior*, 19.2, 195–211.

Psathas, G. 1980: Approaches to the study of everyday life. *Human Studies*, 3.1, 3–17.

—— (ed.) 1979: *Everyday Language*. New York: Irvington.

—— (ed.) 1990: *Interaction Competence*. Lanham: University Press of America.

Quirk, R., Greenbaum, S., Leech, G. and Svartvik, J. 1985: *A Comprehensive Grammar of the English Language*. New York: Longman.

Rifkin, J. 1982: Toward a theory of law and patriarchy. In P. Beirne and R. Quinney (eds), *Marxism and Law*, New York: John Wiley, 295–301.

Ritzer, G. 1988: *Sociological Theory*. New York: Random House.

—— 1990a: Micro–macro linkage in sociological theory: applying a metatheoretical tool. In G. Ritzer (ed.), *Frontiers of Social Theory*, New York: Columbia University Press, 347–70.

—— (ed.) 1990b: *Forontiers of Social Theory*. New York: Columbia University Press.

Roger, D. and Bull, P. (eds) 1989: *Conversation*. Philadelphia: Multilingual Matters.

Rowland, J. 1985: *The Ultimate Violation*. Garden City, N.Y.: Doubleday.

Rubin, L. 1983: *Intimate Strangers*. New York: Basic.

Rubinstein, D. 1986: The concept of structure in sociology. In M. Wardell and S. Turner (eds), *Sociological Theory in Transition*, Boston: Allen and Unwin, 80–94.

Russell, D. 1975: *The Politics of Rape*. New York: Stein and Day.

—— 1984: *Sexual Exploitation*. Beverly Hills: Sage.

Sacks, H. 1967: Unpublished lecture notes. See also *Harvey Sacks: Lectures on Conversation*, 2-vol. set, ed. G. Jefferson (Lectures 1964–72), Oxford: Blackwell, 1992.

Sacks, H. 1972: An initial investigation of the usability of conversational data for doing sociology. In D. Sudnow (ed.), *Studies in Social Interaction*, New York: Free Press, 31–74.

—— 1974: An analysis of the course of a joke's telling in conversation. In R. Bauman and J. Sherzer (eds), *Explorations in the Ethnography of Speaking*, New York: Cambridge University Press, 337–53.

—— 1984a: Notes on methodology. In J. Atkinson and J. Heritage (eds), *Structures of Social Action*, New York: Cambridge University Press, 21–7.

—— 1984b: On doing being ordinary. In J. Atkinson and J. Heritage (eds), *Structures of Social Action*, New York: Cambridge University Press, 413–29.

—— 1985: The inference making machine. In T. van Dijk (ed.), *Handbook of Discourse Analysis*, vol. 3, New York: Academic, 13–23.

—— 1987: On the preference for agreement and contiguity in conversation. In G. Button and J. Lee (eds), *Talk and Social Organizations*, Philadelphia: Multilingual matters, 54–69.

Sacks, H., Schegloff, E. and Jefferson, G. 1978: A simplest systematics for the organization of turn-taking for conversation. In J. Schenkein (ed.), *Studies in the Organization of Conversational Interaction*, New York: Academic, 7–55.

Sanday, P. 1981: The socio-cultural context of rape. *Journal of Social Issues*, 37, 5–27.

Sanders, W. 1980: *Rape and Woman's Identity*. Beverly Hills: Sage.

Scheff, T. 1984: *Being Mentally Ill*, 2nd edn. New York: Aldine.

Schegloff, E. 1972: Sequencing in conversational openings. In J. Gumperz and D. Hymes (eds), *Directions in Sociolinguistics*, New York: Holt, 346–80.

—— 1980: Preliminaries to preliminaries. *Sociological Inquiry*, 50, 104–52.

—— 1982: Discourse as an interactional achievement. In D. Tannen (ed.) *Analyzing Discourse, Text and Talk*, Washington D.C.: Georgetown University Press, 71–93.

—— 1984: On some questions and ambiguities in conversation. In J. Atkinson and J. Heritage (eds), *Structures of Social Action*, New York: Cambridge University Press, 28–52.

—— 1986: The routine as achievement. *Human Studies*, 9.2–3, 111–52.

—— 1987: Between macro and micro: contexts and other connections. In J. Alexander et al. (eds), *The Macro–Micro Link*, Berkeley: University of California Press, 207–34.

—— 1988a: Goffman and the analysis of conversation. In P. Drew and A. Wooton (eds), *Erving Goffman*, Boston: Northeastern University Press, 89–135.

—— 1988b: On an actual virtual servo-mechanism for guessing bad news. *Social Problems*, 35.4, 442–57.

—— 1991: Reflections on talk and social structure. In D. Boden and D. Zimmerman (eds), *Talk and Social Structure*, Cambridge: Polity, 44–70.

Schegloff, E. and Sacks, H. 1974: Opening up closings. In R. Turner (ed.) *Ethnomethodology*, New York: Penguin, 233–64.

Schegloff, E., Jefferson, G. and Sacks, H. 1977: The preference for self correction in the organization of repair in conversation. *Language*, 53, 361–82.

Schenkein, J. 1980: A taxonomy for repeating action sequences in natural conversation. In B. Butterworth (ed.), *Language Production*, vol. 1, New York: Academic, 21–47.

—— (ed.) 1978: *Studies in the Organization of Conversational Interaction*. New York: Academic.

Schiffrin, D. 1987: *Discourse Markers*. New York: Cambridge University Press

Schultz, L. (ed.), 1975: *Rape Victimology*. Springfield, Ill.: Charles Thomas.

Schur, E. 1984: *Labeling Women Deviant: Gender, Stigma, and Social Control* New York: Random House.

—— 1988: *The Americanization of Sex*. Philadelphia: Temple University Press.

Schwartz, H. and Jacobs, J. 1979: *Qualitative Sociology*. New York: Free Press.

Schwendinger, J. and Schwendinger, H. 1983: *Rape and Inequality*. Beverly Hills: Sage.

Scott, W. 1987: *Organizations*, 2nd edn. Englewood Cliffs: Prentice-Hall.

Scully, D. 1988: Convicted rapists' perception of self and victim. *Gender and Society*, 2.2, 200–13.

—— 1990: *Understanding Sexual Violence*. Boston: Unwin Hyman.

Scully, D. and Marolla, J. 1984: Convicted rapists' vocabulary of motive. *Social Problems*, 31, 530–44.

—— 1985a: Rape and psychiatric vocabulary of motive: alternate perspectives. In

A. Burgess (ed.), *Rape and Sexual Assault*, vol. 1, New York: Garland, 294–312.

—— 1985b: Riding the bull at Gilley's: convicted rapists describe the rewards of rape. *Social Problems*, 32, 251–61.

Sharrock, W. 1979: The problem of order. In Peter Worsley (ed.), *Introducing Sociology*, 2nd edn, New York: Penguin, 477–566.

Sharrock, W. and Anderson, B. 1986: *The Ethnomethodologists*. New York: Tavistock.

—— 1987: Epilogue. In G. Button and J. Lee (eds), *Talk and Social Organization*, Philadelphia: Multilingual Matters, 290–321.

Sharrock, W. and Turner, R. 1978: A conversational environment for equivocality. In J. Schenkein (ed.), *Studies in the Organization of Conversational Interaction*, New York: Academic, 173–97.

Sharrock, W. and Watson, R. 1988: Autonomy among social theories. In N. Fielding (ed.), *Actions and Structure*, Beverly Hills: Sage, 54–77.

Shibutani, T. 1986: *Social Processes*. Berkeley: University of California Press.

Short, J. (ed.) 1986: *The Social Fabric*. Beverly Hills: Sage.

Skidmore, W. 1979: *Theoretical Thinking in Sociology*, 2nd edn. New York: Cambridge University Press.

Smart, C. 1989: *Feminism and the Power of Law*. London: Routledge.

Smelser, N. 1986: From structure to order. In James F. Short Jr (ed.), *The Social Fabric*, Beverly Hills: Sage, 33–8.

—— 1988: Social structure. In N. Smelser (ed.), *Handbook of Sociology*, Beverly Hills; Sage, 103–30.

Smith, D. 1978: K is mentally ill. *Sociology*, 12, 23–53.

—— 1983: No one commits suicide. *Human Studies*, 6.4, 309–59.

—— 1990: *The Conceptual Practices of Power*. Boston: Northeastern University Press.

Spencer, C. 1987: Sexual assault: the second victimization. In L. Crites and W. Hepperle (eds), *Women, the Courts, and Equality*, Beverly Hils: Sage, 54–73.

Stinchcombe, A. 1975: Merton's theory of social structure. In L. Coser (ed.), *The Idea of Social Structure*, New York: Harcourt, Brace and Jovanovich, 11–34.

Suchman, L. 1987: *Plans and Situated Actions*. New York: Cambridge University Press.

Sudnow, D. 1965: Normal crimes: sociological features of the criminal code. *Social Problems*, 12, 255–70.

Sztompka, P. 1986: *Robert K. Merton: An Intellectual Profile*. New York: St Martins.

Tanford, J. 1983: *The Trial Process: Law, Tactics and Ethics*. Charlottesville: Michie.

Tannen, D. 1984: *Conversational Style*. Norwood: Ablex.

—— 1989: *Talking Voices*. New York: Cambridge University Press.

Temkin, J. 1986: Women, rape and law reform. In S. Tomaselli and R. Porter (eds) *Rape*, New York: Blackwell, 16–40.

Terasaki, A. 1976: Pre-announcement sequences in conversation. Unpublished MS.

Thompson, J. 1984: *Studies in the Theory of Ideology*. Berkeley: University of California Press.

Thorne, B. and Luria, Z. 1986: Sexuality and gender in children's daily world. *Social Problems*, 33, 176–90.

Tieger, T. 1981: Self-rated likelihood of raping and the social perception of rape. *Journal of Research in Personality*, 15, 147–58.

Todd, A. 1989: *Intimate Adversaries*. Philadelphia: University of Pennsylvania Press.

Toner, B. 1977: *The Facts of Rape*. London: Arrow.

Tong, R. 1984: *Women, Sex, and the Law*. Totowa: Rowman and Allanheld.

Treichler, P., Frankel, R., Kramarae, C., Zoppi, K. and Beckman, H. 1984: Problems and problems: power relationships in a medical encounter. In C. Kramarae et al. (eds), *Language and Power*, Beverly Hills: Sage.

Turner, J. 1986: *The Structure of Sociological Theory*. Homewood, Ill.: Dorsey.

—— 1988: *A Theory of Social Interaction*. Stanford: Stanford University Press.

Turner, J. and Collins, R. 1988: Towrad a microtheory of structuring. In Jonathan Turner (ed.), *Theory Building in Sociology*, Newbury Park: Sage, 118–30.

Van Dijk, T. 1989: Structures of discourse and structures of power. In J. Anderson (ed.), *Communication Yearbook*, vol. 12, Newbury Park: Sage, 18–59.

—— (ed.) 1985: *Handbook of Discourse Analysis*, vol. 3. New York: Academic.

Van der Zanden, J. 1987: *Social Psychology*. New York: Random House.

Walby, S. 1989: Theorising patriarchy. *Sociology*, 23.2, 213–34.

—— 1990: *Theorising Patriarchy*. Oxford: Blackwell.

Walker, A. 1985: The two faces of silence: the effect of witness hesitancy on lawyers' impressions. In D. Tannen and M. Saville-Troike (eds), *Perspectives on Silence*, Norwood: Ablex, 55–76.

—— 1987: Linguistic manipulation, power, and the legal setting. In L. Kedar (ed.), *Power through Language*, Norwood: Ablex, 57–80.

Wallace, W. 1983: *Principles of Scientific Sociology*. New York: Aldine.

Warr, M. 1985: Fear of rape among urban women. *Social Problems*, 32.3, 238–50.

Warshaw, R. 1988: *I Never Called It Rape*. New York: Harper and Row.

Watson, R. 1978: Categorization, authorization, and blame negotiation in conversation. *Sociology*, 12, 105–13.

—— 1987: Doing the organization's work. In S. Fisher and A. Todd (eds), *Discourse and Institutional Authority*, Norwood: Ablex, 91–120.

—— 1990: Some features of the elicitation of confessions in murder interrogations. In G. Psathas (ed.), *Interaction Competence*, Lanham: University of America, 263–95.

Weedon, C. 1987: *Feminist Practice and Poststructuralist Theory*. Oxford: Blackwell.

Weiser, A. 1974: Deliberate ambiguity. *Chicago Linguistic Society*, 10, 721–30.

West, C. 1979: Against our will: male interruptions of females in cross-sex conversations. In J. Orsanu, M. Slater and L. Adler (eds), *Language, Sex, and Gender*, Annals of the New York Academy of Sciences, vol. 327, 81–97.

——— 1984: *Routine Complications*. Bloomington: Indiana University Press.

West, C. and Garcia, A. 1988: Conversational shift work. *Social Problems*, 35.5, 551–75.

West, C. and Zimmerman, D. 1977: Women's place in everyday talk. *Social Problems*, 24, 521–29.

——— 1982: Conversation analysis. In K. Scherer and P. Ekman (eds), *Handbook of Methods in Nonverbal Behavior Research*, New York: Cambridge University Press, 506–41.

——— 1983: Small insults: a study of interruptions in cross-sex conversations with unacquainted persons. In B. Thorne, C. Kramarae and N. Henley (eds), *Language, Gender, and Society*, Rowley: Newbury House, 102–17.

——— 1985: Gender, language, and discourse. In T. van Dijk (ed.), *Handbook of Discourse Analysis*, vol. 4, New York: Academic, 103–25.

——— 1987: Doing gender. *Gender and Society*, 1.2, 125–51.

Whalen, J., Zimmerman, D. and Wahlen, M. 1988: When words fail: a single case analysis. *Social Problems*, 35.4, 335–62.

Whalen, M. and Zimmerman, D. 1987: Sequential and institutional calls for help. *Social Psychology Quarterly*, 50.2, 172–85.

Wiley, N. 1988: The micro–macro problem in social theory. *Sociological Theory*, 6.2, 254–61.

Williams, L. 1984: The classic rape: when do victims report? *Social Problems*, 31.4, 459–67.

Williams, R. 1983: *Keywords*. New York: Oxford University Press.

Wilson, J. 1983: *Social Theory*. Englewood Cliffs, NJ: Prentice-Hall.

Wilson, K., Faison, R. and Britton, G. 1983: Cultural aspects of male sex aggression. *Deviant Behavior*, 4, 241–55.

Wilson, T. and Zimmerman, D. 1980: Ethnomethodology, sociology and theory. *Humboldt Journal of Social Relations*, 7, 52–88.

——— 1986: The structure of silence between turns in two-party conversation. *Discourse Processes*, 9.4, 375–90.

Wilson, T., Wiemann, J. and Zimmerman, D. 1984: Models of turn taking in conversational interaction. *Journal of Language and Social Psychology*, 3.3, 159–83.

Wilson, W. J. 1987: *The Truly Disadvantaged*. Chicago: University of Chicago.

Wittgenstein, L. 1952: *Philosophical Investigations*. New York: Macmillan.

Woodbury, H. 1984: The strategic use of questions in court. *Semiotica*, 48.3–4, 197–228.

Wootton, A. 1989: Remarks on the methodology of conversation analysis. In D. Roger and P. Bull (eds), *Conversation*, Philadelphia: Multilingual Matters, 238–58.

Wright, E. 1978: *Class, Crisis and the State*. New York: Verso.

—— 1989: Models of historical trajectory: an assessment of Giddens's critique of Marxism. In D. Held and J. Thompson (eds), *Social Theory of Modern Societies*, New York: Cambridge University Press, 77–102.

Wrightsman, L. 1987: *Psychology and the Legal System*. Belmont, Calif.: Wadsworth.

Wrong, D. 1979: *Power*. New York: Basic.

Wuthnow, R. 1987: *Meaning and Moral Order*. Berkeley: University of California Press.

Zelditch, M. 1986: The problem of order. In James Short (ed.), *The Social Fabric*, Beverly Hills: Sage, 107–14.

Zimmerman, D. 1978: Ethnomethodology. *American Sociologist*, 13, 6–15.

—— 1988: On conversation: the conversation analytic perspective. In J. Anderson (ed.), *Communication Yearbook*, vol. 11, Beverly Hills: Sage, 406–32.

Zimmerman, D. and West, C. 1975: Sex roles, interruptions and silences in conversation. In B. Thorne and N. Henley (eds), *Language and Sex*, Rowley, Mass.: Newbury House, 105–29.

Index